Harvard Studies in Medieval Latin

2

Guillelmus de Aragonia

De nobilitate animi

Guillelmus de Aragonia

De nobilitate animi

William D. Paden and Mario Trovato

Department of the Classics, Harvard University
Distributed by Harvard University Press
Cambridge, Massachusetts, and London
2012

THIS BOOK IS PRINTED ON ACID-FREE PAPER. ITS BINDING
MATERIALS HAVE BEEN CHOSEN FOR STRENGTH AND DURABILITY.

PRINTED IN THE UNITED STATES OF AMERICA

Library of Congress Cataloging-in-Publication Data

Guillelmus, de Aragonia, active 1280-1310
De nobilitate animi / Guillelmus de Aragonia ; edited by William D. Paden and Mario Trovato.
pages. cm. -- (Harvard studies in medieval Latin ; 2)
Includes bibliographical references and index.
ISBN 978-0-674-06812-4
1. Nobility of character--Early works to 1800. 2. Mind and body--Early works to 1800. 3. Nobility--Early works to 1800. I. Paden, William D. (William Doremus), 1941- II. Trovato, Mario. III. Guillelmus, de Aragonia, active 1280-1310. De nobilitate animi. Latin. 2012. IV. Guillelmus, de Aragonia, active 1280-1310. De nobilitate animi. English. 2012. V. Title. VI. Series: Harvard studies in medieval Latin ; 2.
BJ1533.N6G85 2012
128′.02--dc23

2012018996

For Frances and Ornella

Contents

Abbreviations

AL	*Aristoteles Latinus*, ed. Lorenzo Minio-Paluello and others, 33 vols., Corpus philosophorum Medii Aevi (Bruges, Brussels: Desclée de Brouwer; Leiden, Brill, 1953–).
ALD	*Aristoteles Latinus Database*, ed. Josef Brams and Paul Tombeur [electronic resource] (Turnhout: Belgium Union académique internationale, *Aristoteles Latinus* Centre, Institute of Philosophy [Katholieke Universiteit Leuven], Centre "Traditio Litterarum Occidentalium").
AHMA	*Archives d'histoire doctrinale et littéraire du Moyen Âge.*
Auctoritates	*Les auctoritates Aristotelis: Un florilège médiéval; Étude historique et édition critique*, ed. Jacqueline Hamesse (Louvain: Publications universitaires, 1974).
Cappelli	Adriano Cappelli, *Dizionario di abbreviature latine ed italiane*, 6th ed. (Milan: Hoepli, 1967).
Colker	Martin L. Colker, ed., "De nobilitate animi," *Mediaeval Studies* 23 (1961): 47–79.
CW	*The Complete Works of Aristotle: The Revised Oxford Translation*, ed. Jonathan Barnes, 2 vols., Bollingen Series 71.2 (Princeton: Princeton University Press, 1984).
Díaz y Díaz	Manuel C. Díaz y Díaz, *Index scriptorum latinorum medii aevi hispanorum, pars altera*, Acta Salmanticensia, Filosofía y Letras, 12/2 (Salamanca: Universidad de Salamanca, 1959).
Du Cange	Charles Du Fresne Du Cange, *Glossarium mediae et infimae latinitatis*, 7 vols. (Paris, 1840–1850).
DV	Douay-Rheims Bible.
Glorieux	Palemon Glorieux, *La faculté des arts et ses maîtres au XIIIe siècle*, Études de philosophie médiévale 59 (Paris: J. Vrin, 1971).

Handbook — *A Handbook of the Troubadours*, ed. F. R. P. Akehurst and Judith M. Davis (Berkeley and Los Angeles: University of California Press, 1995).

Hauréau — Barthélemy Hauréau, "Notice sur le numéro 16089 des manuscrits latins de la Bibliothèque Nationale," *Notices et extraits des manuscrits de la Bibliothèque Nationale et autres bibliothèques* 35 (1896): 209–239.

LLT — *Library of Latin Texts* [electronic resource] (Turnhout: Brepols, Centre "Traditio Litterarum Occidentalium").

Meirinhos — José Francisco Meirinhos, "A atribução a Petrus Yspanus das 'Sententie super libro de physonomia,'" *Mediaevalia* (Porto) 7–8 (1995): 329–359.

Morawski — Joseph Morawski, *Proverbes français antérieurs au XVe siècle* (Paris: Champion, 1925).

OED — *Oxford English Dictionary*, 2nd ed. (Oxford, 1989).

OLD — *Oxford Latin Dictionary*, ed. P. G. W. Glare (Oxford, 1968–1982).

Ostwald — Aristotle, *Nicomachean Ethics*, trans. Martin Ostwald, Library of Liberal Arts (Indianapolis, Bobbs-Merrill, 1962).

Otto — August Otto, *Die Sprichwörter und sprichwörtlichen Redensarten der Römer* (Leipzig: Teubner, 1890). *Nachträge*, ed. Reinhard Häussler (Hildesheim: Olms, 1968).

Pack — R. A. Pack, "De pronosticatione sompniorum, libellus Guillelmo de Aragonia adscriptus," *AHMA* 33 (1966): 237–293.

PC — Alfred Pillet and Henry Carstens, *Bibliographie der Troubadours* (Halle: Niemeyer, 1933).

PL — *Patrologiae cursus completus, Series latina*, ed. Jacques-Paul Migne, 221 vols. (Paris, 1841–1864); *Patrologia Latina: The Full Text Database*. ProQuest Information and Learning Company, 1996.

Plato, *CD* — Plato, *Collected Dialogues*, ed. Edith Hamilton and Huntington Cairns (New York: Pantheon Books, 1961).

Terbille — Charles Ignatius Terbille, "William of Aragon's Commentary on Boethius' *De Consolatione Philosophiae*," 2 vols. (PhD diss., University of Michigan, 1972).

Thomas (A.) — Antoine Thomas, "Le *Liber de nobilitate animi* et les troubadours," *Studi medievali*, n.s., 2 (1929): 163–172.

Thomas (M.)	Marcel Thomas, "Guillaume d'Aragon, auteur du *Liber de nobilitate animi,*" *Bibliothèque de l'École des Chartes* 106 (1945–1946): 70–79.
TLL	*Thesaurus linguae latinae* (Leipzig: Teubner, 1900–).
TPMA	*Thesaurus proverbiorum medii aevi: Lexikon der Sprichwörter des romanisch-germanischen Mittelalters*, ed. Kuratorium Singer der Schweizerischen Akademie der Geistes- und Sozialwissenschaften, 14 vols. (Berlin: W. de Gruyter, 1995–2002).
Troubadours	*The Troubadours: An Introduction*, ed. Simon Gaunt and Sarah Kay (Cambridge: Cambridge University Press, 1999).
Walther	Hans Walther, *Proverbia sententiaeque latinitatis medii aevi: Lateinische Sprichwörter und Sentenzen des Mittelalters*, 9 vols. (Göttingen: Vandenhoeck & Ruprecht, 1963–1986).
Werner	Jakob Werner, *Lateinische Sprichwörter und Sinnsprüche des Mittelalters aus Handschriften gesammelt*, 2nd ed., rev. Peter Flury (Heidelberg: C. Winter, 1966).

Preface

GUILLELMUS DE ARAGONIA was a physician and philosopher from Aragon, in northeastern Spain, who was active around the turn of the thirteenth and fourteenth centuries. He wrote the treatise on nobility of mind that is edited here, *De nobilitate animi*, about 1280–1290. By 1300 he had written a commentary on Boethius, the *Commentum in Boetium*, and by 1310 a study of Aristotle's physiognomy, the *Summa supra Physionomiam Aristotelis*. The last of these works is attributed to Guillelmus Hispanus, presumably a variant form of his name. He also wrote on prognostication by dreams (*De pronosticacione sompniorum*) and on Ptolemaic astronomy (*Super Centilogium Tolomei*) in works that have not been dated. His writing combines the qualities of a practical physician with those of a speculative philosopher in the recently reinvigorated Aristotelian tradition.

Guillelmus probably received his training as a physician at the renowned faculty of medicine in Montpellier, since that city, now in France, belonged to the king of Aragon and since Aragon could not boast of another university. In the *Summa supra Physionomiam Aristotelis* he says he traveled to Catalonia and over the Pyrenees to Narbonne, and he shows acquaintance with the language of the *Gallici*, perhaps meaning both Occitan, the language of the troubadours, and French. In *De pronosticacione sompniorum* he says he once spoke with "a certain king" under circumstances that suggest that the king may have been Pedro III, who ruled Aragon from 1276 to 1285. No doubt he also served Alfonso III (1285–1291) and Jaime II (1291–1327). He may have been the beneficiary of an act by Alfonso, who in 1288 returned certain possessions that had been confiscated in a time of civil war to "Master Guillelmus, our physician."

De nobilitate animi was written in a time of stress over the changing nature of nobility. In the thirteenth century nobility was not defined with the clarity of law, as it had been in republican Rome and would be again at the end of the Middle Ages. The evolving status of nobility provoked a body of writings, including this one, that attempted to theorize the idea. A noble was a notable (as Guillelmus pointed out)—a person who was well known by reason of birth, wealth, or power. In Aragon the problem was especially difficult because there were four different strains of nobility, none of them clearly distinct from the others, and because the nobles had been embroiled throughout the thirteenth century in conflict with the king. Their efforts to gain power culminated when Pedro III granted the *Privilegio General* in 1283, founding a long parliamentary tradition, and again in 1285, when Alfonso III granted the *Privilegios de la Unión*, which for a brief period gave the nobility authority to depose a king deemed unsatisfactory. The civil war from which these events emerged was the immediate background of Alfonso's act returning property to Master Guillelmus, his physician. In the fourteenth century kings in Spain and France sought to expand their control over their nobles by creating new ones, a strategy that incidentally turned nobility, which had been a sociological notion, into a precisely formulated legal concept.

Philosophers at this time saw nobility in relation to dynamic changes in their discipline. Averroës' commentaries on Aristotle, disseminated among universities in the early thirteenth century, had fomented a revolutionary anthropological naturalism. Averroës placed rational truth on a par with theological truth; his view of the world and mankind saw them both as objects of reason rather than faith. Under this impulse Aristotelian thinkers turned from the notion of *homo christianus* to that of *homo naturalis*, seeking to understand the value of man as a natural being. Following their lead, Guillelmus sought to promote a healthy society by showing that moral education is the only remedy for the disease of human nature. Nobility for him is a *habitus acquisitus*, a habit acquired by practicing virtuous deeds. He argues that one must cultivate one's intelligence by enhancing speculative activity through practical experience; nobility is the culmination of these two exercises, *sapientia in speculando* (wisdom in exploring the truth) and *studiositas in agendo* (studiousness in action). His approach may be contrasted with those of Andreas Capellanus, a naturalist like Guillelmus but not an Aristotelian, and Brunetto Latini, an Aristotelian like him but not a naturalist. Comparison with three radical Aristotelians who were his contemporaries, Boethius of Dacia, Jacobus de Pistorio, and the Italian poet Guido Guinizelli, shows the complexity of philosophical discourse at the time, and by contrast the intellectual independence of *De nobilitate animi*.

Guillelmus chose a title, *On Nobility of Mind*, that reflects a rhetorical commonplace that true nobility springs from mind or merit rather than body or birth. This topos may be traced from Seneca, Juvenal, and other writers in Greek and Roman antiquity through a tradition that continues into the Middle Ages. In the late thirteenth century the question was a lively one, and not empty rhetoric, because the social issue had not yet been settled in legal terms as it soon would be. Guillelmus's claim was undoubtedly idealistic: the argument for nobility of mind implied a realization that a noble station in society often arose from less lofty considerations. Other, more realistic topoi claimed that nobility was based on birth, wealth, or power. In the Latin translations of his work, Aristotle embraced the realistic perspective. By making the claim for nobility of merit Guillelmus took a stand against the Philosopher, who dominated his thought in other ways. Doing so in a time of uncertainty and strife, he assumed the role of a philosophical activist.

His treatise invokes a throng of other thinkers—Greeks, Arabs, and Latins, philosophers, physicians, astronomers, historians, naturalists, orators, poets, and rustics pronouncing proverbs—who perform variations on the claim and help make the argument persuasive. *De nobilitate animi* attracted attention in the twentieth century because Guillelmus included citations by a number of troubadours, lyric poets from the south of France. The troubadours composed and sang in Occitan, their vernacular; Guillelmus must have translated excerpts from their work into Latin. It is not surprising that some of the quotations are difficult if not impossible to trace back to their sources, the more so because Guillelmus cites creatively, adapting his authorities to his own argument, as Quintilian had taught the orator to do. He enlists the troubadours for sentences expressing worldly wisdom about the body, noble or ignoble, and about servants. Two citations refer to Peire Vidal; others concern Folquet de Marseille, Jaufre Rudel, Guilhem de Montanhagol, and a certain Arnaut, perhaps Arnaut de Mareuil. The most disconcerting one quotes Odantagalus, whose name is otherwise unknown; perhaps this name conceals the troubadour Daude de Pradas, hypothetically *Daude gallus*, "Daude, the Frenchman," who expressed the thought that Guillelmus attributes to Odantagalus. Daude de Pradas and Guilhem de Montanhagol were active in the mid-thirteenth century, only a few years before Guillelmus wrote; the others in the twelfth century, early (Jaufre Rudel) or late. Guillelmus treats the troubadours as philosophers, anticipating their place of honor in Dante's *De vulgari eloquentia* about twenty years later.

The present edition of *De nobilitate animi* represents six manuscripts written from the late thirteenth century to the fifteenth. It is based on the oldest of them, P_1 (Paris, Bibliothèque Nationale de France, MS lat. 16089), which must have been composed within twenty years or so of the completion of the work. The treatise was transmitted from one manuscript to another by a process of open recension in which scribes participated actively and innovative readings were frequent. All six manuscripts derive from an original that was already corrupt. They array themselves in three affiliations, one of which exerted influence on another. We present the text of P_1, corrected as necessary, with addenda from other manuscripts in the variants; we include within the text citations found in other manuscripts but not in P_1 because we have internal evidence that one of them is original. We add an English translation that aims to be idiomatic while following the original closely. We provide a full listing of variants and an extensive collection of sources and analogues.

Mario Trovato (1923–2009) was a professor of Italian at Northwestern University. A fine scholar, known especially for his work on Dante's theory of the good, he was a magnetic teacher, a devoted colleague, and a warm friend. We collaborated on *De nobilitate animi* intermittently over several decades. The discussion of the philosophical context is his alone.

We are indebted to the Hill Monastic Manuscript Library of Saint John's University, Collegeville, Minnesota, for informing us of manuscripts *K*, *R*, and *S* and providing photocopies of *R* and *S*. We thank Dr. Ulrich Fischer of the Historisches Archiv der Stadt Köln for sending a color photocopy of *K*. We are grateful to Miriam Cabré of the Universitat de Girona for calling our attention to the study by Val Naval on the *Summa supra Physionomiam Aristotelis*. For photographs of the proverbs in Ptolemy's *Almagest* (Venice, 1515), we are obliged to F. R. P. Akehurst of the University of Minnesota. Julian Yolles made valuable suggestions for our translation.

After my collaborator passed away, our edition benefited from an expert reading by Marvin L. Colker of the University of Virginia. I am grateful for his meticulous attention. Whatever flaws remain must be my responsibility.

William D. Paden
Professor Emeritus of French
Department of French and Italian
Northwestern University

Introduction

De nobilitate animi was first described by Barthélemy Hauréau in 1896, using one manuscript witness (here referred to as P_1). In 1929 Antoine Thomas brought the treatise to wider attention, providing an edition of extracts based on two manuscripts (P_1 and *B*) and focusing on the citations from several troubadours. In 1945–46 Marcel Thomas published the attribution to Guillelmus de Aragonia contained in a third manuscript (P_2). In 1961 Marvin Colker provided a full edition, based on P_1 and *B*, with extensive annotation of the citations, although he was unaware of the attribution and the third manuscript. In 1959 the canon of works by Guillelmus de Aragonia was listed by Manuel Díaz y Díaz, and in 1971 it was reviewed and corrected by Palémon Glorieux.[1] Since then, several of these works, most notably the *Commentum in Boetium*, have occupied a number of scholars. The present work offers a new edition of *De nobilitate animi*, based on six manuscripts, with a translation, and studies of the date of *De nobilitate animi*; the life and works of the author; the historical, philosophical, and rhetorical contexts; the Latin and Occitan citations; and the manuscript sources and their affiliations.

Date

The date of *De nobilitate animi* can be narrowed to the years between the composition of its latest sources and the earliest known copy, which is in manuscript P_1, compiled in the late thirteenth century. The treatise cites several Latin translations of Aristotle that were completed in the 1260s, principally those by Guillelmus de Moerbeke. Possibly the latest of these was the translation of Aristotle's *Rhetorica* that Moerbeke completed before 1269 and presumably after

1 Glorieux (163) deleted the *Officium in diem festum Assumptionis B. Mariae*, which had been included, perhaps inadvertently, by Díaz y Díaz (no. 1596). Glorieux also added the *Commentum in Boetium*. Despite many uncertainties, the canon according to Glorieux is generally accepted today; see below, "Life and Works of Guillelmus de Aragonia."

1260, when his known career as a translator began.[2] *De nobilitate animi* quotes the *Rhetorica* directly:[3]

> De hac nobilitate loquitur Philosophus primo *Rethorice*, dicens quod "Nobilitas est genti et civitati sui iuris antiquos esse presides," quia sine dubio populares et cives sine aliqua nobilitate loqui nescirent. (1.6.12)
>
> Of this nobility the Philosopher speaks in the first book of the *Rhetoric*, saying, "Nobility is to be, by right, ancient guardians for the people and the city," since without doubt common people and citizens without any nobility would not know how to speak.

Sui iuris and *presides* occur in the translation by Moerbeke but not in the earlier anonymous translation. *De nobilitate animi* repeats the citation, including these terms, in 1.16.6.

Moerbeke translated the *Politica* twice, first in an incomplete version, then in a complete one that he finished about 1265. The latter translation is quoted distinctively in *De nobilitate animi:*

> Unde Philosophus in primo *Politicorum* dicit quod talium iniusticia sevissima gerit arma. (1.11.8)
>
> The Philosopher says in the first book of the *Politics* that the injustice of such people bears most cruel arms.

Sevissima gerit arma occurs in the complete version; in the earlier version Moerbeke had written *gravissima.*[4]

> Optime dicit Philosophus septimo *Politicorum*: "Omnis doctrina et omnis [disciplina] quod nature deficit vult supplere ..." (1.14.14)
>
> The Philosopher says excellently in the seventh book of the *Politics*: "All teaching and all discipline want to supply what is lacking in nature."

2 See W. Vanhamel, "Biobibliographie de Guillaume de Moerbeke," *Guillaume de Moerbeke: Recueil d'études à l'occasion du 700e anniversaire de sa mort (1286)*, ed. J. Brams and W. Vanhamel (Leuven, 1989), 301–383.

3 For bibliographical details on the citations, see "Sources and Analogues."

4 It is also possible that these words come from the *Auctoritates Aristotelis*, but it is uncertain that the *Auctoritates* were composed before *De nobilitate animi* (see below).

In the complete translation Moerbeke wrote, "Omnis enim ars et disciplina quod deficit naturae vult supplere." The earlier, incomplete version did not include Book 7, where this passage occurs.[5]

Guillelmus de Aragonia refers to two Aristotelian texts, *De historia animalium* and *De generatione animalium*, by the same title, *De animalibus*. This is the title used by Michael Scot in the translation that he completed in Toledo around 1120. Guillelmus de Aragonia seems, however, to have used the translations by Moerbeke. He refers to these texts six times, including two references to a passage for which he repeats language from Moerbeke:

> Unde Philosophus in septimo *De animalibus* dicit quod "Anima puerorum nichil differt ab anima bestiarum secundum tempus hoc ..." (1.3.27)

> The Philosopher says, in the seventh book of *On Animals*, "The soul of children differs not at all from the soul of animals, as is appropriate for this time in its development ..."

Moerbeke wrote substantially the same words: "... differt autem nichil ... anima [viz., puerorum] a bestiarum anima secundum tempus hoc." The version by Michael Scot is not as close: "Non est differentia inter animam pueri et animalium" (There is no difference between the soul of children and of animals).

> Ut dicit Philosophus in libro *De animalibus*, vita puerorum ut est dicere a vita bestiarum non differt. (1.13.2)

> As the Philosopher says in the book *On Animals*, the life of children scarcely differs from the life of animals.

Two other passages, 1.15.4 and 1.18.3, are not as clear but seem to indicate indebtedness to Guillelmus de Moerbeke. One passage, 1.11.20, provides no reason to lean either way, and one, 1.15.2, seems closer to Michael Scot but may be explained by a more general absorption of the version by Moerbeke:

> Ut dicit Philosophus in libro *De animalibus*, pater dat formam, hoc est virtutem informantem propinquam, et mater dat materiam corporalem ... (1.15.2)

> As the Philosopher says in the book *On Animals*, the father gives form, that is, the close formative virtue, and the mother gives bodily material ...

[5] *De nobilitate animi* refers to Book 7 again, but implicitly, in 1.3.3.

Michael Scot uses both *forma* and *materia* in the same way: "Vir dat formam et principium motus et femina dat corpus et materiam" (The man gives form and the principle of movement and the woman gives body and matter). Guillelmus de Moerbeke does not use *forma* in this passage: "Masculus quidem exhibet speciem et principium motus, femella autem et corpus et materiam" (The male indeed shows the outward appearance and the principle of movement but the female both body and matter). Elsewhere, however, he associates *forma* with the father as well as *materia* with the mother.

The Pseudo-Aristotelian *Physiognomica* was translated by Bartholomaeus de Messana, who was active around 1258–1266. *De nobilitate animi* seems to refer implicitly to this translation:

> Hoc idem probatur aliter, quia in natura omne perfectius est nobilius; sed vir est muliere perfectior, ergo nobilior. (1.12.3)
>
> The same thing can be proved another way, since in nature every more perfect thing is nobler; and man is more perfect than woman, therefore nobler.

Bartholomaeus de Messana wrote, "Demonstratus est mas femina iustior et fortior et universaliter dicere melior" (It has been shown that the male is more just than the female and stronger, and to say it all, better).

The Pseudo-Aristotelian *Rhetorica ad Alexandrum* is extant in two thirteenth-century versions known as Alpha and Beta. Both are anonymous. Martin Grabmann attributed Alpha to Guillelmus de Moerbeke.[6] If this attribution were accepted, one could posit that Alpha was completed around 1260–1286, the period when Moerbeke engaged in translation; other specialists, however, have rejected this attribution.[7] Moreover, the source used for *De nobilitate animi* could also have been Beta, for which no date more specific than the thirteenth century has been proposed. *De nobilitate animi* quotes the *Rhetorica ad Alexandrum* at 2.5.3 and 2.8.2.

Finally, the *Ethica Nicomachea* was translated four times, including versions known as the *Ethica vetus* and the *Ethica nova*, one completed by Robertus Grosseteste around 1246–1247, and an anonymous revision of Grosseteste from around 1260–1270. *De nobilitate animi* refers several times to passages in the *Ethica* that were not included in the two earliest translations. The source may

6 M. Grabmann, *Eine lateinische Übersetzung der pseudo-aristotelischen Rhetorica ad Alexandrum aus dem 13. Jahrhundert* (Munich, 1932), 19–22.

7 G. Lacombe, *Aristoteles Latinus: Codices*, vol. 1 (Rome, 1939), 79. P. A. Stapleton, "A Latin Translation of the Rhetorica ad Alexandrum from the Thirteenth Century" (PhD diss., University of Illinois, 1977), 5.

have been either Grosseteste or the anonymous reviser. See 1.0.1, 1.3.10, 1.3.23, 1.11.25a, 1.11.27a, 1.12.6, 1.14.8, and 1.14.11.

Antoine Thomas dated the hand of manuscript P_1 to the end of the thirteenth century.[8] Colker described it as "a crabbed French hand of the late thirteenth century."[9] *De nobilitate animi* may therefore be dated by the citations and the earliest hand to around 1270–1290. As discussed below, evidence from Guillelmus's other works suggests the second of these decades, around 1280–1290.

It follows that other texts that were written at the same time or later should not be considered as sources of *De nobilitate animi* but as analogues, if not as descendants. Such may be the case of the *Auctoritates Aristotelis*, which, as Jacqueline Hamesse has argued,[10] may be dated on internal evidence to 1267–1325 and attributed to Marsilio di Padua, who was born about 1275. It also seems likely to be the case of the *Liber de vita et moribus philosophorum*, formerly but no longer attributed by most scholars to Walter Burley, who was born in 1274–1275. This *Liber* was certainly written before 1326.[11] We list parallels to *De nobilitate animi* in these two works without determining whether they are sources, analogues, or descendants.

Life and Works of Guillelmus de Aragonia

The attribution of *De nobilitate animi* to Guillelmus de Aragonia is based on the colophon in manuscript P_2:

> H[e]c lectura petit quisnam sit lector et unde,
> Ne careat titulis ut peregrin[a] suis;
> Hic est Wille[l]mus medicine sorte magister;
> Regis Arrogonie de dicione fuit.[12]

> This reading asks who may be the reader, and where from,
> Lest it lack its titles like a stranger;

8 Thomas (A.), 164.

9 Colker, 50.

10 *Auctoritates*, 38–43.

11 J. Ottman and R. Wood, "Walter Burley: His Life and Works," *Vivarium* 37 (1999): 1–24. The *Commentum in Boetium* mentions a *Libellus de vita philosophorum* that was not identified by Terbille (2:16, 153) but that might seem to refer to the *Liber de vita et moribus philosophorum*. If so, it would appear that the latter work did serve as a source for Guillelmus de Aragonia. However, we have not found the opinion that the *Commentum* attributes to the *Libellus* in Pseudo-Walter Burley, *Liber de vita et moribus philosophorum*, ed. H. Knust (Tübingen, 1886). (The *Auctoritates Aristotelis* refer to Walter Burley: see *Auctoritates* 27.0.)

12 Cited by Thomas (M.), 71; see our edition.

> He is Willelmus, by profession a master of medicine;
> He was from the domain of the king of Aragon.[13]

The quatrain recurs more correctly in the *Commentum in Boetium*, also by Guillelmus.[14] Manuscript *R* supports the attribution:

> Explicit liber *De nobilitate animi* editus a magistro Guillermo de Arrogonia.
>
> Here ends the book *De nobilitate animi* put forth by Master Guillelmus de Aragonia.

Manuscripts *B* and *K* have explicits but no attributions: "Explicit *De nobilitate animi* liber," in *B*; "Explicit libellus *De nobilitate animi*," in *K*. Manuscripts P_1 and *S* have neither explicit nor attribution.[15]

The attributions in P_2 and *R* establish that the author of *De nobilitate animi* was named Guillelmus de Aragonia. The presence of the colophon in P_2 and the *Commentum in Boetium* implies that their author was the same, a possibility that is further supported by the texts' similarity of thought, expression, and sources.[16] The date of the *Commentum* was long considered to be around 1330 on the basis of a note following the colophon in the Erfurt manuscript: "Completa Mon. a. D. MCCCXXXV post Reminiscere feria V," that is, "Completed at Mon." (presumably Montpellier) "in 1335, on the Thursday after 'Reminiscere' Sunday," March 16, 1335.[17] Although it was once uncertain whether this date referred to the completion of the work or that of the manuscript containing the note, we may now be sure that it means the latter since the prologue to the *Commentum* has been identified as the source of Jean de Meun's prologue to his translation of the *Philosophiae consolatio*.[18] Jean died in 1305; he appears to have completed

[13] Discussion of the quatrain in Terbille, 1:2–6. We take *lectura*, "reading," as referring to the *Commentum in Boetium* or *De nobilitate animi*, respectively, and *lector*, "reader," as referring to the author.

[14] Pack, 238 n. 8.

[15] The title, which is confirmed within the text at 1.0, recurs in the same form in *K* and, in a later hand, in *R*. In P_1 it is abbreviated *De nobilitate* in the margin at the beginning; in *S* it occurs in the upper margin of the second page of the work as *Tractatus de nobilitate anime* [sic].

[16] Terbille 1:6–7; see note 70 below for resemblances in the argument. The *Commentum* as edited by Terbille cites the following authorities that also figure in *De nobilitate animi*: the *Disticha Catonis*, Galen's *Tegni*, Hermes Trismegistus, Haly, Isidore's *Etymologiae*, proverbs, Ptolemy's *Almagest*, and the biblical book of Wisdom. On the *Libellus de vita philosophorum* see above, note 11.

[17] Pack, 238 n. 8; Terbille, 1:3; cf. Glorieux, 163.

[18] R. Crespo, "Il prologo alla traduzione della 'Consolatio Philosophiae' di Jean de Meun e il commento di Guglielmo d'Aragona," in *Romanitas et Christianitas, Studia Iano Henrico Waszink ... Oblata* (Amsterdam, 1973), 55–70.

this translation by about 1300.[19] The *Commentum* was also used in a Picard translation of the *Philosophiae consolatio* written shortly after 1315.[20] It has been the object of several studies, but as of this writing no complete edition is readily accessible.[21]

A third work attributed to Guillelmus de Aragonia is the *Summa supra Physionomiam Aristotelis* that immediately follows *De nobilitate animi* in manuscript P_1 and ends with an attribution: "Explicit summa magistri Guillelmi Hispani supra Physionomiam Aristotelis cum questionibus ejusdem" (Here ends the *Summa* of Master Guillelmus Hispanus *Supra Physionomiam Aristotelis* with questions of the same).[22] Marcel Thomas pointed out that some of the ideas

19 "Towards the end of the thirteenth century, *ca.* 1300": A. J. Denomy, "The Vocabulary of Jean de Meun's Translation of Boethius' De Consolatione Philosophiae," *Mediaeval Studies* 16 (1954): 20.

20 J. K. Atkinson, "A Fourteenth-Century Picard Translation-Commentary of the Consolatio Philosophiae," *The Medieval Boethius: Studies in the Vernacular Translations of "De consolatione philosophiae,"* ed. A. J. Minnis (Cambridge, 1987), 32–62.

21 The *Commentum in Boetium* begins "Sicut scribit Philosophus primo Politicorum: 'Omnia appetunt bonum'." Glorieux, 163. Meirinhos, 350–351. Terbille used the Erfurt manuscript to edit the commentary on Book 1, entire; Book 2, prose and meter 6–7; Book 3, prose and meter 9, excerpts from meter 12; and Book 5, prose and meter 2. W. Senner, "Der vollständige Kommentar des Guillelmus de Aragonia über die *Consolatio Philosophiae*," *Bulletin de philosophie médiévale* 22 (1980): 98–100, pointed out that the *Commentum* also occurs in Cambridge, University Library, Ii.3.21, together with the translation of Boethius by Chaucer. This manuscript has been published in facsimile: *Boetii De Consolatione Philosophiae, with the English Version Ascribed to Chaucer ... A Reproduction of MS Ii.3.21 in the Cambridge University Library*, 2 vols. (Washington, D.C., 1928); see *National Union Catalog Pre-1956 Imprints*, 63:496. Crespo published the prologue from three manuscripts, "Il prologo," 55–59. Using five manuscripts, C. Olmedilla Herrero published the prologue in "Un accessus medieval: El comentario de Guillermo de Aragón al *De consolatione philosophiae* de Boecio," *Actas: II Congreso Hispánico de Latín Medieval (León, 11–14 de Noviembre de 1997)* (León, 1998), 2:709–720, and the commentary to Book 3, meter 12 in "Commentaire de Guillaume d'Aragon sur *De Consolatione Philosophiae* de Boèce," *L'Orphée de Boèce au Moyen Âge: Traductions françaises et commentaires latins (XIIe-XV siècles)*, ed. B. M. Atherton and J. K. Atkinson (Verona, 2000), 181–196. The commentary to Book 4, meter 7.13ff., was published by Atkinson, *A Fourteenth-Century Picard Translation-Commentary*, 60–62. English translations of the prologue and the commentary to Book 3, meter 12 appeared in A. J. Minnis, A. B. Scott, and D. Wallace, *Medieval Literary Theory and Criticism c. 1100–c. 1375: The Commentary Tradition*, rev. ed. (Oxford, 1988), 328–335. We have not seen C. Olmedilla Herrero, "Edición crítica de los comentarios de Guillermo de Aragón al *De consolatione Philosophiae* de Boecio" (diss., Universidad Complutense de Madrid, 1997).

22 The *Summa supra Physionomiam Aristotelis* begins, "Sicut dicit philosophus primo Rethoricorum (seu Rhetorice) Nobilitas est ..." L. Thorndike and P. Kibre, *A Catalogue of Incipits of Mediaeval Scientific Writings in Latin*, rev. ed. (Cambridge, Mass., 1963), col. 1488 (attributed to William of Spain; six manuscripts, that of Erfurt dated in the thirteenth century). Thomas (M.) (76, n. 2) quotes the attribution in P_1. Díaz y Díaz, no. 1594. Glorieux, 163. Terbille, 1:7–8. Meirinhos, 346–350, 355–359 (thirteen manuscripts; uses the title *Sententie super libro de physonomia*). This *Summa* should not be confused with an anonymous physiognomic work that has been attributed to Aristotle, Avicenna, Averroës, or an unknown Christian author. See R. A. Pack, "Auctoris Incerti De Physiognomia Libellus," *AHMA* 41 (1974): 113–138. Nine versions of the *Physiognomia* are described in C. B. Schmitt and D. Knox, *Pseudo-Aristoteles Latinus: A Guide to Latin Works Falsely Attributed to Aristotle Before 1500* (London, 1985).

in the *Summa* resemble those in *De nobilitate animi* and posited that Guillelmus Hispanus was Guillelmus de Aragonia.[23] As for the two names, Charles Terbille elaborated the argument "that a man living outside his native land may use its name as an epithet ... A native of Aragon by the name of William could be called Guillelmus Hispanus."[24] One manuscript of the *Summa* was written before 1310.[25] Its author says he has traveled to Catalonia and the region around Narbonne and shows some acquaintance with the language of the *Gallici*, by which he seems to have meant speakers of both Occitan and French.[26]

A fourth work, called *De pronosticacione sompniorum*, is attributed in the manuscripts to a certain Albertus (perhaps Albertus Magnus), to Arnaldus de Villa Nova, and to Guillermus de Arigonia.[27] M. Thomas, Roger Pack, and Terbille have argued for Guillelmus de Aragonia.[28] M. Thomas proposed that anecdotes in the treatise referring to *rex quidam*, "a certain king," concern events that occurred in 1282, during the reign of Pedro III, king of Aragon from 1276 until his death in 1285.[29] Although Terbille judges some of these interpretations more persuasive than others,[30] we have plausible evidence that Guillelmus de Aragonia was on intimate terms with Pedro III, if it is indeed he who wrote that the king had told him about his dreams: "A certain king told me that in a dream he crowned his wife ..."[31]

23 Thomas (M.), 76–77.

24 Terbille, 1:8. The identification of Guillelmus Hispanus with Guillelmus de Aragonia is "generalmente condivisa," according to J. Agrimi, "La ricezione della Fisiognomica pseudoaristotelica nella Facoltà delli Arti," *AHMA* 64 (1997): 151. It has been supported by P. Val Naval, who dates the *Summa* between 1260 and 1295 or 1309 and conjectures that it may have been written in France. See "Autoría y datación de la Summa supra Phisonomiam Aristotelis," *Studium: Revista de humanidades* 12 (2006): 138.

25 Paris, Bibliothèque Nationale de France, lat. 16158; Agrimi, "La ricezione della Fisiognomica pseudoaristotelica," 151, 187.

26 Thomas (M.) remarks that Guillelmus "devait savoir un peu de provençal et de français" (77) since he mentions that the *Gallici* say *cayla*, "quail" (Occitan *calha* but not French *caille*) and *s'esbaïst*, "he was astonished" (French *s'esbaïst* but not Occitan *s'esbaït*).

27 *De pronosticacione* (or *pronosticationibus*) *sompniorum* begins, "Philosophantes antiquos sive (seu) Indos." Thorndike and Kibre, *A Catalogue of Incipits*, col. 1040 (five manuscripts). L. Thorndike, *A History of Magic and Experimental Science* (New York, 1958), 2:300–302. Thomas (M.), 72–75. Díaz y Díaz, no. 1593. Glorieux, 163. Meirinhos, 352–353. On the attributions see Pack, 256. On the relation between dreams and the stars in this treatise see T. Gregory, "I sogni e gli astri," *I sogni nel medioevo*, ed. T. Gregory (Rome, 1985), 138–141.

28 Thomas (M.), 71–72. Pack, 237–238. Terbille, 1:9–10.

29 Thomas (M.), 74–75.

30 Terbille, 1:10–13.

31 Terbille, 1:10. "Retulit etiam michi rex quidam quod coronaret in sompno uxorem suam" (Pack, 280).

A fifth work, called *Super Centilogium Tolomei*, is subtitled *Scripta magistri Gwillelmi de Arragonia.*[32] Ptolemy's *Centilogium* also figures among the sources of *De nobilitate animi*, *De pronosticacione sompniorum*, and the *Summa supra Physionomiam Aristotelis.*[33] Terbille considers the style of this work consistent with that of Guillelmus de Aragonia.[34] The *Super Centilogium Tolomei* has been neither dated nor edited.

Other attributions are less persuasive. Lynn Thorndike proposed to identify Guillelmus de Aragonia with Guillelmus Anglicus, a citizen of Marseille who wrote a treatise *De urina non visa* (*Of Urine Unseen*) in 1219; but Thorndike himself conceded that the suggestion seems unlikely since it would require the same Guillelmus to be English, Aragonese, and Marseillais.[35] A misleading and perhaps inadvertent attribution was implied by Manuel Díaz y Díaz concerning an *Officium in diem festum Assumptionis Beatae Mariae* but was ignored for good reason by Glorieux.[36] The *Officium* provides no support for the attribution.[37] Thinking that the *Commentum in Boetium* was composed around 1330, Terbille introduced a document dated 1335 that mentions three *magistros* named Guillermus in the Faculty of Medicine at Montpellier.[38] None of them, however, is called either *de Aragonia* or *Hispanus*. Since we now know that the *Commentum* was composed before 1305 and probably around 1300, this document may be set aside.

We conclude that Guillelmus de Aragonia, sometimes called Guillelmus Hispanus, was a physician from Aragon who was active in the period from the 1280s or possibly the 1270s until before about 1310. As a philosopher, he wrote on physiognomy, oneirology, astrology, and ethics. He completed *De nobilitate animi* by about 1290, the *Commentum in Boetium* by 1300, and the *Summa supra Physionomiam Aristotelis* by 1310. His writings show a spirit both practical and speculative, as is fitting in a physician-philosopher.[39] They were transmitted in manuscripts that grow in number as research continues. The commentary on Boethius was translated into French by Jean de Meun about 1300 and

32 *Super Centilogium Tolomei* begins, "Sicut dicit Ptolomeus in proverbiis Almagesti ..." Thorndike and Kibre, *A Catalogue of Incipits*, col. 1489 (two manuscripts). Thorndike, *A History of Magic and Experimental Science*, 2:301. Thomas (M.), 78. Díaz y Díaz, no. 1595. Glorieux, 163. Terbille, 1:13–14.

33 The last according to Meirinhos, 353.

34 Terbille, 1:14.

35 Thorndike, *History of Magic and Experimental Science*, 2:301, 487.

36 Díaz y Díaz, no. 1596, under "Guillelmus de Aragonia medicus." Glorieux, 163.

37 F. Fita [y Colomé], ed., "Rezo antiguo de la Inmaculada Concepción," *Monumentos antiguos de la Iglesia Compostelana* (Madrid, 1882), 92–104. Fita makes no reference to the author.

38 Terbille, 1:14–25.

39 "As conexões entre a medicina, a astrologia e a filosofia, com uma intenção prática mas também especulativa e edificante, apresentam-se como a marca mais saliente do pensamento de Guilherme Hispano" (Meirinhos, 353).

again by an anonymous Picard about 1315. It was translated into Catalan about 1360; this version was revised about 1390, translated into Castilian, and used by a translator of Nicolas Trevet's commentary on Boethius.[40] In the fifteenth century the *Commentum in Boetium* was studied in England alongside the translation of Boethius by Geoffrey Chaucer.[41]

Guillelmus held the title of *medicine magister* according to the colophon of *De nobilitate animi* in P_2 and the *Commentum in Boetium*, echoed by *magister* in the explicit of *R*, the attribution of the *Summa supra Physionomiam Aristotelis*, and that of the *Super Centilogium Tolomei*. The master's was a teaching degree, in contrast to the bachelor's, which was practical.[42] It seems likely that Guillelmus received his title from the Faculty of Medicine in Montpellier since Montpellier was ruled by the king of Aragon and there was no other university in the king's domain.[43] Medical study at Montpellier had been first mentioned about 1137; in 1289 Pope Nicholas IV granted the university the rank of *studium generale*.[44] With Paris and Bologna it was one of three great medical schools, Salerno having entered a period of decline.[45]

Guillelmus de Aragonia was probably the same as Guillelmus Hispanus, who says in the *Summa supra Physionomiam Aristotelis* that he traveled to Catalonia and Narbonne. He may have spoken with Pedro III, surnamed "the Great." He probably also served under Alfonso III, the Liberal (1285–1291), and Jaime II, the Just (1291–1327). The kings of Aragon, with its capital at Zaragoza, held Montpellier from 1204 to 1349. They were also the counts of Catalonia, with its

40 The Catalan translation by P. Saplana was completed between 1358 and 1362 and revised by Ginebreda around 1390. It is now lost, but a Castilian version survives. C. Olmedilla Herrero, "Commentarios a la Consolatio Philosophiae de Boecio: Guillermo de Aragón y la versión castellana anónima del comentario de Nicolás de Trevet," *Cuadernos de filología clásica* (Madrid) 2 (1992): 277–288.

41 M. J. Gleason, "Clearing the Fields: Towards a Reassessment of Chaucer's Use of Trevet in the *Boece*," *The Medieval Boethius: Studies in the Vernacular Translations of "De consolatione philosophiae,"* ed. A. J. Minnis (Cambridge, 1987), 93 n. 13.

42 V. L. Bullough, "The Development of the Medical University at Montpellier to the End of the Fourteenth Century," in Bullough, *Universities, Medicine and Science in the Medieval West* (Aldershot, 2004), 22.

43 Montpellier was the only university in the domain of the king of Aragon until another was founded at Lérida (Catalonia) in 1300. On Lérida, said to be the site of the first university in the Crown of Aragon, see J. N. Hillgarth, *The Spanish Kingdoms 1250-1516*, vol. 1 (Oxford, 1976), 284. Hillgarth overlooks Montpellier.

44 Bullough, "Development of the Medical University at Montpellier," 16, 24.

45 Ibid.; see also Terbille, 1:26–42. Olmedilla Herrero declares as fact that Guillelmus de Aragonia was a master of medicine at the University of Montpellier ("Un accessus medieval," 714). She does not document this opinion, which may be due to Terbille, who, unaware that the *Commentum in Boetium* was written by 1305, believed that it was written in Montpellier in 1335. The same assumption is made by Val Naval in "Autoría y datación de la Summa supra Phisonomiam Aristotelis," 133, 138.

capital at Barcelona, as a result of a marriage in 1137. In the thirteenth century their power spread to include Valencia on the southern coast and the islands of Majorca, Minorca, and Sicily.[46] As we shall see in the next section, it may be possible to identify Guillelmus de Aragonia with another master of medicine, a subject of Alfonso III whom the king mentioned in a document in 1288.

Nobility in History

The words *nobilis* and *nobilitas* derive from the root of *noscere*, "to know"; a noble is a person who is notable, worthy to be known, as Guillelmus de Aragonia was aware.[47] Nobility had been a well-defined legal concept in Republican Rome and would become one again throughout Europe in the fourteenth and fifteenth centuries. During the long interval between these two times, however, after the decline of authority that marked the beginning of the Middle Ages and before its revival, nobility was a looser notion. It was not precisely defined in legal terms but comprised an unsteady balance of notable birth, wealth, and power, especially the power to make war, which was the preoccupation of the aristocracy.[48]

Throughout this period, as Martin Aurell has written, "The contours of the aristocratic group change to the rhythm of political, social, and economic transformations."[49] David Crouch has identified a turning point in northern France when the aristocracy (which he uses as a sociological term) became a nobility (a legal term), precisely in the reign of Philip IV (1285–1314), who created an instrument called the letter patent of ennoblement by which the king could transform a commoner into a noble.[50] Events in Italy followed a

46 On "The Crown of Aragon, 1229–1327: A Mediterranean Empire?" see J. N. Hillgarth, *The Spanish Kingdoms*, 1:233–286; and T. N. Bisson, *The Medieval Crown of Aragon: A Short History* (Oxford [illegible]). The expanded personal possessions of the king were called the Crown of Aragon, in contrast to the kingdom proper, from 1296 onward. See J. M. Del Estal, "Antigüedad del concepto y denominación 'Corona de Aragon,'" *Medievalia* (Barcelona) 10 (1992): 133–168.

47 *OLD* s.v. *nobilis, nobilitas. De nobilitate animi* 1.0.1, 1.0.6. Prosser notes that "the link between notability and *noblesse* was basic." G. Prosser, "The Later Medieval French Noblesse," *France in the Later Middle Ages, 1200–1500* (Oxford, 2002), 207.

48 M. Aurell, *La noblesse en occident (Ve-XVe siècle)* (Paris, 1996), 5. Compare C. B. Bouchard, *Strong of Body, Brave and Noble: Chivalry and Society in Medieval France* (Ithaca, 1998), 2–3: "Nobility did not in the eleventh and twelfth centuries constitute a distinct or even clearly definable group ... Nothing like modern consciousness of social class existed before the fourteenth century." Combining wealth and power as one idea, Guillelmus de Aragonia (*De nobilitate animi* 1.1.8) defined nobility more idealistically in terms of ethics, birth, and power.

49 Aurell, *La noblesse en occident (Ve-XVe siècle)*, 5 (our translation).

50 D. Crouch, *The Birth of Nobility: Constructing Aristocracy in England and France 900–1300* (Harlow, 2005), 3. See also *Encyclopedia of the Middle Ages*, ed. André Vauchez (Cambridge, 2000), s.v. "Nobles, Nobility": "It has been said that nobility did not exist until the moment when the prince was able to make a non-noble into a noble, officially endowed with a number of honours, privileges and pre-eminences. In France this moment corresponded to the first three decades of the

similar chronology.[51] In fourteenth-century Aragon and Castille, beginning with Jaime II of Aragon (1291–1327), kings created a new titled nobility as a means to strengthen royal power.[52] In Catalonia nobles had held the title of count or viscount since time immemorial; they continued to hold only those titles until the fourteenth century, which saw a blossoming of *marqueses*, dukes, and barons.[53]

These developments raised a new criterion for nobility: one could be a noble because a prince had made one noble. But one could pass for noble by displaying a notable lifestyle. As Maurice Keen observes, "Though the traditional regard for lineage had hardened into legal doctrine, the barriers that the law erected proved very far from insurmountable":

> What the tighter and better defined rules did do, however, in combination with the observable fact that they were so commonly breached, was to focus attention more sharply than before on the question, what the real essence of nobility was ... The question was important, to the heralds perhaps especially as the registrars of the insignia of nobility, but to the chivalrous world generally as well. A great deal of ink came to be spilt in its discussion, and the writers who considered it drew on all the resources of their erudition.[54]

Keen discusses two writers who studied this theme: Bartolus of Sassoferrato, a professor of law at Perugia, in the fourteenth century, and Olivier de la Marche, a French knight, in the fifteenth.[55] In the thirteenth century the physician Guillelmus de Aragonia anticipated the growing importance of the subject.

14th century." Concerning the south of France as well as the north, see also G. Prosser, "The Later Medieval French Noblesse," in *France in the Later Middle Ages, 1200–1500*, ed. D. Potter (Oxford, 2002), 182–209. The troubadour Johan Esteve, who was active from 1270 to 1289, remarked (PC 266.2 v. 20) that his lady made him as happy as "a lord who can give nobility" (*senhor que pot donar nobleza*). See *Le poesie del trovatore Johan Esteve*, ed. S. Vatteroni (Pisa, 1986), 53–54, no. 1. Vatteroni translates *nobleza* as "ricchezza."

51 "While in thirteenth century Florence the family ... was a clearly recognisable social unit, the nobility was not. It was only at the end of the thirteenth century ... that a legal definition of nobility was introduced ... Neither were there, before the end of the thirteenth century, legal attributes which distinguished the nobility from the *popolo*." N. Rubinstein, *Studies in Italian History in the Middle Ages and the Renaissance*, vol. 1, *Political Thought and the Language of Politics* (Rome, 2004), 167.

52 F. de Moxó Montoliu, "Jaime II y la nueva concesión de títulos nobiliarios en la España del siglo XIV," *Anales de la Universidad de Alicante: Historia medieval* 9 (1992–1993): 133–143.

53 A. de Fluvià Escorsa, "Los títulos nobiliarios en el Principado de Cataluña (siglo IX–1716)," *Hidalguía: La revista de genealogía, nobleza y armas* 36.207 (1988): 249–255.

54 M. Keen, *Chivalry* (New Haven, 1984), 148.

55 Ibid., 148–151.

The situation of the nobility in Aragon in the decade of the 1280s was complicated and turbulent. Nobles comprised not one homogenous group but four varieties that had different though not clearly distinguished names.[56] The language of the *Privilegio General* of 1283 (on which more below) consistently referred in hierarchical order to the *ricoshombres*, "powerful men," that is, the ancient nobility, a handful of great families; the *mesnaderos*, "men-at-arms"; the *cavalleros*, "knights"; and lastly the *infançones*, an urban patriciate that had sprung up in the twelfth century.[57] The *mesnaderos*, *cavalleros*, and *infançones* were overlapping orders of military nobility. The *Cortes*, sessions of parliament summoned irregularly by the king, would later comprise four *brazos*, or "arms," representing the *ricoshombres*, the *eclesiásticos*, the *cavalleros*, and the *universidades* (not the university—there was no university in the kingdom of Aragon at this time—but the universality of all other good men, the *ciudadanos* from villages, towns, and cities). The two arms of the *Cortes* representing the *ricoshombres* and the *cavalleros*, the greater and lesser nobility, contrasted with just one branch reserved for the nobility in neighboring Catalonia and elsewhere, as for the Lords in England.[58]

All four types of nobles had turbulent relations with the king. The history of aristocratic rebellions reached back as far as the 1220s, peaked in the 1240s, and culminated in the 1280s, when they reached the pitch of civil war.[59] Among the causes of this perennial unrest may be cited the end of the main phase of the Reconquest (of Muslim territory), which left men-at-arms without a war to fight and the king without a steady supply of new lands to distribute to his followers. Another cause was the dynastic advancement of the kings of Aragon, who gained the title of count of Barcelona by marriage in 1137 and continued to expand their interests abroad—to Valencia, the Midi, and Sicily. When Pedro III conquered

56 See L. González Antón, *Las uniones aragonesas y las Cortes del reino (1283-1301)* (Saragossa, 1975), 1:436: "En los comienzos de la etapa la indefinición es completa." In the *Cortes* of October 1283 that produced the *Privilegio General* twenty-two nobles were present, but it is impossible to know if more than twelve were *ricoshombres* or when an individual began to be a *ricohombre* (ibid.).

57 E. Sarasa Sánchez, *El Privilegio general de Aragón: la defensa de las libertades aragonesas en la Edad Media, estudio y edición* (Saragossa, 1984), 79–80, 81, 88, 89. "No podemos distinguir a los mesnaderos de los caballeros" (González Antón, *Uniones*, 1:437). On the overlapping terms *caballero* and *infanzón*, see R. Conde y Delgado de Molina, "La salva de la infanzonía aragonesa: fueros, praxis documental y archivo," *Aragón en la edad media* 14–15.1 (1999): 314. Further on the *infançones*, see J. L. Corral Lafuente, "Cambios estructurales en Aragón a mediados del siglo XIII," *Aragón en la edad media* 5 (1983): 95–112; and C. Laliena Corbera and M. T. Iranzo Muñío, "Poder, honor y linaje en las estrategias de la nobleza urbana aragonesa: siglos XIV–XV," *Revista d'història medieval* 9 (1998): 41–80.

58 On the development of *brazos* for the greater and lesser nobility under Jaime II (1291–1327), see L. González Antón, "Las Cortes aragonesas en el reinado de Jaime II," *Anuario de historia del derecho español* 47 (1977): 626–656.

59 J. A. Sesma Muñoz, *La Corona de Aragón: Una introducción crítica* (Saragossa, 2000), 110–116.

Sicily in 1282, the nobles of landlocked Aragon, unlike those of Catalonia on the sea, found his adventure without interest and were incensed that their king had set off to conquer the island without seeking their aid and counsel. Another unfortunate effect was that Pope Martin IV, who was a Frenchman, excommunicated Pedro for conquering Sicily from the French and pronounced an interdict upon his lands. Martin awarded Aragon to Charles de Valois, the son of Philippe III of France, and Charles threatened to assert his claim by invasion.[60] The nobles of Aragon, who considered themselves freed of their bonds of loyalty to their king because he was excommunicate, joined together in the *Unión*, as their alliance was called, and demanded a meeting to resolve their differences. At the *Cortes* of Zaragoza in 1283 Pedro had no alternative but to make specific concessions to each of the types of nobility. The *Privilegio General* that he issued became the cornerstone of a long parliamentary tradition in Aragon, like the legacy of the *Magna Carta* in England.

When Pedro III died in 1285, the crown passed to his son Alfonso III. Soon rebellion broke out at assemblies in Daroca and Zaragoza. Taking the offensive, Alfonso plunged Aragon into a civil war, which he promptly lost. On December 28, 1287, he signed the *Privilegios de la Unión*, granting to the nobility, among other rights, the power to remove him from the throne if he did not rule to their satisfaction. Having thus effectively abdicated his royalty, he set about at once to ingratiate himself with his recent enemies by returning properties that had been confiscated during the troubles. Among the beneficiaries were the bishop of Zaragoza, who had been the leader of the *Unión*; a throng of *ricoshombres*; and, at a more humble level, the king's personal physician. In a document of January 10, 1288, Alfonso, in Zaragoza, instructed the authorities in Daroca to return to *magistro Guillelmo, fisico nostro*, "Master Guillelmus, our physician," whatever property of his they held by reason of the recent war.[61]

This *Magister Guillelmus*, a personal physician to Alfonso III, was undoubtedly from Aragon. Was he identical to Guillelmus de Aragonia, *medicine sorte magister*? We have seen the evidence from *De pronosticacione sompniorum* that its

60 Charles made this threat good in 1285, when he was crowned king of Aragon in Llers (Catalonia). On the events of this year and the cycle of Occitan political poems about them, see M. de Riquer, *Los trovadores: Historia literaria y textos* (Barcelona, 1975), 3:1590–1600.

61 "Justicie et juratis Daroce: Mandamus vobis quot incontinenti, visis presentibus, restituatis et desemparetis magistro Guillelmo, fisico nostro quidquid ei emparatum vel occupatum tenetis racione guerre preterite; cum nolimus quod aliqui[d] sibi detineatur emparatum seu eciam occupatum occasione dicte guerre. Datum Cesaraguste, IIIIo idus januari." (To the justice and jurors of Daroca: We command you that as soon as you see these present [words] you restore and release to Master Guillelmus, our physician, whatever you hold seized from him or occupied by reason of the recent war, since we do not wish that anything be held, seized from him or occupied, on the occasion of the said war.) González Antón, *Uniones*, 2:347, document 217 (reads *aliqui*); comments, 1:213.

author conversed in 1282 with Pedro III. Apparently Guillelmus enjoyed close relations with his monarch. The philosopher and the beneficiary of Alfonso's act were both physicians, and both were styled *magister*. The match in time and place are as good as may be hoped. Of course there may have been other masters of medicine in Aragon named Guillelmus. Nevertheless, while acknowledging that the evidence for seeing the philosopher Guillelmus de Aragonia in this royal document falls short of decisive, we shall entertain it as plausible.

If this identification is correct, it adds to our meager knowledge of the author of *De nobilitate animi* and other works that he held property in Daroca, which was presumably his home. Daroca was and is located eighty-four kilometers south of Zaragoza on the road to Valencia, and was the site of one of the early sparks that had enflamed Aragon. A wall dating from the twelfth century enclosed Daroca and serves to this day as a reminder that the medieval town was always on a wartime footing.[62] The act of restitution casts Guillelmus in a complex role in difficult times. Even though he was Alfonso's personal physician, he must have joined the *Unión* in rebellion; like his fellow rebels, however, he was soon forgiven by his versatile king.

Against the background of political machinations on all sides, the effort in *De nobilitate animi* to determine the philosophical basis of nobility departs from the particularity of history in order to ascend to the broader realm of truth. We imagine that the physician and philosopher must have found the nobility of Aragon, and the king as well, lacking in the habit of virtuous action. If this interpretation is sound, it provides another reason to think Guillelmus wrote the treatise in the 1280s.

It is possible that the language of *De nobilitate animi* at its sharpest expresses condemnation of abuses that provoked Guillelmus to rebel against Alfonso. In a document of 1280 outlining his procedures as heir apparent, Alfonso, then about fifteen years old, made a commitment to hear pleas on Mondays and to hold council on Tuesday and Friday mornings; but unless there was pressing business he reserved the rest of the week "a son deport e a sa volentat" (for his sport and whatever he wished to do).[63] Guillelmus may have had such a policy in mind when he declared (1.18.7) that if a noble takes so much pleasure in recreation that he postpones the work that pertains to his nobility, "Dico talem usum ad [vi]litatem et bestialem fatuitatem converti" (I say that such usage changes into ignobility and bestial fatuousness). It is possible that Guillelmus was thinking of Alfonso when he condemned sons who destroy the good work of their noble fathers (1.4.15–16). He may have been thinking of Alfonso again

62 "Una sociedad en pie de guerra," according to M. L. Rodrigo Estevan, *La ciudad de Daroca a fines de la edad media: Selección documental, 1328–1526* (Daroca, 1999), 11.

63 F. Soldevila, *Vida de Pere el Gran i d'Alfons el Liberal* (Barcelona, 1963), 346.

when he modified a text from Ecclesiastes (10:16), "Vae tibi terra cuius rex est puer" (Woe to you, land whose king is a boy), by replacing *puer* with *iuvenis*, "youth, unmarried man" (1.6.9); Alfonso remained a *iuvenis* because he never married, and he died at age 26 in 1291. This passage occurs in the chapter "On Nobility of Power" (1.6), immediately after a reflection on the foolishness of kings who "undertake and commit things without reason, and the opposite of what they thought would come about befalls them because of their misguided desire" (1.6.8). Such language could refer to the conflict of 1287.

At the end of the prologue to *De nobilitate animi* Guillelmus expressed the hope that his treatise would inspire readers to a higher ethical standard:

> Intitulatur autem iste liber *De nobilitate animi*, eo quod illa sit potior inter omnes ... (1.0.14)
>
> This book is titled *On Nobility of Mind* in order that nobility may be stronger among all men ...

The word *potior*, "stronger," implies the critical judgment that nobility of mind as Guillelmus witnessed it around him was weak. At the end of the work he repeated his original purpose to enable each man to recognize whether he is noble or ignoble (1.0.13, 2.10.6). Surely, he must have felt, such recognition would strengthen virtuous habits.

Nobility in Philosophy

The medieval notion of nobility was polysemic: applied to mankind, it was taken variously as a theological quality inherent in the human form, a generative property that produced a privileged class of people, a moral way of living and behaving, or the highest degree of human perfection. Nobility was also equated with perfection of nonhuman beings, both organic and inorganic.

De nobilitate animi reflects the transformation of philosophy in the twelfth and thirteenth centuries, when scholars impelled by Averroës' commentaries on Aristotle were drawn to his theory of anthropological naturalism. The Sicilian court of Frederick II was at the origin of this upheaval. Michael Scot, a member of Frederick's court, was both a scientist (an astrologer) and a philosopher; with other members of a team, he translated Averroës' commentaries on Aristotle into Latin. During the 1220s copies of these Latin versions reached the universities at Bologna, Paris, and Oxford.[64] These classic Arab works encouraged

[64] R. A. Gauthier, "Notes sur les débuts (1225–1240) du premier 'averroïsme,'" *Revue des sciences philosophiques et théologiques* 66 (1982): 321–374.

scholars to attend to the cosmos as a natural reality, an object of reason, rather than as an object of faith, as it is in the Bible and patristic theology. Indeed, Averroës declared reason independent of the Koran and placed rational truth on a par with theological truth.[65] By 1250 Averroës' commentaries and the translations of Aristotle that were made in Toledo had brought naturalistic hermeneutics of the cosmos, and particularly of mankind, to the center of European philosophical consideration.

Aristotelian philosophers, physicians, and poets turned away from the traditional notion of man as *homo christianus* or *renatus*, whose natural reality was undervalued in contrast with grace, since his nobility was considered a divine attribute shared with humanity by God. They turned instead toward man as *homo naturalis*, who had his origin and purpose on earth.[66] Deviating from Neoplatonic theories, these thinkers concentrated on what constitutes the value of man as a natural being.[67] Their investigations focused on the *De anima*, Aristotle's study of the form that makes man human, and particularly on the specific activities of the mind—both theoretical activity directed toward truth and practical activity, defined by the Philosopher as "the activity of the soul in conformity with excellence or virtue."[68] But which of the two, theoretical or

65 "Le Coran est pour lui un mode d'accès à la vérité. Pas une vérité. Et là est son programme: décrypter le Coran, y découvrir le moyen de comprendre l'univers, d'en extraire la vérité ... Science et foi sont pour lui autonomes; le rationnel et le révélé ne s'expliquent pas l'un par l'autre, car ils sont extérieurs l'un à l'autre; ils disent chacun à leur manière la vérité ... Pour Averroès, il n'y a en effet qu'une vérité, scientifique, et le Coran n'est pas une vérité en soi mais un guide vers la vérité, qui est scientifique." J. Attali, *Raison et foi: Averroès, Maïmonide, Thomas d'Aquin* ([Paris], 2004), 24–25. For Averroës, see R. Arnaldez, *Averroes: A Rationalist in Islam* (Notre Dame, 2000), 88–89, 116: "Men capable of reflection do not need Qur'anic revelation to know what falls into the category of demonstrative proofs ... It is, however, always the same truth that is apprehended through different channels ... We should fully understand that the testimony of the Book adds nothing to the certitude of demonstrative proof."

66 W. Ullmann, "Some Observations on the Medieval Evaluation of the Homo Naturalis and the Christianus," *L'homme et son destin d'après les penseurs du Moyen Age: Actes du Premier Congrès International de Philosophie Médiévale, Louvain-Bruxelles 28 août-4 septembre 1958* (Louvain, 1960), 145–151.

67 The *Elementatio theologica* by Proclus and the *Liber de causis* by Ibn Daoud, translated by Gherardo da Cremona in the twelfth century, were the most direct sources of emanative Neoplatonic theory, in which God, or *prima Bonitas*, the source of nobility, shares his goodness in all things, although each thing receives it according to its material container. Dante adheres to this theory. "Every substantial form proceeds from its first cause, who is God, as is stated in the *Book of Causes*; each form becomes diverse in individuals not through that cause, which is utterly simple, but through secondary causes and through the matter into which the form descends" (*Convivio* 3.2.4). *Dante: The Banquet*, trans. C. Ryan (Saratoga, Calif., 1989), 81.

68 Aristotle, *Nicomachean Ethics* 1.7 (Bekker 1098a), trans. Ostwald, 17. The turn from theory to practice was motivated by the axiom "Unumquodque operatur secundum quod est" (Manner of action corresponds to manner of being). Scholars asked which object of the soul's activities should be evaluated as the noblest in order to discover the nature of the soul.

practical activity, should be seen as the higher value, capable of bestowing a degree of nobility on men? Even though the notion of nobility by birth, *nobilitas generis*, was widely rejected, philosophers debated whether nobility of mind, *probitas animi*, could exist without being supported by wealth.[69] Scholars who knew Aristotle's notion of *theoria*, or "self-sufficiency," identified nobility with natural beatitude or happiness, an effect of contemplation of truth, the object of theoretical intellectual activity.

The treatise by Guillelmus de Aragonia arose in the midst of this complex evolution. His little book is composed of two parts. In the first, by using arguments drawn from the *Nicomachean Ethics*, he defines nobility of mind as comprising nobility of soul, body, and fortune and shows the superiority of nobility of soul to the other two types. In the second part, employing the rhetorical *argumentum ex auctoritate*, he cites a range of eminent authors in order to demonstrate that his thesis is rooted in their teachings and to enable his reader to distinguish the noble from the ignoble. Like other works attributed to Guillelmus, *De nobilitate animi* is radically Aristotelian.[70] He ignores the concept of nobility expressed by

69 M. del Giudice, "La Contentio de nobilitate generis et animi probitate secondo il codice di Fitalia," *Centro di Studi Filologici e Linguistici Siciliani: Bollettino* 14 (1980): 393–404; comments by M. Corti, *Scritti su Cavalcanti e Dante: La felicità mentale, percorsi dell'invenzione e altri saggi* (Turin, 2003), 76.

70 In the proemium to his commentary on Boethius, Guillelmus synthesizes the ideas that guide his argument in *De nobilitate animi*, including the end of both irrational and rational beings, the specific difference in their activities, and the necessity of education or moral training to enable people to act as humans. The commentary takes the form of an *accessus ad auctores*. Thus the end, or purpose, of Boethius's book (*finis operis*) coincides, for Guillelmus, with Aristotle's principle "Omnia appetunt bonum" (Terbille, 2:1)—"All things seek the good." This same principle is at the foundation of *De nobilitate animi* (1.0.1): "Ex naturali appetitu ad bonum ... movemur" (Out of natural desire ... we are moved to the good). However, the appetitive activity of animals works differently from that of humans: "Alia enim entia determinate et sine errore videntur appetere et persequi bonum suum, homo enim indeterminate et confuse appetit et movetur in bonum" (Terbille, 2:2) [For other beings seem to seek and pursue their good in a defined way and without error, but man seeks the good and is moved to it in an undefined way and confusedly]. In *De nobilitate animi* the author points out (1.3.21) the cause of moral confusion, which is the combination of irrational and rational activities in the same subject, and states that in order to eliminate confusion the sensitive part of man must submit to intellectual power: "Pars sensitiva in homine ... debet intellectui deservire" (The sensitive part in man ... must serve the intellect). Guillelmus goes on (1.3.23) to identify the sensitive activity in man with an action in itself defective or unhealthy that is generated from ignorance: "Defectus in accione circumstancie non est nisi ex defectu electionis in contemplacione ipsarum circumstantiarum, que nichil aliud est quam ignorantia in agendo." (A defect in action can only result from a defect of some circumstance or circumstances that inform action; and a defect of a circumstance in an action can only result from a defect of choice in the contemplation of those same circumstances, which is nothing other than ignorance in acting.) Although the wording is different, the two works agree about the corrective of *confusio* or *ignorantia*. In the commentary this corrective is described as follows: "Unde inter alia entia solus homo indiget exercitio in agendo et doctrina in eligendo ut directe et sine errore in bonum proprium moveatur" (Terbille, 2:2) [Whence among other beings only man lacks exercise in acting and doctrine in choosing so that he might be moved directly and

the Neoplatonic philosophers and theologians,[71] and he welcomes Plato's principles insofar as Aristotle adopted them.[72] Although he does not identify the addressee of his treatise, we may speculate that as a physician he intended to promote a morally healthy society. His motivation appears to have been sociopolitical: to show that moral education is the only remedy for the disease of human nature.

without error toward his own good]. In *De nobilitate animi* it is described (1.3.15) as "sapientia in speculando et studiositas in agendo" (wisdom in reflection and studiousness in action). In both works the author reveals his Aristotelian convictions. In the commentary he states, "Ad utilitatem igitur talium librum Boethii ... proposui legere ... quae in eo disputantur evidenter edocent quemlibet inter bona discernere et ad quod bonum debent homines dirigere corpus et mentem" (Terbille, 2:3) [Therefore for the utility of such men I have proposed to read the book of Boethius ... (since) the things that are discussed in it evidently teach anyone to discern among good things and to what good thing men must direct body and mind"]. In *De nobilitate animi* (1.3.26) he writes, "Oportet hominem esse bonum et bene in actibus moralibus connutritum antequam possit vel debeat dici sapiens" (A man must be good and well nourished in moral acts before he can or should be called wise). On the proemium, see also Pack, 239–240; Crespo, "Il prologo"; Olmedilla Herrero, "Un accessus medieval," 715–717; English translation in Minnis et al., *Medieval Literary Theory and Criticism*, 328–331.

71 According to Thomas Aquinas (*Summa Contra Gentiles* 1.70), "Gradus nobilitatis et vilitatis in omnibus entibus attenditur secundum propinquitatem et distantiam a Deo, qui est in fine nobilitatis" (The degree of either nobility or ignobility in all things must be measured according to their propinquity or distance from God, who is at the summit of nobility). At the end of *De nobilitate animi* (2.10.7) Guillelmus prays, "Laudetur altissimus ... a quo fluit omnis nobilitas et in quem omnis actio nobilis terminatur" (Praised be the Highest ... from whom flows all nobility and in whom every noble action has its end).

72 In the commentary on Boethius, Guillelmus meticulously analyzes Prose 9 of the *Philosophiae consolatio* in order to reverse the Platonic Christian reading, probably that of Chartrean readers. Thus for Guillelmus the *omnium Patrem*, "Father of all things," is not the biblical God, but the *virtus regulativa*, the "regulating force," of all beings (Terbille, 2:123), the author of nature, the Aristotelian *causam efficientem omnium*, "efficient cause of all things" (124). This principle continues throughout the analysis. The commentator underlines that Boethius interpreted Plato's ideology correctly—that is, as it was understood and explicated by Aristotle. Guillelmus concludes the analysis as follows: "Ita legendo declarationem illam, littera est satis plana et sententia non obscura. Nec imponemus Boethio Platonicorum crimina, quia valde bene Aristotelem intellexit" (Terbille, 2:135). [So, reading that declaration, the letter is plain enough and the sentence not obscure. Let us not impose upon Boethius the crimes of the Platonic (philosophers), since he understood Aristotle very well.] See also P. Courcelle, "Étude critique sur les Commentaires de la Consolation de Boèce (IXe–XVe siècles)," *AHMA* 12 (1939): 101. Guillelmus accepts Platonic principles if these are included in Aristotle's philosophic system, as in the Aristotelian reference at *De nobilitate animi* 1.3.23: "Malus est ignorans ita quod per ignorantiam contigit actionum malicia" (An evil man must be ignorant because evil actions occur through ignorance). It is true, as Nardi points out, that Aristotle in his *Ethics* deals with the soul's *aegritudines* caused by natural passions; however, Plato had used this medical language in the *Timaeus*. See B. Nardi, "L'amore e i medici medievali," *Saggi e note di critica dantesca* (Milan, 1966), 245.

The originality of Guillelmus's thesis lies in his concept of nobility as a *habitus acquisitus*, an "acquired habit."[73] From the beginning of the treatise he states firmly that nobility is not an innate virtue, a natural property of the soul, but a habit earned by practicing virtuous deeds. Nobility is an outcome of moral education: beginning in childhood, people must go through a process of learning the value of moral virtues and then exercise them freely and consistently in order to achieve the *habitus*, the golden crown of human worthiness. The effective function of the *habitus* is presented (1.1.4) as an Aristotelian active agent, or *actus*, that has the power of actualizing the soul's potential, disposing it toward achieving its proper good: "Per habitum autem quilibet dispositus est ad bene operandum" (Out of habit one is disposed to acting well). Nobility is like a garment (*habitus*, "a style of dress" [*OLD*]) whose fabric is woven of all the moral virtues that enrich and direct the mind by inclining it to act rationally and honestly. The opposite of nobility is ignobility (*vilitas*). Both are habits acquired by acting, whether virtuously or viciously. Both stimulate practical activity and solicit the actor to move, respectively, toward good or evil: "Habitus movet potentiam ad opus" (Habit moves potential to action). This diagnosis of ignobility shows that it is a pathological disorder, *ignorantia*, caused by the *pars sensitiva*, both internal and external sensation, which clouds the light of the mind and instigates it to act viciously.[74]

The critical issue of nobility seen as a *habitus acquisitus* comes under close scrutiny in the chapter entitled "De nobilitate anime" (1.3) and throughout the ten *questiones* (1.9–18). The author clarifies the notion of *habitus* as related to

73 This notion of nobility as a habit rather than an innate property of the human form can be traced directly to the *Nicomachean Ethics* 2.1 (Bekker 1103a25): "The virtues are implanted in us neither by nature nor contrary to nature: we are by nature equipped with the ability to receive them, and habit brings this ability to completion and fulfillment" (trans. Ostwald, 33). Aristotle answers "the problem raised at the opening of Plato's *Meno* (70a) whether excellence is acquired by teaching, by practice, or by nature" (Ostwald, 33 n. 1).

74 Expanding on the citation from Algazel in 1.3.20, Guillelmus writes (1.3.21–23), "Et causa huius est quia pars sensitiva in homine, que est proprium subjectum et principium passionum, debet intellectui deservire, passiones relinquens. Unde si passiones insequitur et ad se trahit intellectum et in bestialem operationem declinat, tunc cessat operatio intellectus, quare nec acquiritur sapientia passionibus non domatis. E contrario etiam intelligit Aristoteles tertio *Ethycorum* ubi dicit quod malus est ignorans, ita quod per ignorantiam contingit actionum malicia." (And the cause of this is that the sensitive part in man, which is the proper subject and source of feelings, must leave feelings aside to serve the intellect. So if it obeys feelings and draws the intellect to itself and declines into animal activity, then the activity of the intellect ceases, which is why wisdom is not acquired unless the feelings have been tamed. In the third book of the *Ethics* Aristotle explains this by the contrary when he says that an evil man must be ignorant because evil actions occur through ignorance, and the cause of this is that a defect in action can only result from a defect of some one or of some circumstances that inform action; and a defect of a circumstance in an action can only result from a defect of choice in the contemplation of those same circumstances, which is nothing other than ignorance in acting.)

various categories of people (children, women, politicians) and adds an explanation of nobility in animals (1.18). Regarding human nobility, he finds that among the three immanent activities of the soul, practical activity (*operari*) and speculative intelligence (*sapientia* or *intelligere*) are "the noblest and best" (1.3.10). He concludes (1.3.11–12) that those must be judged noble who "rejoice in intellectual operations and live by them" (Vere nobiles debent iudicari qui intellectualibus operationibus gaudent et vivunt), and adding, "Such are philosophers and wise men" (Tales autem sunt philosophantes et sapientes). Guillelmus avers with his master that intellectual excellence consists in contemplative activity, the theoretical knowledge whose object is absolute truth. However, he seems to give his own interpretation of Aristotle's statement, "A man whose activity is guided by intelligence, who cultivates his intelligence and keeps it in the best condition, seems to be most beloved by the gods."[75] For Guillelmus, too, a man must "cultivate his intelligence and keep it in the best condition." He holds that speculative activity is so closely connected to practical wisdom that one cannot be accomplished without the other. He defines *nobilitas* as the combination of these two activities and labels them, respectively, "wisdom in exploring the truth" and "studiousness in action": "Nobilitas igitur anime nichil aliud est quam sapientia in speculando et studiositas in agendo" (1.3.15). But which of these two activities should be given priority? Guillelmus stands for *studiositas in agendo*, which he presents as the *sine qua non* of *sapientia in speculando*.[76] The references to Plato, Boethius, and Algazel help the reader to understand the view that intelligence cannot explore the truth unless it is clean of "filthy morals." They are made clean by the acquired habit of acting rationally ("vitam regulare secundum rationem"), which enables the intellect to "speculate unimpeded, to seek truth in things, and finally to attain wisdom": "ut intellectus non impeditus valeat speculari, et in entibus querere veritatem et finaliter attingere sapientiam" (1.3.28). Guillelmus portrays an ideal society of citizens whose worthiness results from serious moral education. By consistently acting according to reason from childhood onward, people acquire a moral habit that helps them to see the light of practical wisdom, to follow it, and through it to gain theoretical wisdom.

This vision involves ideas shared with other writers, such as nobility seen as a virtuous way of living and behaving. In order to suggest the position of

[75] *Nicomachean Ethics* 10.9 (Bekker 1179a23–24), trans. Ostwald, 294; compare *De nobilitate animi* 1.3.3.

[76] The word *studiositas* maintained the classical meaning of Latin *studere* or *studiosus*, which describe a person who is thoughtful in manner. *Studiositas* corresponds to Aristotle's *spoudaios*, describing "a person who has a sense of the importance of living his life well and of fulfilling his function in society in accordance with the highest standards" (Ostwald, 314).

De nobilitate animi in its field of discourse, we shall sketch its relation to other texts on the same subject, beginning with Andreas Capellanus, who was a naturalist like Guillelmus but not an Aristotelian, and was active in northern France around 1185, and Brunetto Latini, who was an Aristotelian but not a naturalist, an Italian who wrote in French but died in Florence in 1294.

For Andreas, natural love (*passio innata*) is the source of moral virtue, which is a common theme of the troubadours.[77] He describes such love as a pedagogical device, providentially designed to make "the hirsute barbarian as handsome as can be: it can even enrich the lowest-born with nobility of manners."[78] In other words, people are endowed by nature with eroticism, an educational, innate energizer that stimulates a man to acquire excellence and to behave chivalrously in order to conquer a noble lady, or a lady to win the love of a deserving man. The ultimate purpose of acquiring nobility, as portrayed in the first part of the *De amore*, is to conquer a partner and develop an extramarital relationship. This concept of nobility differs from what it means for Guillelmus. In *De nobilitate animi* nobility stems not from a *passio innata* that involves two persons of differing sex but from an ethical obligation of the political state, which is compelled to help society acquire nobility through moral training. This pedagogical system must start operating on the social body from childhood in order to generate citizens who act honestly out of habit. Ethical education is specifically aimed at taming natural drives or *passio innata*, which people have in common with beasts (1.3.2): "Communes sunt quibus [anima] communicat plantis et bestiis universis" (The common [activities of the soul] are those by which it communicates with all plants and beasts).[79]

77 "The claim that artfully fashioned words of love are a source of value goes back to the beginnings of Occitan poetry" in Guilhem de Peitieu, *Pos vezem de novel florir*, according to L. Paterson, "*Fin'amor* and the Development of the Courtly Canso," *Troubadours*, 28. According to P. Cherchi, *Andreas and the Ambiguity of Courtly Love* (Toronto, 1994), ix, "Andreas was not a codifier of courtly love but an adverse interpreter who, in order to carry out his polemic, chose to mimic courtly lovers in the hope of unmasking their supposed deceitfulness." On Andreas's intention to construct "a discourse on love in the new, emerging scholastic mode," a discourse that inevitably undermined "the very elements of troubadour idealism," see D. A. Monson, *Andreas Capellanus, Scholasticism, and the Courtly Tradition* (Washington, D.C., 2005), 4, 343.

78 P. G. Walsh, ed., *Andreas Capellanus on Love* (London, 1982), 39, §1.

79 Later in his treatise Andreas reverses his previous assumption about *passio innata*, splitting his concept of love into two ideas: *purus amor*, which has "such virtue that the source of all moral worth derives from it" (Walsh, *Andreas Capellanus*, 181, §472), and *amor mixtus*, "which affords its outlet to every pleasure of the flesh" (181, §474). Although he emphasizes the negative aspect of *amor mixtus*, Andreas states that it is "true and merits praise" (ibid.). Only in the third book, *De reprobatione amoris*, does Andreas recant his previous ideology and extol the value of *purus amor.*

Like Guillelmus de Aragonia, Brunetto Latini makes effective use of Aristotle's *Ethics* in order to establish a solid foundation for human worth.[80] Brunetto sets forth the Aristotelian notion of nobility as an outcome of "all instruction which exhorts a man to perform works of virtue" and "to keep away from vice."[81] However, contrary to Guillelmus's naturalism, Brunetto reads Aristotle in the light of biblical and theological tradition. Thus the soul "was created at the very moment it enters the body," so that its "good is worthier ... because it is a good from God, and its form is known only through virtuous works."[82] For Brunetto the virtuous person is someone whose virtues are implanted naturally rather than acquired and performed as a habit. His concept of contemplative virtue is described theologically as having "three parts, that is, faith, hope, and charity."[83] The noble man described in the *Livres dou Tresor* is a *homo christianus* whose intrinsic worthiness consists in acting honestly according to Christian faith.

Finally we shall compare *De nobilitate animi* to the work of three authors who were contemporaries of Guillelmus de Aragonia and, like him, radical Aristotelians: Boethius of Dacia, Jacobus de Pistorio, and the poet-philosopher Guido Guinizelli. The first two identify nobility with Aristotelian *theoria* and agree that the supreme beatitude results from theoretical and practical activities that involve the sensitive faculties and the soul. According to Boethius of Dacia, nobility culminates in "the knowledge of truth, the performance of good works, and the enjoyment of both" (cognitio veri et operatio boni et delectatio in utroque).[84] This high achievement turns man into a true noble and makes him worthy of honor. Jacobus de Pistorio comes closer to Guillelmus de Aragonia in his theory of the relationship between the sensitive faculties and the soul. Referring to the *Nicomachean Ethics*, Jacobus holds that in order to contemplate the truth clearly, humans must have a "healthy body" (corpus sanum) free from the affections of the sensitive faculties.[85] Jacobus's discourse is speculative

80 An Aragonese translation of Brunetto's *Livres dou Tresor* is extant in a single copy (not the original), dated 1425–1450. See D. Prince, ed., *Text and Concordance of the Aragonese Translation of Brunetto Latini's "Li livres dou tresor": Gerona Cathedral, MS 20-a-5*, four microfiches with a Guide (Madison, Wis., 1990). On the date of the copy, see the Guide, 6–7.

81 Brunetto Latini, *Li Livres dou Tresor* 2.54, ed. S. Baldwin and P. Barrette (Tempe, Ariz., 2003), 207. Brunetto Latini, *The Book of the Treasure (Li Livres dou Tresor)*, trans. P. Barrette and S. Baldwin (New York, 1993), 196.

82 *Li Livres dou Tresor* 1.14.3, 2.7.1, ed. Baldwin and Barrette, 12, 156; trans. Barrette and Baldwin, 11, 148. See also Brunetto's notion of religion in *Li Livres dou Tresor* 2.98.

83 *Li Livres dou Tresor* 2.56.1, ed. Baldwin and Barrette, 209; trans. Barrette and Baldwin, 198.

84 M. Grabmann, ed., "Opusculum Magistri Boetii Daci: De summo bono sive de vita philosophi," *Mittelalterliches Geistesleben* (Munich, 1936), 2:211.

85 "Licet autem omnes affectiones et passiones appetitus sensiviti sint precipua impediencia." P. O. Kristeller, ed., "A Philosophical Treatise from Bologna Dedicated to Guido Cavalcanti: Magister Jacobus de Pistorio and His Questio de Felicitate," *Medioevo e Rinascimento: Studi in onore di Bruno Nardi* (Florence, 1955), 1:454. Jacobus refers to Aristotle's *Ethics*, Books 2, 7, and 10.

rather than practical; his focus falls on *theoria*, the noblest human activity that makes a man happy. For him the contemplation of truth turns earthly life into an ecstatic reality.

In his poem *Al cor gentil*, which is a small treatise on nobility, Guido Guinizelli follows the Averroistic philosophers who claimed that nature is independent from grace and philosophy from theology.[86] Nature is the mother of human forms; human activities, both theoretical (symbolized as *il sole*, the sun) and practical (virtue, which descends from the sun), are portrayed as the instruments by which humans reach their proper actualization. However, the poet stresses the distinction between noble and depraved nature. The former is enlightened by the sun of Aristotelian *theoria* and receives power from it; the latter is deprived of the light of science and virtue, indeed diametrically opposed to them both. Guinizelli's theory includes a kind of determinism: nobility is an exclusive privilege of those who were born of a healthy Mother Nature. The poet rejects the possibility for less privileged individuals to move from an inferior to a superior state in life.

In *De nobilitate animi* Guillelmus de Aragonia develops a thesis substantially different from the arguments made by these contemporaries. Contrary to Boethius of Dacia and Jacobus de Pistorio, he is not concerned with nobility as *theoria* or beatitude, the highest degree to which human nature is capable of being actualized. His emphasis falls instead on nobility through practical wisdom, which he sees as the result of ethical education. Whereas Jacobus de Pistorio is concerned with ethics as a way to emancipate human nature from the disorder of the senses in order to enjoy the vision of truth, Guillelmus acknowledges that moral discords are impediments but goes to their root and proposes a remedy: an education that must evolve constantly until it produces the habit of nobility. Finally, contrary to Guido Guinizelli, Guillelmus regards nobility not as a privilege restricted to a few but as a potential shared among all members of society. In his view, not only those born of noble nature but also those born of depraved nature may be trained from childhood so as to acquire the habit of living and acting nobly.

Nobility in Rhetoric

Because of the dominant role of aristocracy in society, the ongoing changes in its structure, and the intellectual and ethical challenges posed by those changes, the concept of nobility held compelling interest. This interest motivated the cultivation of topoi, or rhetorical commonplaces. The topos to which Guillelmus

86 G. Contini, ed., *Poeti del Duecento* (Milan, 1960), 2:460–464.

de Aragonia subscribed was that of *nobilitas animi*, also called *nobilitas animae* or *mentis* or *morum*, nobility of mind or soul or conduct, which can be traced back to Greek antiquity and forward to Dante and beyond.[87] In Latin the thought occurs among the *Sententiae* of Publilius Syrus:

> Virum bonum natura, non ordo facit. (5.15)
>
> Nature, not rank, makes a man good.

in the epistles of Seneca:

> Animus facit nobilem. (44.5)
>
> Mind makes a noble.

in the satires of Juvenal:

> Tota licet veteres exornent undique cerae
> atria, nobilitas sola est atque unica virtus. (8.19)
>
> Even though old waxen images [of ancestors] may everywhere adorn halls, the sole and unique nobility is virtue.

and in Boethius:

> Iam uero quam sit inane, quam futtile nobilitatis nomen, quis non uideat? ... Quodsi quid est in nobilitate bonum, id esse arbitror solum, ut imposita nobilibus necessitudo uideatur ne a maiorum uirtute degeneret. (3.6.7)
>
> Who seeth not what a vain and idle thing it is to be called noble? ... But if there be anything good in nobility, I judge it only to be this, that it imposeth a necessity upon those which are noble, not to suffer their nobility to degenerate from the virtue of their ancestors.[88]

87 Colker, 47, referring to Epicharmus, Euripides, and others quoted by Stobaeus, *Florilegium*, ed. A. Meineke, vol. 3 (Leipzig, 1856), 154–155. On the topos, see Colker 47–49; E. R. Curtius, *European Literature and the Latin Middle Ages* (New York, 1963), 179–180; W. C. McDonald, "The Nobility of Soul: Uncharted Echoes of the Peraldean Tradition in Late Medieval German Literature," *Deutsche Vierteljarhrsschrift für Literaturwissenschaft und Geistesgeschichte* 60 (1986): 543–571. Rubinstein (*Studies in Italian History*, 1:189), referring to *Convivio* 4, notes that "for Dante true nobility is nobility of the soul."

88 *The Consolation of Philosophy*, trans. I. T. (1609), rev. H. F. Stewart (Cambridge, Mass., 1962), 249.

Seneca's brief formulation generated the concise phrase *nobilitas animi*, which echoed in Rabanus Maurus in the ninth century, Alphanus of Salerno in the tenth, and, in the twelfth, in Marbod of Rennes, Alan of Lille, and Matthew of Vendôme.[89] Juvenal's assertion that virtue is the only nobility was remembered in the twelfth century by Hildebert of Tours, Petrus Cantor, and by the authors of sentences and proverbs.[90] Petrus Cantor blended the Senecan phrase into Juvenal's line, producing a more quotable version than the original since he made it fit into a hexameter:

> Nobilitas animi sola est atque unica virtus.[91]
>
> Nobility of mind is the sole and unique virtue.

In the fourteenth century the topos would enter Occitan:

> Veraya nobleza ven ad home de cor franc.[92]
>
> True nobility comes to a man from a noble heart.

By his choice of theme and title Guillelmus de Aragonia inscribed his work in an honorable tradition.

89 Rabanus Maurus, *Commentaria in Exodum* 4.23, *PL* 108: 244d: "Non enim Deus nobilitatem carnis, sed nobilitatem animi pensat" (For God does not weigh nobility of flesh but nobility of mind). Alphanus of Salerno, *Carmina* 31, *Sermo ad clerum in laudem Vincentii martyris*, *PL* 147: 1248b: "Nos instruat ista virilis / nobilitas animi" (Let that manly nobility of mind instruct us). Marbod of Rennes, *Carmina* 22, *M. episcopus R. archidiacono* 1566, *PL* 171: 1659b: "Tu bonus ... / quem sic commendat nobilitas animi" (You, a good man, ... whom thus nobility of mind commends). Alan of Lille, *Anticlaudianus* 9.7, *PL* 210: 573b: "Cur bella movere / quaeris in imbelles? satis est potuisse, nec ultra / nobilitas animi quaerat, nisi vincere posse." (Why do you seek to make war against those unfit for war? It is enough to have been able; let nobility of mind not seek further than to be able to conquer.) Matthew of Vendôme, *Ars versificatoria* 1.27, ed. E. Faral, *Les arts poétiques du XIIe et du XIIIe siècle* (Paris, 1962), 116: "Virtus nobilitat animum" (Virtue ennobles the mind).

90 Hildebert, *Moralis philosophia, Quaestio* 3, *PL* 171: 1043b: "Si autem veram requiris nobilitatem, audi poetam Juvenalem: Nobilitas [animi] sola est atque unica virtus." (But if you seek true nobility, hear the poet Juvenal: "Nobility of mind is the sole and unique virtue.") Walther 17031: "Nobilitas sola est atque unica virtus." Walther 17037a: "Nobilitat virtus" (Virtue makes [one] noble).

91 Petrus Cantor, *Verbum abbreviatum* 10, *PL* 205: 47d. Dante quotes this version of Juvenal in *Monarchia* 2.3.4, ed. P. G. Ricci (Milan, 1965), 176.

92 *Vices et vertus*, in *TPMA*, s.v. "Adel," 6.2.1.138; on the date, see K. Baldinger, *Complément bibliographique au "Provenzalische Supplementwörterbuch" de Emil Levy: Sources—Datations* (Genève, 1983), 380. Anticipated in the thirteenth century by the troubadour Sordel, who contrasted the *noble cor*, or "noble heart," with *gentillesa*, "high birth," in his *Ensenhamen d'onor*, vv. 632–640, ed. M. Boni, *Sordello: Le poesie* (Bologna, 1954), 217.

The claim for nobility of mind is intrinsically idealistic. It is dialogic by implication, responding to the more realistic claim for nobility of birth, wealth, or power, as Publilius Syrus made clear (see above) with his reference to *ordo*, "rank," and as Juvenal did with his mention of *veteres cerae*, "old waxen images," both referring to nobility by birth. The topos of nobility of mind confronted its opposite, called *nobilitas carnis* or *corporis* or, most frequently, *generis*, nobility of the flesh, body, or birth.[93] The latter claim is as ancient as the claim for nobility of mind. *Nobilitas* always ranged in meaning from the realistic to the idealistic, from "nobility of rank or birth" or "the aristocracy, the nobles," to "loftiness of character, nobility, heroism," or "superior quality, nobility, excellence" (*OLD*). Seneca uses *nobilitas* for nobility in the pragmatic sense:

> Vides autem divitiis, nobilitate, viribus quam multi male utantur. (*Epistles* 120.3)
>
> But you see how many people make poor use of wealth, nobility, and strength.

Both Seneca and Juvenal relate the noble class by metonymy to their spacious courts:

> Non facit nobilem atrium plenum fumosis imaginibus. (*Epistles* 44.5)
>
> A hall full of grimy old images does not make one noble.

> Tu nobilium magna atria curas? (*Satires* 7.90)
>
> Do you frequent the great halls of nobles?

The implication is double: one should not care about the wealth of nobles, but at the same time those whom we call noble do indeed have wealth.

In the time of Guillelmus de Aragonia there were sentences or proverbs proclaiming that wealth makes nobility:

93 *Nobilitas carnis*: Rabanus Maurus, above. *Nobilitas corporis*: Martin of Braga, *De moribus* 4, *PL* 72: 30d: "Nobilitas animi est generositas sensus; nobilitas corporis, generosus animus." (Nobility of mind is generosity of sense; nobility of body, a generous mind.) *Nobilitas generis*: Augustine (auctor incertus), *Ad fratres in eremo commorantes* 23, *PL* 40: 1274: "Ad regnum enim coelorum non conducit nos gloria mundi, non multitudo divitiarum, non nobilitas generis, non scientia, non sapientia, non facundia verborum" (Not glory of the world, not a multitude of wealth, not nobility of birth, not knowledge, not wisdom, not eloquence leads us to the kingdom of heaven).

Nobilitant gazae privatos nobilitate. (Werner N 85)

Riches ennoble citizens with nobility.

Nobilitas cum re pro nobilitate tenetur;
Nobilitas sine re pro rusticitate tenetur. (Werner N 86)

Nobility with possessions is considered nobility;
nobility without possessions is considered rusticity.

Nobilitas sine re non est nisi nomen inane. (Werner N 90)

Nobility without possessions is but an empty name.

There was even the odd proverb to the effect that nobility could be gained by cultivating the approval of the crowd:

Nobiliter vives, si placabis tibi cives. (Werner N 94)

You will live nobly, if you reconcile citizens to yourself.

In the Latin translations of Aristotle that Guillelmus de Aragonia knew well, it is the realistic view of nobility that predominates. Thus in *Politica* 3.13 (Bekker 1283a37), according to the translation by Guillelmus de Moerbeke:

Ingenuitas enim est virtus generis.[94]

For good birth is virtue of birth.

To this the *Auctoritates Aristotelis* (15.63) added a gloss:

Ingenuitas est virtus generis, id est nobilitas.

Good birth is virtue of birth, that is, nobility.

Guillelmus de Moerbeke returns to *ingenuitas* in *Politica* 4.8 (Bekker 1294a21–22):

Ingenuitas enim est virtus et divitiae antiquae.[95]

Good birth is virtue and ancient wealth.

This passage was also glossed in the *Auctoritates* (15.72):

94 *AL* 29.2, p. 203, line 11: "Good birth is excellence of race" (*CW* 2036).

95 *AL* 29.2, p. 409, lines 10–11: "The fourth, what is called good birth, is the result of the two last, being only ancient wealth and excellence" (*CW* 2054).

> Ingenuitas et nobilitas sunt virtutes et divitiae antiquae.
>
> Good birth and nobility are virtues and ancient wealth.

And again *Politica* 5.1 (Bekker 1301b40–1302a1):

> Nobilitas enim et virtus in paucis.[96]
>
> For nobility and virtue [are] in few.

Echoed in the *Auctoritates* (15.84):

> Nobilitas et virtus in paucis inveniuntur.
>
> Nobility and virtue are found in few.

Guillelmus de Moerbeka also translated the *Rhetoric*:

> Est enim nobile quidem secundum generis virtutem, generosum autem secundum non degenerasse a natura; quod quidem ut in pluribus non accidit nobilibus, sed sunt multi levis valori.[97]
>
> For one is noble by the virtue of birth and generous if one has not degenerated from nature; which does not happen in many nobles, but many are of slight value.

The Pseudo-Aristotelian *Rhetorica ad Alexandrum*, which Guillelmus de Aragonia attributed to Aristotle,[98] refers in the original Greek to the themes of personal nobility and good birth:

> If there is nothing reputable in the ancestry of the subject of your eulogy, you must insist on his personal nobility and suggest that all those who have a natural predisposition for excellence are well born ...[99]

But the Latin versions avoid referring to *nobilitas animi*:

96 *AL* 29.2, p. 501, line 1: "Good birth and excellence are rare" (*CW* 2067).

97 Aristotle, *Rhetoric* 2.5 (Bekker 1390b20), *AL* 31.1–2, p. 250, line 31 to p. 251, line 1: "Being well-born, which means coming of a fine stock, must be distinguished from nobility, which means being true to the family nature—a quality not usually found in the well-born, most of whom are poor creatures" (*CW* 2215).

98 *De nobilitate animi* 2.5.3, 2.8.2.

99 *Rhetoric to Alexander* 36 (Bekker 1441a6), *CW* 2305. Mentioned by Colker, 47.

> Si vero nihil gloriosum a progenitoribus sit, dic quod ipse est bene meritus ostendens, quod benefici sunt omnes, qui ad virtutem adherent. (Version Alpha)[100]
>
> But if there is nothing glorious from the ancestors, say that he himself [the subject of your praise] is deserving by showing that they are all generous who cleave to virtue.
>
> Si vero nihil a parentibus gloriosum existat, dic, quod ipse est strenuus, concordando, quod bene facti sunt, qui bene virtutem sequuntur. (Version Beta)[101]
>
> But if nothing glorious from the ancestors appears, say that he himself is vigorous by agreeing that they are well made who follow virtue well.

In this passage the Greek text refers to "personal nobility," that is, *nobilitas animi*, and the quality of being "well born," that is, *nobilitas generis*. But the Latin versions avoid any such reference: Alpha substitutes *bene meritus* for "personal nobility," and *benefici* for being "well born"; similarly, Beta substitutes *strenuus* and *bene facti*. In neither Alpha nor Beta is there a palpable concept of nobility by merit or birth. We conclude that the Aristotle known to Guillelmus de Aragonia expressed the view of nobility by birth but not by merit. In making his central claim Guillelmus departed from his master's teaching.[102]

Though the notion of *nobilitas animi* was idealistic, it would be a mistake to consider it empty rhetoric, a superficial ornament draped over a firmly established reality of nobility by birth in contemporary society.[103] We may be tempted to assume that in late thirteenth-century Aragon and throughout Europe at this time nobility was already stable and sharply defined in the law, as it would become in the fourteenth and fifteenth centuries and remain until the age of revolutions. In the time of Guillelmus de Aragonia, however, nobility was neither stable nor sharply defined in the law. By arguing that nobility accrues from mind, Guillelmus laid a claim on his reader's sense of social ethics at a time when the issue had not yet been settled in practice.

100 Ed. Grabmann, 69–70: *meritus*, "deserving, meritorious" (*OLD*); *beneficus*, "beneficent, kind, generous" (*OLD*).

101 Ed. Stapleton, 226.

102 Rubinstein (*Studies in Italian History*, 190) notes that "Aristotle, who did not consider nobility as such a separate element of the state, did not intend to formulate a theory of nobility, but for thirteenth-century schoolmen, he did precisely that."

103 *Pace* McDonald, "The Nobility of Soul," 546, and Rubinstein, *Studies in Italian History*, 193.

As we have said, in relation to the agitated philosophical scene, Guillelmus was a vigorous debater. In relation to the turbulent social scene, he was an idealist and an activist. No wonder he joined the revolt.

Citations

De nobilitate animi is studded with citations that name a wide range of authorities.[104] Defining his subject in the first part, Guillelmus develops his argument by citing Aristotle most frequently, but he also refers to other thinkers who wrote in Hebrew, Greek, Latin, and Arabic. In the second part he cites various authors to show that his thesis echoes their thought. Taking both parts together, he mentions the philosophers Aristotle, Plato, Socrates, and Boethius; the wise King Solomon; the physician Galen; the astronomers Ptolemy, Alfraganus, and Algazel; the naturalist Pliny; the historian Sallust; the orators Demosthenes and Cicero; and the poets David (author of the Psalms), Horace, Juvenal, Boethius, "Cato" (that is, Pseudo-Cato, the unknown author of the *Disticha Catonis*), and several troubadours. All these sources except the troubadours were available to him in Latin versions that we assume he used.

His sources are primarily writers of Greek or Roman antiquity and the early Middle Ages. The Arabic writers he cites lived from the ninth century (Alfraganus) to the twelfth (Algazel). The troubadours lived in the twelfth century, either early (Jaufre Rudel) or late, at the apex of the movement (Folquet de Marseille, Arnaut de Mareuil, Peire Vidal), or in the thirteenth century: Guilhem de Montanhagol was active from 1233 to 1268.[105] Guillelmus cites no Spanish writer except Isidore of Seville. Nor does he cite any writer by name who wrote in Spanish, Italian, or French, although he may allude to Brunetto Latini, the Florentine philosopher who wrote in French during his exile from 1260 to 1267, including a stay in Montpellier. He quotes Latin proverbs from anonymous rustics; he bows to popular usage in his definition of nobility (1.1.8), although he is wary of popular misconceptions (1.16.4–5).

Guillelmus embeds his authors within his own discourse in a manner that varies from precise citation, in which the quotation retains its independent status, to dynamic interaction, in which it blends into its new context. In this variety of treatment he is typical of his age. Narrative works composed in Occitan in the thirteenth and fourteenth centuries cited troubadours as authorities analogous to traditional ones from the Bible, the Latin classics, or

[104] See "Index of Sources and Analogues."

[105] Riquer, *Los trovadores*, 1:148, 1:583, 2:647, 2:858, 3:1429.

the allegory of love (*fin'amors*, "true love").[106] Early in the thirteenth century Raimon Vidal of Besalù, in Catalonia, integrated troubadour lyrics logically and naturally into his own narrative verse to illustrate a point, to justify one, or to serve as moral guides.[107] Guillelmus's contemporary Matfre Ermengaud of Béziers wrote his encyclopedic *Breviari d'amor* (Breviary of Love) from 1288 to about 1292. Quoting hundreds of passages from the troubadours, Matfre blurred the distinction between his their voices and his own:

> He speaks of the troubadours, and for them, and makes them speak, but they also speak for him. He shapes their words and they his ... The boundaries between text and quotations are far less important than the concourse of subjects.[108]

The freedom with which Guillelmus treats quotations reflects rhetorical doctrine. Quintilian advised the orator to adapt the proverb or sentençe to his own purpose.[109] Alan of Lille, in the twelfth century, was no doubt thinking of writing on wax tablets when he declared, "An authority has a wax nose; that is, it can be bent in various directions."[110] The distinction between self and other underlies the modern distinction between proverb and sentence, two notions that were largely continuous in the Middle Ages, as we see in the title of Hans Walther's compendium *Proverbia sententiaeque latinitatis medii aevi*. When Lord Russell, in the nineteenth century, defined the proverb as "One man's wit and all men's wisdom," he amalgamated sentence and proverb even as he distinguished wittily between them.[111]

106 F. Vielliard, "Auteur et autorité dans la littérature occitane médiévale non lyrique," *Auctor et auctoritas: Invention et conformisme dans l'écriture médiévale, Actes du colloque tenu à l'Université de Versailles-Saint-Quentin-en-Yvelines, 14–16 juin 1999* (Paris, 2001), 375–389.

107 H.-E. Keller, "*La Cort d'Amors* de Raimon Vidal et ses citations," *Literatur, Geschichte und Verstehen: Festschrift für Ulrich Mölk zum 60. Geburtstag* (Heidelberg, 1997), 185–192.

108 S. Kay, "How Long is a Quotation? Quotations from the Troubadours in the Text and Manuscripts of the *Breviari d'amor*," *Romania* 127 (2009): 22.

109 "Proverbia opportune aptata": Quintilian, *Institutio Oratoria* 6.3.98, ed. D. A. Russell. Russell translates as "Proverbs which are to the point" (3:114); we prefer "Proverbs fittingly adapted": *apto*, "to bring into position for use, bring to bear, apply; to form or modify so as to suit, adapt, accommodate, fit" (*OLD*). Elsewhere (8.5.6) Quintilian writes, "Maiorem vim accipiunt [sententiae rectae] et mutatione figurae ... et tralatione a communi ad proprium"; Russell translates, "[Direct *sententiae*] acquire greater force (1) by a change of Figure ... (2) by a move from the general to the particular" (3:410). We prefer to render the last words, "by a move from the common to one's own."

110 "Auctoritas cereum habet nasum, id est, in diversum potest flecti sensum": Alanus de Insulis, *De fide catholica* 1.30, *PL* 210.333, quoted by M. Bolduc, "Naming Names: Matfre Ermengaud's Use of Troubadour Quotations," *Tenso* 22 (2007): 50.

111 "One morning at breakfast Lord John Russell, the English statesman ..., is said to have defined a proverb by saying it is 'One man's wit and all men's wisdom'": A. Taylor, "The Wisdom of Many

In general, Guillelmus's manner of citation resembles ours, but it shows one persistent trait that blurs our distinction between direct and indirect discourse. Like us, he commonly introduces indirect discourse with *quod* "that." Unlike us, however, he also introduces direct discourse the same way:

> Cato dicit quod "Dives avarus habet nummos, sed non habet corpus." (2.7.6)

Literally,

> Cato says that "A rich miser has coins, but does not have himself."

Because the language cited closely matches that of the original (in this case verbatim), as editors we treat citations such as this one as direct discourse. The present translation elides the slightly confusing *quod* since it violates today's usage: "Cato says, 'A rich miser ...'" So rendered in today's language, the sentence makes a clear distinction between the voice of Guillelmus and that of Cato, although in Latin this distinction is overridden as Cato's words enter Guillelmus's speech. More often Guillelmus too elides the *quod* and produces direct discourse like today's.[112]

Guillelmus blends citations into his own discourse in other ways too. In numerous passages he quotes even Aristotle indirectly and with relative freedom.[113] He treats Boethius, Horace, and Ptolemy similarly. Usually his citations provide the title of a work and often the chapter number, but sometimes he writes simply that another authority is supposed "to have said" (*dixisse*) something, as when he quotes Plato by way of a quotation in Galen (1.3.17). Others whom he quotes without titles include Socrates, Diogenes, Demosthenes, Porphyry—all Greeks, whom he did not read in the original—and the troubadours, who provided no titles for their songs. Like Matfre Ermengaud, he often adds a comment after the quotation, bridging the transition back to his own thought. Sometimes the comment comes first. He interrupts a quotation from the Psalms by inserting glosses (1.6.10). He usually quotes the *Disticha Catonis*, a school text that pupils learned by heart, with verbatim accuracy, but once he departs from the text of a distich by appending an elaboration that he may have found in Cicero (2.5.5). Citing Algazel in support of a generalization that he shares, he represents the astronomer first in indirect discourse, shifts to

and the Wit of One," in Taylor, *Selected Writings on Proverbs*, ed. W. Mieder (Helsinki, 1975), 68.

112 Direct discourse occurs with *quod* in twenty-seven citations, without it in forty-eight. Manuscript *B* frequently omits *quod*.

113 He quotes Aristotle ten times directly and faithfully, despite minor variants, but twenty times indirectly and more freely.

direct discourse, injects a clarification, and completes the citation in direct form (1.3.20). He quotes Juvenal with no indication that he is making a citation at all, so that the opinion quoted seems to become entirely his own (2.8.7).

These various techniques echo the ways Matfre Ermengaud quotes troubadours in his Occitan verse encyclopedia. They imply that Guillelmus, like Matfre and other writers of their period, did not distinguish the self from others quite as we do. Indeed, the word "citation" took on today's meaning as recently as the seventeenth century. Latin *citatio*, postclassical and medieval, meant "summons" as in law; its reflexes in various languages took on the meaning "citation of an authority, quotation" in the early modern period.[114] Guillelmus did not have this meaning attached to *citatio*,[115] nor did his practice conform entirely to this meaning. When quoting an authority, he made it his own more readily than we do today.

Proverbs override the distinction between vernacular and Latin, as did Guillelmus's treatise with its sources in both. His citations of proverbs and sentences blend qualities that are oral and literary, traditional and original. Some of the proverbs he quotes, such as the one at 2.8.4, are attested elsewhere in effectively identical Latin form; others are more idiosyncratic and may reveal the hand of the author. He may have shown his own wit in the following saying, either proverb or sentence:

> Willanus dicit quod "Stultus est qui ponit pedes ante oculos," eo quod stulti improvide operantur. (2.2.3)
>
> The peasant says, "A fool is a man who puts his feet before his eyes," because fools act without forethought.

We have found parallels to the contrast between feet and seeing in Ennius, Cicero, and Lactantius—not exactly peasants—but not the sharp distinction between feet and eyes. Whether the metaphor is his own or someone else's, Guillelmus added his own gloss to clarify its meaning. Another proverbial expression echoes the Bible:

> Sapiens terram respicit et celum considerat. (2.1.9)
>
> The wise man watches the earth and considers the sky.

[114] In the sixteenth century in Italian and English, in the seventeenth in Catalan and French. See S. Battaglia, *Grande dizionario della lingua italiana*, s.v. "citazione"; *OED*, s.v. "citation"; J. Coromines, *Diccionari etimològic i complementari de la llengua catalana*, s.v. "citació"; *Trésor de la langue française*, s.v. "citation."

[115] The word does not occur in *De nobilitate animi.*

In Proverbs we read that the Lord watches the ways of man and considers all his steps, which may have provided syntactic and lexical elements of this sentence (*respicit, considerat*).[116] But Guillelmus has changed the thought entirely. He has put the wise man, the philosopher, in the place of God, even though God looks down on man and the wise man more modestly looks out on the earth and up to the sky (or heaven). If Guillelmus invented this saying, he made the biblical proverb into a sentence of his own.

Troubadours

The sphere of Occitan culture spread beyond the south of France, where the language was the mother tongue.[117] Troubadours traveled from the Midi to Italy and Spain. Italian and Spanish poets traveled to the Midi; both appeared in a satirical gallery by Peire d'Alvernhe, about 1161, that included *us veilletz lombartz*, "an old Lombard," and Peire de Monzo, from Aragon.[118] Italian poets from Sordello, in the thirteenth century, to Dante, in the fourteenth, composed original verse in Occitan.[119] Catalan poets used Occitan to write lyric verse from the twelfth century to the fifteenth, even though Catalan prose appeared in the fourteenth.[120] Ausias March, in the mid-fifteenth century, was the first to write Catalan poetry free of Occitan elements. In the time of Guillelmus de Aragonia the troubadours were part of his own culture.

In Aragon, wedged between the dominant languages of Catalan and Castilian, kings welcomed troubadours who celebrated their glory in Occitan.

116 "Respicit Dominus vias hominis et omnes gressus illius considerat" (Proverbs 5:21).

117 Poets in northern France and Germany imitated the troubadours in French and German. W. D. Paden, "Old Occitan as a Lyric Language: The Insertions from Occitan in Three Thirteenth-Century French Romances," *Speculum* 68 (1993): 36–53; D. H. Nelson, "Northern France," *Handbook*, 255–261; S. Huot, "Troubadour Lyric and Old French Narrative," *Troubadours*, 263–278; S. C. Van D'Elden, "The Minnesingers," *Handbook*, 262–270.

118 Peire d'Alvernhe, *Chantarai d'aquestz trobadors*, PC 323.11, vv. 43, 73; ed. A. Fratta, *Peire d'Alvernhe: Poesie* (Rome, 1996), 47–59, 188–196, no. 8; notes on Peire de Monzo, p. 192, and the old Lombard, p. 195. *Monzo* could also refer to a place in Castile: Riquer, *Los trovadores*, 1:332–341.

119 Ronald Martinez, "Italy," *Handbook*, 279–294. H.-E. Keller, "Italian Troubadours," *Handbook*, 295–304. M. Cabré, "Italian and Catalan Troubadours," *Troubadours*, 127–140.

120 I. Cluzel, "Princes et troubadours de la maison royale de Barcelone-Aragon," *Boletín de la Real Academia de Buenas Letras de Barcelona* 27 (1957–58): 321–373; M. de Riquer, "Els Trobadors catalans," *Història de la literatura catalana: Part antiga* (Barcelona, 1964), 1:24–196; C. Di Girolamo, "L'eredità dei trovatori in Catalogna," *Filologia antica e moderna* 9 (1995): 7–21; J. T. Snow, "The Iberian Peninsula," *Handbook*, 271–278; I. de Riquer, "Presencia trovadoresca en la Corona de Aragón," *Anuario de estudios medievales* 26 (1996): 933–966; S. Asperti, "I trovatori e la Corona d'Aragona: riflessioni per una cronologia di riferimento," *Mot, so, razo* 1 (1999): 12–31; Cabré, "Italian and Catalan Troubadours." M. Cabré, "Mécènes et troubadours dans la Couronne d'Aragon," *Europe* 86, nos. 950–951 (2008): 126–136; J. Moran i Ocerinjauregui, "Inicio y desarrollo del Catalán escrito," *Medioevo romanzo* 27 (2003): 311–319.

Jaime I, the Conqueror (1213–1276), was served by Guilhem de Montanhagol in 1238 and met Guiraut Riquier in 1265.[121] He rewarded Cerverí de Girona, a Catalan troubadour who wrote in Occitan, for poetic service with a grant of property; expressing his gratitude, Cerverí addressed Jaime as *nobles reys cortes*, "noble, courtly king."[122] Paulet de Marselha praised Jaime's son and heir, the *infante* Pedro, calling him "noble" and providing a noble physical description: "Ric, jove, fort, e gran / lo troba hom, e bel e bo" (People find him powerful, young, strong, and great, / and fair and good.)[123] When Jaime died, Matieu de Quercy grieved for the *noble rey*.[124] Cerverí too lamented Jaime's death even as he celebrated Pedro III, his successor, as yet another *noble rey*.[125] Cerverí also praised Pedro's son and successor, Alfonso III, when he was still *infante*.[126] This is the Alfonso whose personal physician was Guillelmus de Aragonia.

For four centuries, from the twelfth to the fifteenth, Aragonese kings, princes, and a princess wrote Occitan verse themselves.[127] The first to do so was Alfonso II (ruled 1162–1196), who left us two compositions.[128] Guillelmus de Aragonia probably served two kings, Pedro III and Jaime II, who poetized in Occitan.[129] Kings of Aragon employed several vernaculars—Aragonese, Catalan, Castilian—for general purposes as well as Occitan for poetry and Latin for affairs of state.[130] No one wrote lyric poetry in Aragonese.

The troubadours are exceptional among the authorities cited in *De nobilitate animi* since one must suppose, in the absence of other Latin versions of their work, that Guillelmus found their texts in Occitan and translated them himself. They are the only vernacular poets he quotes, despite the existence of vigorous lyric poetries in French since about 1180, Galician-Portuguese since about 1200,

121 P. T. Ricketts, *Les poésies de Guilhem de Montanhagol, troubadour provençal du XIIIe siècle* (Toronto, 1964), 14; Guiraut Riquier, *Guilhem de Mur, que cuia far*, PC 248.37, ed. M. P. Betti, "Le tenzoni del trovatore Guiraut Riquier," *Studi mediolatini e volgari* 44 (1998): 7–193, no. 9.

122 Cerveri de Girona, *Entre Caldes e Penedes*, PC 434.7b, v. 3, ed. M. de Riquer, *Obras completas del trovador Cerverí de Girona* (Barcelona, 1947), no. 12.

123 Paulet de Marselha, *L'autrier m'anav'ab cor pensiu*, PC 319.6, vv. 61–62, ed. I. de Riquer, *Paulet de Marselha: Un provençal a la cort dels reis d'Aragó* (Barcelona, 1996), no. 5. *Nobl'enfan*, vv. 86, 126.

124 Matieu de Quercy, *Tant suy marritz*, PC 299.1, ed. C. Appel, *Provenzalische Inedita aus Pariser Handschriften* (Wiesbaden, 1892), 193–196.

125 Cerveri de Girona, *Si per tristor*, PC 434a.62, ed. Riquer, *Obras completas*, no. 40. Cerverí calls Pedro "noble" in *Qui bon frug*, PC 434.11, v. 33, ed. Riquer, no. 101; *Eras veiretz*, PC 434a.23, v. 36, ed. Riquer, no. 21; *Nulhs hom savis*, PC 434a.41, v. 32, ed. Riquer, no. 81.

126 Cerveri de Girona, *Meig vers*, PC 434a.32, ed. Riquer, no. 100, according to Riquer's revised opinion in *Los trovadores*, 3:1556 n.3.

127 Cluzel, "Princes et troubadours," 321–322.

128 Ibid., 324–334. Riquer, *Història de la literatura catalana*, 1:41–55.

129 Pedro III: Cluzel, "Princes et troubadours," 349–354; Riquer, *Història de la literatura catalana*, 1:165–170. Jaime II: Cluzel, 354–358; Riquer, 1:170–173.

130 Pérez Lasheras, *La literatura del reino de Aragón hasta el siglo XVI*, 44.

and Italian since about 1230. He treats them as pioneers in the vernacular who engaged in dialogue with great thinkers—as poets who made their vernacular illustrious. He likens them to philosophers (2.3.1). His work may be seen as an antecedent of the *De vulgari eloquentia*, in which, twenty years later, Dante would trace the origin of the illustrious Italian vernacular to the Occitan poets whom he called "doctores," or "teachers."[131]

Guillelmus adapts sayings from Latin and Occitan so freely that some of his citations have defied the best efforts to identify their sources.[132] Seven citations may be attributed to troubadours with degrees of confidence that range from persuasive to speculative. They are not found in the first part of the treatise, where Guillelmus constructs his argument, but in the second, where he illustrates it. Most of them are concentrated in the chapter on nobility of the body (2.3); one is in the chapter on ignoble bodies (2.4) and another in the chapter on proverbs about servants (2.6). Guillelmus turned to the troubadours for insights about the body, noble or ignoble, and about servants, but not for understanding the soul or lords. His citations of proverbs are distributed similarly: all of the proverbs but one occur in the second part, where they are scattered more broadly. He draws on the troubadours for worldly wisdom and proverbs for common sense. In the first part of the book he favors the philosophers—Aristotle, Boethius, Horace—for more fundamental guidance.[133]

It is particularly difficult to identify Guillelmus's sources among the troubadours since he represents them in Latin prose.[134] Despite this difficulty, however, as a means to trace his creative adaptations we shall make a working assumption that his troubadour citations correspond to something in the known canon, an assumption that has recently become more practical because we now possess an electronic concordance of all the extant troubadour texts.[135] By examining the complete canon we should, according to this assumption, be able to deter-

131 "Petrus de Alvernia et alii antiquiores doctores" (Peire d'Alvernha and other ancient masters). *De vulgari eloquentia* 1.10.2, ed. Steven Botterill (Cambridge: 1996), 22–23. *De vulgari eloquentia* was written between 1303 and 1305. See *Enciclopedia Dantesca*, s.v. "De vulgari eloquentia."

132 Thus 1.14.16 (Galen), 2.1.6, 2.1.7, 2.1.10, 2.2.6 (Demosthenes), 2.5.8, 2.6.3; and see the discussion of Odantagalus (2.3.8) below.

133 He cites Aristotle more than thirty times in the first part, only five times in the second; Boethius seven times in the first, three in the second; Horace five times in the first, twice in the second. The balance tips for the *Disticha Catonis*, with five citations in the first part and six in the second; and for Solomon, with one in the first part and three in the second.

134 Among the troubadours themselves intertextuality was keyed to verse form: a *sirventes*, or satire, that imitated a *canso*, or love song, would reproduce the model's rhyme scheme, the syllabic count of its lines, and its rhyme sounds. See F. M. Chambers, "Imitation of Form in the Old Provençal Lyric," *Romance Philology* 6 (1953): 104–120; and M. L. Meneghetti, "Intertextuality and Dialogism in the Troubadours," *Troubadours*, 181–196.

135 P. Ricketts, *Concordance de l'occitan médiéval: COM2, Les troubadours, Les textes narratifs en vers* (Turnhout, 2005).

mine the source of any citation from the troubadours. It remains true, of course, that extensive materials composed by the troubadours have been lost.[136]

Only one citation from a troubadour has been identified to universal satisfaction:

> De curialitate servi Petrus Vitalis dicit quod "Prudentia servi et valor est magnus si dominus fuerit silvester et iracundus, quod ab ipso sine infamia separetur." (2.6.6)

> Regarding the courtliness of a servant Peire Vidal says, "The prudence and courage of a servant are great if his lord is crude and wrathful, and he manages to leave him without a scandal."

Joseph Anglade, who edited Peire Vidal, provided the source:

> Quar sens es e grans valors
> Qui de brau senhor felo
> Se lonha ses mal resso.[137]

> For it shows good sense and great worth if one takes leave of a cruel, nasty lord without a scandal.[138]

In context, Peire is speaking of himself as the victim of his lady's harshness; in comparison to himself, he invokes the tact and skill of a vassal who manages to escape a nasty lord without creating public embarrassment. Guillelmus transplants the citation into a chapter on slaves and masters, *De proverbiis servorum*. Peire's metaphorical vassal turns into a real domestic servant.

Guillelmus cites Peire Vidal again in the chapter on nobility of the body, in a passage that was punctuated and understood by Antoine Thomas and Anglade in this way:

> Petrus Vitalis dicit quod "Pulcritudo corporis est magnum precium, nisi intrinsecus paciatur defectum." (2.3.5)

> Peire Vidal says, "Beauty of body is a great merit, unless the body suffers an inner flaw."

[136] K. Klingebiel, "Lost Literature of the Troubadours: A Proposed Catalogue," *Tenso* 13.1 (1997): 1–23.

[137] J. Anglade, "Peire Vidal et le *Liber de Nobilitate Animi*," *Studi Medievali*, n.s., 2 (1929): 445–446. Peire Vidal, *Atressi co.l perilhans*, vv. 28–30, PC 364.6, ed. J. Anglade, *Les poésies de Peire Vidal*, 2nd ed. (Paris, 1966), no. 2.

[138] "Car c'est le fait d'un homme intelligent et distingué de s'éloigner sans éclat d'un seigneur dur et fourbe": trans. Anglade, *Les poésies*.

Anglade suggested a partial parallel:

> Domna, vostra beutatz
> E.l finz pretz mentaubutz
> Mi fai semblar sabenc
> Tot autre joi ...[139]

> Lady, your beauty and your perfect reputation make every other joy seem despicable to me ...[140]

As Anglade saw,[141] the beginning of the Occitan passage corresponds to the beginning of the Latin: *beutatz* and *pretz* match *pulcritudo* and *precium*. But the Occitan then changes the subject. Considering the way Guillelmus adapts his sources to his own thought, as we have noticed particularly in the citation from the *Disticha Catonis* at 2.5.5, it seems reasonable to accept Anglade's suggestion for the first part of the phrase ("Pulcritudo corporis est magnum precium"), even though the rest follows the philosopher's own line of argument. Peire is the source of the first part of what follows but not the second. Therefore we punctuate as follows, identifying the first words as the citation, followed by Guillelmus's comment:

> Petrus Vitalis dicit quod "Pulcritudo corporis est magnum precium," nisi intrinsecus paciatur defectum. (2.3.5)

> Peire Vidal says, "Beauty of body is a great merit," unless it suffers an inner flaw.

The voices of Peire Vidal and Guillelmus blend.

The chapter on nobility of the body begins with a citation of Folquet de Marseille:

> Fulco Marsiliensis dicit, "Si corpus bene formetur et eidem cor bene proportionetur sive in viro sive in muliere, nobilitatem ostendit." (2.3.1)

> Folquet de Marseille says, "If the body is well formed and the heart is well proportioned to it, in either a man or a woman, it shows nobility."

139 Peire Vidal, *Son ben apoderatz*, vv. 61–64, PC 364.45, ed. Anglade, *Les poésies*, no. 15.

140 "Dame, votre beauté et votre parfaite renommée me font paraître méprisable toute autre joie ...": trans. Anglade, *Les poésies*.

141 Anglade, "Peire Vidal et le *Liber de Nobilitate Animi*." In his more recent edition of Peire, D'Arco Silvio Avalle denied that Guillelmus could have referred to this source but failed to suggest a better one.

Colker[142] pointed out a vague resemblance in Folquet:

> E ja.l cors non se deu clamar
> de re que.l cor li puosca far,
> que tornat l'a al plus onrat seingnor.[143]

> I [*literally* the body, *i.e.*, my body] must not complain / of anything my heart may do to me, / for it has turned me [my body] toward the most honored lord.[144]

In both languages play on the words for body (Latin *corpus*, Occitan *cors*) and heart (*cor*) is resolved by the appearance of *nobilitatem*, that is, the "onrat seignor." Folquet employs ambiguous language: the definite article in "lo cors ... lo cor" takes on the meaning of the possessive pronoun, as it often does in Old Occitan; the "plus onrat seingnor," masculine, applies to the lady by the convention of the feudal metaphor. The latter ambiguity echoes in Guillelmus, in the clause "sive in viro sive in muliere," but the meaning has changed. The troubadour's suffering in love has become the basis for a generality about physiognomy. Guillelmus uses the scaffolding of Folquet's poetic thought to sustain his own distinctive argument, much as we noticed him doing with a biblical text from Proverbs at 2.1.9.

The same chapter contains a reference to Jaufre Rudel:

> Gaufridus Rodel dixit, "Multi laudant magnitudinem cum fortitudine, et ego laudo si racio gerat frenum." (2.3.7)

Literally,

> Jaufre Rudel said, "Many people praise magnitude with strength, but I give praise if reason holds the reins."

This opaque proposition corresponds to nothing in the works of the troubadour Jaufre Rudel. We can make sense of it (whoever the author) by supposing that *magnitudinem* takes on an extended meaning of generosity, Occitan *largeza*,[145]

142 Colker, 73.

143 Folquet de Marseille, *En chantan*, vv. 31–33, PC 155.8, ed. S. Stronski, *Le troubadour Folquet de Marseille* (Cracovie, 1910), no. 5; ed. P. Squillacioti, *Le poesie di Folchetto di Marsiglia* (Pisa, 1999), no. 11. We quote from Squillacioti.

144 "Le corps ne doit pas, cependant, faire grief au coeur, quel que soit le mal que celui-ci puisse lui causer, car il l'a dirigé vers le plus honorable seigneur ...": trans. Stronski, 122.

145 *Magnus*, "(of the mind or spirits) ... generous, lofty" (*OLD*). *Largueza*, "largesse"; cf. *larc*, "large; libéral, généreux," Levy, *Petit dictionnaire provençal-français*, 222.

and *fortitudine* here means merit, Occitan *proeza.*[146] Adopting these meanings, we translate:

> Jaufre Rudel said, "Many people praise generosity with merit, but I give praise if reason holds the reins."

Guillelmus credits Jaufre with saying that he approves of reasonable moderation in generosity. Compare this passage from an anonymous troubadour:

> Ges eu no tenc toz los larcs per fort pros,
> Car no sabon chausir on s'es bes mes,
> Per q'eu prez mais escars sabi cortes,
> E mais me plaz de lui us petiz dos
> Qe s'us larcs fols mi donava dos tanz.[147]
>
> I surely do not consider generous men (*larcs*) as very noble (*pros*),
> for they know not how to tell where the good is found;
> I think more highly of a wise, courtly man who is frugal,
> and a small gift from him pleases me more
> than if a generous fool (*us larcs fols*) gave me twice as much.

The unknown troubadour praises moderation in financial behavior, contrary to others who celebrate generosity unbound. Guillelmus speaks of moderation in size and strength, transferring the theme to the domain of the physical body, as is suitable in a chapter on bodily nobility. His false attribution of the sentiment to Jaufre Rudel resembles his false attribution to Seneca of an opinion held by Plato (2.10.5). His general freedom in handling citations extends in these cases to careless attribution, whether his own or that of his source.

Up to this point the names of troubadours in Guillelmus have not been problematic: we have no hesitation in understanding *Petrus Vitalis* as Peire Vidal, *Fulco Marsiliensis* as Folquet de Marseille, or *Gaufridus Rodel* as Jaufre Rudel. *Montaneolus* is not quite so transparent, but we may easily see in it the Occitan *Montanhagol.*

146 The denotation of *fortis* ranges from physical strength to honorable conduct, courageous disposition, or heroic action (*OLD*). *Proeza*, "deeds of arms, prowess; merit," W. D. Paden, *An Introduction to Old Occitan* (New York, 1998), 462; the root is *pro*, "good, noble," ibid.

147 PC 461.129, ed. A. Kolsen, "25 bisher unedierte provenzalische Anonyma," *Zeitschrift für romanische Philologie* 38 (1914–1917): 290. For the theme of measure in generosity, see also Guilhem de Montanhagol, *Qui vol esser agradans e plazens*, PC 225.13, vv. 25–32, ed. P. T. Ricketts, *Les poésies de Guilhem de Montanhagol, troubadour provençal du XIIIe siècle* (Toronto, 1964), no. 13. Compare Werner P 124: "Prodigus esse cave vel avarus! sis, rogo, largus, / Sis et in aede tua centeni luminis Argus!" (Fear to be prodigal or greedy; I ask you to be generous, / And in your home to be an Argus with a hundred eyes!)

> Dicit Montaneolus quod "Pulcri corpore sine cordis vigore sunt ymagines sine vita," quod optime dictum est, utrobique enim apparet quod non existiterit. (2.4.17)
>
> Montanhagol says of them, "The beautiful in body without strength of heart are images without life," which is very well said, for such a person seems to be alive in neither [body nor heart].

This is a loose paraphrase of a passage in Guilhem de Montanhagol:

> Mas ja melhur'om e gensa
> en raubas e en guarnir
> e en manhta captenensa,
> e.s vol hom trop gent tenir.
> Mas en dar ni en servir
> no vei far melhuramen.
> E doncx que.us faretz, manen?
> Ja morretz vos, can que can;
> gardatz que.l temps no.us engan.[148]
>
> But everyone grows better and more elegant
> in garments and adornment
> and in many a comportment,
> and wishes to be stylish.
> But as for giving and service,
> I see no one doing better.
> Then what will you become, rich men?
> You will die at one time or another;
> watch out that time does not surprise you.[149]

Guilhem sings about elegant people who become, in Guillelmus, *pulcri corpore*. They are lacking, says Guilhem, "en dar ni en servir" (in giving and service), which Guillelmus elides. Guilhem warns them that they will die; Guillelmus elaborates, saying they are "sine cordis vigore" and "ymagines sine vita." Guilhem's censure of wealthy misers turns into another physiognomic observation. Guillelmus is less interested in social criticism than philosophical reflection.

[148] Guilhem de Montanhagol, *On mais a hom de valensa*, PC 225.11, vv. 28–36, ed. Ricketts, *Les poésies de Guilhem de Montanhagol*, 70.

[149] "Mais on fait mieux et on est plus élégant / en ce qui concerne les vêtements, la parure / et l'extérieur en général; / on tient à être bien mis. / Mais pour ce qui est de la libéralité et du service, / je ne vois aucun progrès. / Que deviendrez-vous donc, riches? / Vous mourrez un jour ou l'autre; / prenez garde de ne pas être surpris par le temps" (trans. Ricketts).

The name *Arnoldus* calls up only too many people, including Arnoldus de Villa Nova, the Catalan physician and astrologer who lived for some time at the court of Aragon. Among the troubadours we find no less than nine Arnauts, including Arnaut Daniel and Arnaut de Mareuil. Guillelmus cites a certain Arnoldus:

> Arnoldus dicit quod "Pulcritudo corporis sine cordis pulcritudine et absque nobilitate est vilitas et flos transiens sine fructu." (2.3.6)
>
> Arnoldus says, "Beauty of body without beauty of heart and without nobility is ignobility, and a flower passing away without fruit."

Perhaps Guillelmus was thinking of this passage from Arnaut de Mareuil:

> A dona non s'eschai beutatz,
> si no ten en car sa valor,
> qu'avol gent e folh parlador
> fan cujar als melhors tal re
> per que dechai son pretz e se,
> que.l semblans adutz l'ochaizo,
> si tot del fag se ditz de no.[150]
>
> Beauty does not befall a lady / unless she holds dear her reputation; / for nasty people and foolish tongues / make better people think things / that make her reputation decline, and herself; / for even if she denies it, / the appearance brings on the accusation.[151]

In a cynical mood Arnaut de Mareuil says that beauty brings on accusations, implying that many people are envious. Guillelmus criticizes not envious people who surround a beauty but those who, possessing physical beauty themselves, lack beauty of heart or nobility. He pronounces such merely physical beauty "flos transiens sine fructu" (a flower passing away without fruit), recalling, perhaps, another source entirely, the Song of Songs (1:12): "Mane surgamus ad vineas, videamus si floruit vinea, si flores fructus parturient" (Let us arise early to the vineyards, let us see if the vineyard has flowered, if the flowers bear fruit). If this assessment is correct, Guillelmus has changed a stroke of satire against

150 Arnaut de Mareuil, *Lo gens temps m'abelis e.m platz*, PC 30.18, vv. 28–34, ed. R. C. Johnston, *Les Poésies du troubadour Arnaut de Mareuil* (Paris, 1935), no. 19.

151 "Beauté n'échoit pas à une dame / si elle ne protège jalousement sa renommée; / car les méchants et les mauvaises langues / font croire aux meilleurs des choses / qui détruisent sa réputation et elle-même; / car même si du fait elle dit non, / l'apparence amène l'accusation ..." (trans. Johnston).

the envious crowd into an adverse moral judgment, with a biblical overtone, of those who lack inner beauty and nobility.

The name *Odantagalus* suggests no one—in Latin, Greek, Arabic, or Occitan.

> Odantagalus dicit quod "Promptitudo corporis vel levitas dominium habet pedum, sed laus erit si pedes absque stultitia moveantur." (2.3.8)

> Odantagalus says, "Swiftness or lightness of body has power of the feet, but there will be praise if the feet move without folly."

The manuscripts are not unanimous: three read *Odantagalus* (P_1P_2S), one *Odontagalus* (*K*), one *ad antagalus* (*R*); one scribe (*B*) threw up his hands and wrote, "Item quidem alter" (Again, someone else). These variants do not suggest that the name was difficult to pronounce—five manuscripts agree on its form, except for the play of two vowels—but that the name was unknown. It has not been found elsewhere. A. Thomas suggested that it is a corruption of *Mantagalus*, that is, Guilhem de Montanhagol,[152] but as we have seen, this troubadour is the *Montaneolus* of another citation; moreover, the poems of Guilhem de Montanhagol offer nothing comparable.[153] I have found nothing helpful by pursuing the words *promptitudo*, *levitas*, and *stultitia* in several powerful lexical instruments.[154] But there is a possible source in Occitan, in a narrative romance on the cardinal virtues by Daude de Pradas:

> Qui mou son cors per leugeria,
> cel movementz ven de foillia.[155]

> If one moves his body in frivolity, / that movement comes from folly.

Daude says that frivolous movement of the body comes from folly; Guillelmus observes the logical complement, that bodily movement without folly deserves praise. Occitan *mou* and *movementz* correspond to Latin *moveantur*; *son cors*, to *corporis*; *leugeria*, to *levitas*; *foillia*, to *stultitia*. Guillelmus has adapted Daude's lexicon into a proposition that amplifies Daude's statement.

Daude de Pradas was a cleric and troubadour from Rodez who wrote from 1214 until 1282 and finished the *Roman sur les quatre vertus cardinales* between

152 Thomas (A.), 169.

153 Ricketts supposes that Guillelmus is thinking of a passage in a text that has been lost, but the title of which, *Lou tractat dels vycis et vertus* (The treatise of the vices and vertues), was mentioned by Jean de Nostredame en 1575. See Ricketts, *Les Poésies de Guilhem de Montanhagol*, 12–13, 19.

154 *ALD*; *Bibliotheca Teubneriana Latina*; *LLT*; Otto, with the *Nachträge*; *PL*; *TPMA*; Walther; Werner.

155 P. T. Ricketts, ed., "Le roman de Daude de Pradas sur les quatre vertus cardinales," *La France latine* 134 (2002): 131–183, vv. 1346–1347.

1220 and 1231.[156] Could his name have produced *Odantagalus*? One may conjecture an original reading *Daude gallus*, "Daude the Frenchman," misread as *Dandegallus* and interpreted as *Dantegallus*, whence *Dantagalus*.[157] As for the initial O, might it possibly represent Daude's title as *official* of Rodez?[158] This is a strained solution for a desperate case, but at least it is motivated by a plausible resemblance between Guillelmus's text and its putative source.

These seven identifications range in persuasiveness from conclusive, in the first case only, through varying degrees of plausibility, to highly conjectural in the last. We do not claim to have solved them all beyond cavil, but we doubt that it is possible to do so. The uncertainty stems from the creative manner in which Guillelmus treated his sources, particularly his Latin translations from the Occitan. Although we do not grasp with confidence some of the authorities he invokes, all of the citations serve to enrich his discourse with a chorus of his predecessors, some more recognizable than others. All of them contribute to further his argument.

Manuscripts

The present edition uses six manuscripts of *De nobilitate animi*. They were written from the late thirteenth century to the fifteenth.

P_1 Paris, Bibliothèque Nationale, lat. 16089, f. 238rA.1–242rA.45. End 13th c. Hauréau, 209: "Pièces ... du XIIIe, du XIVe, peut-être même du XVe siècle, et rien n'indique quand elles ont été jointes ainsi les unes aux autres." A. Thomas, 164: "l'écriture [of *De nobilitate animi*] peut être assignée à la fin du XIIIe siècle." Colker, 50: "a crabbed French hand of the late thirteenth century."[159] No title except in 1.0.14, no incipit, no explicit. Includes 127 citations.[160] Constant abbreviations. Marginalia include asterisms, insertions, corrections, guide letters for capitals, and indications of *versus*.

P_2 Paris, Bibliothèque Nationale, nouv. acq. lat. 3074, f. 7r.13–18r.31. 14th c. J. Porcher, "Nouvelles acquisitions latines et françaises du Département des Manuscrits de la Bibliothèque Nationale pendant les années 1941–1945,"

156 Riquer, *Los trovadores*, 3:1545. Ricketts, "Le roman," quotes the colophon, which names the scribe and gives the date 1268; but this date refers to the year when the scribe completed the manuscript.

157 Guillelmus de Aragonia used *Gallici* for the people of Narbonne, if it was indeed he who, as Guillelmus Hispanus, wrote the *Summa supra physionomiam*. See the discussion of his life, above.

158 A. H. Schutz, *Poésies de Daude de Pradas* (Toulouse, 1933), x–xvii.

159 Thorndike and Kibre, *A Catalogue of Incipits*, col. 1488, date P_1 as a whole in the fourteenth century.

160 The citations in our edition that are not in P_1 come from P_2 (2.10.8), P_2KR (1.11.27a, 2.2.9, 2.4.13), *B* (1.15.7), and *K* (1.11.25a, 2.3.4, 2.7.8, 2.7.9).

Bibliothèque de l'Ecole des Chartes 106 (1945–1946): 239. M. Thomas. Incipit and versified colophon. Marginalia include the title of the work and titles of chapters, comments, corrections, names of authorities cited in 2.1–2, 2.4, and 2.7–9, catchwords, asterisms, and doodles. Adds a citation at 2.10.8, omits one at 1.11.13. P_2KR insert citations at 1.11.27a, 2.2.9, 2.4.13. P_2KR fail to recognize *Salamo* at 2.2.2 and substitute *Secundo*; *B* substitutes *Item*.

B Bruges, Bibliothèque municipale, MS 424, f. 312r.1–322v.32. Late 14th or 15th c. Dated 14th century by A. De Poorter, *Catalogue des manuscrits de la Bibliothèque publique de la ville de Bruges* (Gembloux, 1934), 474–477, and by A. Thomas ("l'écriture ne paraît pas antérieure au milieu du XIVe siècle," 165). "About the middle of the fifteenth century" for Colker in his edition (51). More recently Colker has argued for late 14th or 15th century, citing comparable hands in A. G. Watson, *Catalogue of Dated and Datable Manuscripts c. 700–1600 in the Department of Manuscripts, the British Library*, vol. 2 (London, 1979), plates 261, 283 (14th century), and 497 (15th century), and M. B. Parkes, *English Cursive Book Hands 1250–1500* (Oxford, 1969), plates 17.i–ii.[161] Incipit and explicit. Insertions and deletions of text. Renders the name of the troubadour Folquet de Marseille as *Fulco magister Siliensis* (2.3.1). Marginalia include corrections, guide letters, and the notation *versus*. Inserts a citation at 1.15.7; omits citations at 1.3.23, 1.11.27a, 2.2.9, 2.4.13, 2.4.15, 2.8.8.

K Cologne, Historisches Archiv der Stadt, HAStK 7002 70 (olim GB 2o 70), f. 193rA.1–201rA.25. Paper. 15th c. G. Gattermann, *Handschriftencensus Rheinland* (Wiesbaden, 1993), 957–958. Incipit and explicit. Some omissions and insertions of text. Uses red ink for the title of the work, incipit, chapter titles, capital letters, and to underline particular passages. Occasional barbarisms: *diversivius* 1.11.18, *famalis* 2.9.5, *physoniones* 1.11.22. Frequently replaces *Philosophus* with *Aristoteles*. Attributes citation at 2.5.6 to Horace instead of Aristotle (as a character in the *Alexandreis*); credits citation at 2.3.7, from *Gaufridus Rodel*, to *Gaufridus Bodel*, perhaps thinking of the trouvère Jehan Bodel. In addition to citations inserted by P_2KR, *K* alone inserts citations at 1.11.25a, 2.3.4, 2.7.8, and 2.7.9; with *B*, *K* deletes citation at 2.4.15. The citation at 1.11.25a is shown to be original, and not an accretion, when it is recalled in 1.14.8.

R Rein (Reun), Stiftsbibliothek, MS 205, f. 231v.15–246r.27. Paper. 15th c. *Die Handschriften-Verzeichnisse der Cistercienser-Stifte Reun in Steiermark* [etc.],

[161] M. L. Colker, personal communication, November 2009.

vol. 1 (Vienna, 1891), 77–78. Explicit. Distinctive spellings: *quit* for *quid*, *quot* for *quod*, *aput* for *apud*, *sicud* for *sicut*, suggest that the scribe spoke a language, such as German, in which voiced stops become voiceless when made final. Marginalia include chapter titles, notes on themes or authors of citations, a manicule, *Nota ben[e] et consid[era]*, *Nota valde bene*, *Nota*. A catchword at 2.8.2. Occasional insertions and deletions.

S Salzburg, Stiftsbibliothek Sankt Peter, MS a.V.14, f. 181vD.20–189vC.25. Parchment. 15th c. (1462). A. Jungwirth, *Beschreibung der Handschriften des Stiftes St. Peter in Salzburg* (1913; photocopy, Ann Arbor, Michigan, 1983), without pagination. Deletions of text damage meaning when, asking "utrum rex sit nobilior comite, vel imperator rege" (whether a king is nobler than a count, or an emperor than a king), *S* deletes *rege* (1.17.1) and produces "whether a king or an emperor is nobler than a count"; again when *vilitatem*, "ignobility," appears as *utilitatem*, "usefulness" (1.18.7, 2.4.10). Renders name of troubadour Folquet de Marseille as *Fulco magister Siluensis* (2.3.1). Ornamental initials of chapters. Text written around a hole in the parchment that extends over seven lines of text, *S* 187, recto A and verso D, lines 13–19 (at sentences 1.14.3, 1.18.7). Title of work appears in a different hand on the upper margin of the second page. Omits citations at 1.11.27a and 2.2.9.

Affiliations

In "Variants" we present all substantial alternative readings in the six manuscripts.[162] Our listing includes nearly 2,400 variants, in each of which an individual reading that varies from the edition is shared by some number of manuscripts. The number of manuscripts that share a given variant ranges from one to six. The frequency of variants represented in only one manuscript is high. Indeed, more than 1,900 of the nearly 2,400 variants involve a single manuscript. Precise figures are given in table 1.

[162] In the following discussion we disregard paratextual materials in the "Variants" such as the title of the work, the titles of chapters, and marginalia; the first words of chapters that lack their initial letter; original readings that were corrected by the scribes; and references to earlier editions.

MS	Variants	Percentage of all variants (2,388)	Percentage of 2,230 variants
P_1	31	1%	1%
P_2	203	9%	9%
B	471	20%	21%
K	713	30%	32%
R	325	14%	15%
S	176	7%	8%
Total	1919	80%	86%

Table 1: Variants in One Manuscript

As the table shows, fully 80% of the variants in the tradition are represented by just one manuscript apiece. Each of these variants was apparently the work of the scribe who wrote it. Evidently the scribes did not regard their task as requiring them to reproduce with punctilious fidelity the exact text of their exemplar; rather, they felt free to vary the verbal detail of the version they produced. We are in the presence of an open recension in which innovative readings are frequent. While such readings may be mechanical errors, as in closed recension, many of them make their own sense, showing that the scribe has invested thought in the task at hand. The scribes participated actively in transmission, which is why they produced so many variants. Therefore variants shared by more than one witness may more easily be coincidental than in a more constricted scribal practice. Because the degree of individual variation among manuscripts is so high, we shall henceforth disregard variant types that are represented in fewer than 1 percent of all occurrences, that is, in fewer than 24. This decision reduces the total number of variants under consideration (from 2,388 to 2,230) and slightly alters the percentages of table 1, as the right column shows.

Table 1 also shows that P_1, compiled in the late thirteenth century, is closer to P_2 (fourteenth century) than to *B* (late fourteenth or fifteenth century). For this reason we present variants in the order P_1P_2BKRS. Slightly closer to manuscript P_1 than P_2, however, appears to be *S*, from the fifteenth century. These observations may be developed further by taking into consideration the variants that involve more than one manuscript (and more than 1 percent of all variants), as in table 2.

Affiliation		Alpha			Beta		Gamma	**Total**
Three MSS (variants)					P_2KR (117)			
Two MSS (variants)				P_2K (31)	KR (50)	P_2R (67)	BK (46)	
One MS (variants)	P_1 (31)		S (176)	P_2 (203)	K (713)	R (325)	B (471)	
Total variants in affiliation		207			1,506		517	2,230
Percent of 2230		9%			68%		23%	100%

Table 2: Variants in Three MSS, Two MSS, or One MS

Manuscripts P_1 and S account for 9 percent of the variant groupings; as we saw in Table 1 they seem to be affiliated, albeit distant in time. A more complex affiliation involves P_2, K, and R. Some readings are shared by P_2K, others by P_2R, others yet by KR, and some are shared among the three manuscripts P_2KR. The variants involved in this affiliation account for 68 percent of the total. Finally, B shares variants with K (BK in Table 2) and appears to be affiliated with it. Since B does not share a significant number of variants with P_2 or R,[163] however,

[163] P_2B account for nine occurrences and BR for nine.

we regard it as standing apart from the P_2*KR* group. *B* and *BK* represent the remaining 23 percent of the 2,230 variants.

We have perceived the outlines of three affiliations. The first, Alpha, joins the late thirteenth-century manuscript, P_1, with fifteenth-century *S*; Beta joins fourteenth-century P_2 with fifteenth-century *K* and *R;* and Gamma joins late fourteenth- or fifteenth-century *B* with fifteenth-century *K*. Gamma, in the form of *B*, appears to be contaminated by an exemplar that led to *K*. Although Beta includes three times as many variants as Gamma, within these affiliations manuscript P_2 has fewer variants than does manuscript *B*. Within Beta we find two manuscripts (P_2 and *R)* that are closer to P_1 than *B* is, and one (*K*) that is more distant.[164] We cannot say that all the manuscripts in a given affiliation are closer to those in another affiliation, or farther from them, because a given manuscript's divergence from its exemplar was not mechanically determined by the tradition but depended on innovations by individual scribes.

These observations provide an overview of the transmission of the text. They do not, however, provide the basis for a detailed stemma since that would require more certainty about specific errors or innovative readings than open recension allows. Furthermore, we have found scattered evidence that none of the manuscripts descends directly from the archetype. This evidence takes the form of readings that are unanimous in all six witnesses and yet erroneous.

> Tunc Salustius respondens obicientibus dixit, "Nova nobilitas isti inest in qua melius est peperisse quam ab aliis habitam corrupisse." (1.4.12)

All the manuscripts read *in*, whether followed by *qua* (P_1*BS*), *quam* (*K*), or *quo* (P_2*R*). But the word *in* distorts the syntax of the citation, as we see in the original text of Sallust: "Mihi nova nobilitas est, quam certe peperisse melius est quam acceptam corrupisse" (I have a new nobility, which it is surely better to have begotten than to have received it and then corrupted it). *Quam* is the object of *peperisse*. The point is not that Marius begot something unspecified while living in a new nobility but that he begot a new nobility. We emend *in qua* (P_1) to *qua[m]*, and translate: "There is in him a new nobility, and it is better to have begotten this nobility than to have corrupted one received from others."

164 Infrequent variants that cross over the three affiliations include the following. Alpha (P_1 and *S*) coincides with Beta (P_2*KR*) when P_1P_2 share two variants, aside from larger groups (such as P_1*KR*); P_2*S* share three variants, *KS* fourteen, and *RS* seven, aside from larger groups (such as P_2*KRS*). Alpha coincides with Gamma (*B* contamined by *K*) when P_1*B* share one variant and when *BS* share fourteen. Beta and Gamma coincide, apart from the contamination represented by *BK*, when *B* shares nine readings with P_2 and nine with *R*. We regard none of these cases as sound evidence of affiliation.

> Ad rationes vero, ad primam dico quod ea que sunt eiusdem speciei, si habent formam in materia, non oportet quod habeant operationem eiusdem nobilitatis vel malitie. Contingit enim talibus quod ex bona vel mala dispositione in materia sint bene vel male in suis operationibus expedita. Unde homines bene dispositi secundum corpus bene disponuntur in mente, ut vult Philosophus in libro *De anima*; dicit enim molles carne aptos mente. (1.11.12–14)

> As for the arguments, on the first I say that even though things that have the same species have the same material form, it is not necessary that they have action of the same nobility or wickedness. It happens that such things may be well or badly directed in their actions because of good or bad disposition in matter. Some men who are well disposed in body are well disposed in mind, as the Philosopher claims in the book *On the Soul*, for he says that those who are soft in flesh are apt in mind.

Aristotle's dictum, "Those who are soft in flesh are apt in mind," does not illustrate the preceding statement as the manuscripts give it: "Men who are well disposed in body are well disposed in mind." Rather, it illustrates the claim that "men who are [badly] disposed in body are well disposed in mind." There can be no doubt that a soft body is badly disposed in contrast to a hard body, which is well disposed, as the *Auctoritates Aristotelis* make clear: "Molles carne mente aptos dicimus, duros vero ineptos" (Those soft in flesh we call apt in mind, but those hard [in flesh] we call inept [in mind]). The contrast between good and bad disposition springs from the argument being made: "Even though things that are of the same species have the [same] material form, it is not necessary that they have action of the same nobility or badness." Although the manuscripts read *bene dispositi* unanimously (in *B*, *bene* was inserted by a corrector), we emend *bene* to *[male]*.[165]

> Unde quibus ita contingit quod corpus bene dispositum et temperatum et bene formatum existit animam habent expeditam, nec malicia complexionis torquentur; immo naturaliter tendunt ad ea que sunt rationis et intellectus tamquam ad operationem propriam inclinatam. (1.11.26)

[165] A more elaborate hypothesis would suppose there had been a *saut du même au même* starting from *Unde homines bene dispositi secundum corpus [male disponuntur in mente, et homines male dispositi secundum corpus] bene disponuntur in mente*, and that the scribe skipped from the first *corpus* to the second. Although this solution has a certain elegance, we prefer the more economical one.

> Those whose body happens to be well disposed, temperate, and well formed have a developed soul, and are not distorted by malice of complexion; rather they naturally tend toward things of reason and intellect, insofar as they are inclined to proper action.

All six manuscripts read *inclinatam*, as though modifying *operationem*. We do not grasp how the *operatio propria* could be "inclined." We therefore emend with Colker to *inclinat[i]*, which modifies the implicit subject of the sentence.

> Oppositum videmus, quod per doctrinam bonam multi meliorantur in actionibus suis. Ad primam questionem dicendum ... (1.14.7–8)

> To the contrary we see that many people are improved in their actions by good teaching. On the first argument one should say ...

Colker emends *questionem*, which occurs in all the manuscripts, to *racionem*. Elsewhere the treatise uses *questio* for each of its principal points and *ratio* for a subordinate argument, for example a little later in 1.14.12: "Ex hiis est facile ad questionem respondere et ad rationes" (It is easy, then, to answer the question and the arguments), where *questio* refers to 1.14.1, "Whether those who are ignoble by nature can become noble by teaching or training," and the *rationes* are the arguments made in response to the question.[166] We emend *questionem* to *[rac]ionem*.

> Et tales sunt generaliter omnes qui aliis bene vivere precipiunt, secundum Senecam, et ipsi ad hoc laborare non curant. Quare [Plato] dicit quod similes sunt naute loquaci de gubernatione navis qui postea navem tempestati dimittit; unde ipse dicit quod homo debet facere et non loqui, quia gloria bonorum virorum non est in propria lingua, sed eorum gloria inter bonos. (2.10.4–5)

> Such people are generally all who tell others to live well, according to Seneca, and do not trouble to work at it themselves. [Plato] says that they are like a sailor who chatters about steering a ship and then sends the ship into a storm; so he himself [*i.e.*, Seneca] says that a man must act and not speak, since, [as Cato says above,] the glory of good men is not in their own speech; rather, their glory is among the good.

Where we conjecture *Plato* the manuscripts read either nothing at all (*quare dicit*, *P_1BS*) or *ipse* (*quare ipse dicit*, *P_2KR*). In either case the subject of *dicit* must refer

[166] Compare 1.17.6: "Ex hiis et predictis patet ad questionem et rationem" (From these considerations and what was said before it is clear as to the question and the argument).

to *Senecam*. As we explain in "Sources and Analogues," however, Seneca did not make such a statement, whereas Plato did, and Plato's statement was remembered by Cicero and John of Salisbury. Positing that Guillelmus de Aragonia remembered it too, we emend.

Our text refers to specific book numbers in its sources on twenty-two occasions.[167] Twenty of these references are accurate. The two that are not accurate concern Aristotle's *De generatione animalium*; both occur in all the manuscripts. One reads *capitulo primo* (1.15.4), with or without abbreviations of *capitulo* to *.c.* and *primo* to *.i.* But the opinion cited, namely, that in generation there are many movements on the part of the father and mother, occurs in Book 4 of *De generatione animalium*. In Book 1 Aristotle states more simply that the father is the origin of movement, the mother of matter, but he does not distinguish among plural movements. (For further details see "Sources and Analogues.") We suspect that an early manuscript read *po* for *primo*, which was a misreading of the Arabic numeral *4* in its exemplar. Arabic *4* in these manuscripts resembles a looped ribbon, and could have been mistaken for the letter *p*.[168] In our edition we correct the manuscripts to read *[quarto]*.

At 1.11.20 we find *15to* in P_1, *15* in P_2BRS, and *xvo* in *K*. The reference to a Book 15 of *De generatione animalium* is surprising since Aristotle's work contains only five books. In the translation from the Arabic by Michael Scot, *De generatione animalium* became the third of three treatises combined under the title *De animalibus*, which is the title used by Guillelmus de Aragonia for both this work and *De historia animalium*. But the present citation corresponds to Book 4 of *De generatione animalium*, which became Book 18 of Michael Scot's version, so the reference to Book 15, though it may be partially explained by Michael Scot's renumbering, remains corrupt. We suspect that an early manuscript read correctly *iv* in Roman numerals, and that this was misread as *15* in Arabic numerals, which was possible because an Arabic 5 resembled *v* in these manuscripts and elsewhere.[169] The confusion between Roman and Arabic numerals that we conjecture in these two passages (1.11.20 and 1.15.4) worked in opposite directions, which is troubling, particularly in view of the early date of P_1 relative to composition. Nevertheless, we believe, in view of the accuracy of book references elsewhere in the work, that Guillelmus de Aragonia intended *[quarto]* here too.

167 Including two when it refers to the *Proverbia Almagesti*, the collection of proverbs that prefaces Ptolemy's *Almagest* in the translation by Gherardo da Cremona.

168 Compare Cappelli, 425, where variations on this form of the Arabic numeral *4* are illustrated from the twelfth century to the fifteenth.

169 Compare Cappelli, 422–426, for examples from the twelfth century to the sixteenth.

Further evidence that all the manuscripts are corrupt is not masked behind unanimous readings, but in the variants on the name *Odontagalus* (2.3.8); see our discussion above, under "Troubadours."

Another insight into the tradition is afforded by a citation in P_1 (1.14.8) that refers back to another (1.11.27a) that is found only in the fifteenth-century witness *K*.

> Dicendum quod Philosophus dicit primo *Ethycorum* quod etiam superius fuit dictum, scilicet quod quidam sunt boni per se. (1.14.8)
>
> One should say what the Philosopher says in the first book of the *Ethics* that was just said above: some people are good in themselves.

Looking back to find what *etiam superius* refers to, we read:

> Unde tales dicuntur boni [primo *Ethicorum*] per se. (1.11.27a)
>
> In the first book of the *Ethics* such people are called good in themselves.

The words *primo Ethicorum* occur only in *K*. We infer that despite its late transmission, this citation is original. Other citations lacking in P_1 that appear to be accretions may be original too. One that is attested first in *K* looks like a word association, when the word *vultus* (2.3.3) leads to *Distortum vultum* (2.3.4). In the chapter on proverbs of the rich, *K* inserts a citation at 2.7.9: "Rusticus dicit quod dives est cui suum sufficit" (The peasant says, "He is rich to whom his own is enough"), perhaps failing to realize that nearly the same proverb will be included not once but twice in the following chapter.[170] Then again, however, since these two citations echo each other within 2.8, perhaps the anticipation in 2.7 is original as well. Similarly, a citation in P_2KR echoes one in P_1 at 1.11.27a: "Dicuntur tales viri inutiles" (Such men are called useless) anticipates "Ad mores tales sunt inutiles" (Such men are useless for good conduct) at 1.14.11. Other citations too are repeated.[171] One citation, in the bottom margin of manuscript *B* (1.15.7), looks so much like a scribal addition that we have relegated it to a note. In the other cases, however, we have incorporated into the text citations lacking in P_1 but present in later manuscripts, on the grounds that they may be either accretions or survivals of the original.

170 "Et hoc intendit rusticus qui dicit quod 'Pauper est cui suum non sufficit'" (2.8.4) [The peasant understands this who says, "A poor man is one to whom his own is not enough"]. "Et Oratius dicit quod 'Non est pauper cui sufficit rerum usus'" (2.8.11) [Horace says, "He is not poor to whom the use of things is enough"].

171 Citations that recur include those from Aristotle at 1.3.27 and 1.13.2, Horace at 1.8.5 and 2.9.4, and the *Disticha Catonis* at 1.8.10 and 2.10.3.

We conclude that all six manuscripts derive from an exemplar that was already at least slightly corrupt. From that exemplar descended three affiliations. Alpha produced a manuscript in the late thirteenth century and another in the fifteenth (P_1 and *S*); Beta produced one in the fourteenth century and two in the fifteenth (P_2 and *KR*); Gamma produced one in the late fourteenth or fifteenth century (*B*) that shares readings with one in Beta (*BK*). If Gamma is regarded as subordinate to Beta the stemma is bifid, but if Gamma is considered independent it is trifid. However that may be, the high rate of scribal innovation and the contamination of Gamma would make any attempt to produce a conflated critical text hazardous.

This Edition

We take P_1 as the base of our edition because it is the oldest extant manuscript, and must have been written within a decade or two of the composition of the work. We correct P_1 for reasons of lexicon, morphology, syntax, and sense on the basis of readings in the other manuscripts or by conjecture, as discussed above, under "Affiliations." We mark with square brackets [ ] departures from the base manuscript, that is, from P_1, within the text or from other manuscripts in the paratext (the title, chapter titles, incipit, explicit).

The division of the work into two parts is indicated in the two prologues (1.0.11, 2.0.1). The divisions into chapters are indicated by capital letters in P_2*BKS*.[172] In P_1 and *R* spaces were left for capital letters that were not added and must be supplied, although guide letters for the rubricator occur sporadically.[173] We have numbered the chapters and the sentences and inserted paragraphing.

P_1 contains no title for the work other than that indicated within the text at 1.0.14; there are no incipit, no explicit, and no chapter titles. *S* differs in these respects only because it provides the title of the work, which occurs in the margin of the second page and is an obvious afterthought. The other four manuscripts provide the title of the work and/or an incipit, an explicit, and chapter titles. The titles for the twenty-eight chapters vary in number from eight in *R* to twelve in *B*, sixteen in P_2, and twenty-five in *K*.[174] They also vary in quality. Two of the titles in *K* are misleading: at 1.6, which concerns proverbs about power (*nobilitas dominiorum*), *K* reads *De nobilitate domini*, "On the nobility of a lord"; at 2.2, on proverbs about the foolish, *K* reads *De proverbiis nobilitatis anime*, "On proverbs of nobility of soul." Although the chapter titles must be accretions,

172 No capital letter occurs in *B* at 2.1, or in *S* at 1.2, 2.1, or 2.10.

173 The capital letter is present in P_1 at 2.10 and in *R* at 1.0, 1.2, and 1.16.

174 Although the prologue (1.0) has no title in any manuscript, a capital letter or the space for one distinguishes it in all the manuscripts except *R*.

we regard them as useful to the reader. Accordingly we provide them, as did A. Thomas and Colker. We draw on *K* for the titles represented there satisfactorily, but not for 1.6, where we turn to *B* and the margin of P_2, or for 2.2, where we conjecture *De proverbiis [insipientum]*, "On proverbs of the unwise." *K* provides no title for 1.3, where we turn to P_2, or for 1.14 and 1.18, where we use the obvious conjectures, *Questio [sexta]* and *Questio [decima]*. *K* also provides the incipit of the work as the title for 1.0, the incipit of the second part as the title of 2.0, and an explicit. We append the anonymous colophon in P_2.

We include the citations from manuscripts other than P_1, marking them with square brackets, except that we place the citation at 1.15.7 among the "Sources and Analogues." When P_1 abbreviates a quotation with *et cetera* and another manuscript of *De nobilitate animi* provides a fuller version, we insert the fuller version. We do not insert the complete citation from the source but provide it in "Sources and Analogues."

In order to create a translation in idiomatic English, we have departed from a strictly literal rendering by reducing certain effects of polysyndeton and redundancy. Contrariwise we have expanded ellipses as we found necessary for clarity, using square brackets [ ] to enclose substantial editorial insertions. Because our translation does not aim to follow the Latin word for word, we do not reproduce in the translation the square brackets that mark departures from the base manuscript in our edition of the Latin text.

Guillelmus de Aragonia

DE NOBILITATE ANIMI

William of Aragon

ON NOBILITY OF MIND

Pars 1

0. Prologus

Incipit quidam tractatus *De nobilitate animi.*

1. [E]x naturali appetitu ad bonum et ex eius cognicione ad bene operandum movemur, et ex bonis operibus boni, noti, et notabiles iudicamur in bonum. 2. Dico notabiles, id est nobiles; *nobilis* enim nichil aliud est quam bene operans. 3. Quod per sui contrarium probatur: vilis enim operatio et mala facit hominem iudicari vilem et malum, ergo per oppositum bona operatio et notabilis faciet hominem nobilem de necessitate. 4. Unde nobilitas nichil aliud videtur esse quam operatio bona, vel saltem habitus vel potentia intrinseca que principium est bone operationis sine qua nullus ad bene operandum movetur, sicut nichil disgregat visum nisi quod albedinem habet. 5. Licet tamen potentia operationem precedat, tamen non cognoscitur nisi per operationem. 6. Unde de aliquo non possumus dicere quod nobilis sit nisi quia notabiliter et bene agit, unde quando hoc videmus, dicimus aliquem nobilem et nobilitatem habere.

7. Nunc autem ita est quod plures in notitia ipsius nobilitatis mirabiliter sunt decepti. 8. Quidam enim credunt eam habere et cognoscere qui nec eam habent nec cognoscunt; alii etiam sunt qui cum eam habeant non tamen eam credunt habere, eo quod eam non cognoscunt; alii sunt qui eam habent et cognoscunt, non tamen ipsa utuntur ut deberent. 9. Perfecte autem nobiles sunt qui eam habent et cognoscunt et secundum eam notabiliter operantur. 10. Ut igitur nobilitas et qui sint vere nobiles cognoscantur, hunc libellum pro posse conabor construere in quo ostendetur quid sit nobilitas et quot sint nobilitatis species secundum ordinem nature et secundum sententiam omnium philosophorum et aliorum qui laboraverunt ad notitiam veritatis.

11. Iste liber duas habebit particulas. 12. In prima ostendetur quid sit nobilitas cum suis speciebus et determinabuntur in ipsa questiones communes quas fieri de nobilitate contingit. 13. In secunda erunt plura proverbia et sententie et sermones succincti in quibus quilibet in suo statu poterit cognoscere, si advertere voluerit, utrum sue operationes sint nobiles sive viles. 14. Intitulatur autem iste liber *De nobilitate animi* eo quod illa sit potior inter omnes, ut in prosecutione libri patebit.

Part 1

0. Prologue

Here begins a certain treatise *On Nobility of Mind.*

1. Out of natural desire we are moved to the good, and out of knowledge of it we are moved to doing well, and out of good acts we are judged good, knowledgeable, and notable in goodness. 2. I say notable, that is, noble; for *noble* means nothing else than doing good. 3. This is proven by its opposite: for ignoble and wicked acts cause a man to be judged ignoble and wicked, so by the contrary, good and notable acts will necessarily cause a man [to be judged] noble. 4. Nobility appears, then, to be nothing else than doing good acts, or at all events it is a habit or intrinsic potential, the principle of doing good acts, without which no one is moved to do good, just as nothing differentiates a visual impression except what has whiteness. 5. Although potential precedes action, it is not known except through action. 6. We cannot say of someone that he is noble unless he acts notably and well, so that when we see this, we call someone noble and say he has nobility.

7. Now it is true that many men are marvelously deceived in their perception of this nobility. 8. Some believe they have it and know it who neither have it nor know it; others, although they have it, do not believe they have it since they do not know it; yet others have it and know it but do not put it to use as they should. 9. Those who are perfectly noble have it and know it and, following it, act notably. 10. Therefore, in order that nobility and those who are truly noble should be known, I shall put together this little book to the best of my ability, showing what nobility is and how many types of nobility there are according to the order of nature and the opinions of all philosophers and others who have toiled for the knowledge of truth.

11. This book will have two parts. 12. In the first will be shown what nobility is, with its types, and common questions that happen to be raised about nobility will be answered. 13. In the second there will be many proverbs and sentences and pithy sayings by which any man may recognize, if he wishes to learn, whether his deeds are noble or ignoble according to his condition. 14. This book is titled *On Nobility of Mind* in order that nobility may be stronger among all men, as will become apparent in the development of the book.

Caput 1

Quid sit nobilitas

1. [N]obilitas est habitus qui movet ad talia opera faciendum que in bonitate communiter cognoscuntur, secundum quod pertinet ad eorum naturam. 2. Dico quod est habitus quia cum in anima et corpore non sit aliud quam habitus vel potentia vel passio, nobilitas non est potentia nec passio quia per potentiam vel passionem homo non laudatur nec vituperatur, homo autem per nobilitatem laudatur. 3. Relinquitur igitur quod sit habitus, quocumque modo nobilitas sit accepta. 4. Per habitum autem quilibet dispositus est ad bene operandum vel operari; unde habitus movet potentiam ad opus, et quia opera quedam sunt que facta sunt per habitum vilitatis et malicie, [et illa sunt in se vilia, quedam vero per habitum nobilitatis et illa sunt bona et laudabilia, ideo bene dictum quod nobilitas est habitus qui movet ad bona opera. 5. Secundum alios nobilitas est secundum quam aliquis dicitur habere bonas dispositiones naturales ad suscipiendum habitus virtuosos; et si ista bona dispositione aliquis bene utatur acquirendo habitus virtutis, iam nobilis dicitur natura et moribus.]

6. Sunt autem tria nomina idem significantia quantum ad propositum, licet in se et proprie accepta quoquomodo differant, scilicet *nobilitas, generositas, altitudo generis*. 7. *Nobilitas* enim proprie significat notabilem operis bonitatem; *generositas* vero notabilem multitudinem unius generis; *altitudo* vero magnitudinem dominii et qualitatem ipsius. 8. Ego autem sub nomine *nobilitatis* intelligo illa tria, sicut et in populari fit usu.

Caput 2

Quot sint species nobilitatis

1. [E]x hoc quod dictum est in descriptione nobilitatis possumus plane ostendere quod tres sunt nobilitatis species, quia habitus qui cum acquisitus, dirigens potentiam in opus, et ipsum opus reddit bonum. 2. Aut dirigit in hiis que pertinent ad potentiam anime [aut in hiis que pertinent ad potentiam corporis] aut in hiis que fortune tribuuntur. 3. Est enim manifestum cuilibet quod quilibet operatur male aut b[e]ne secundum quod sibi inest aut ex parte anime aut ex parte corporis aut ex parte fortune. 4. Erunt igitur generaliter loquendo tres

Chapter 1

What Nobility Is

1. Nobility is a habit that moves people, according to what pertains to their nature, to do acts that are commonly recognized as good. 2. I say that it is a habit because, whereas in the soul and body there is nothing else than habit, potential, and experience, nobility is not a potential or an experience because a man is not praised or blamed for a potential or an experience, but a man is praised for nobility. 3. It remains therefore that nobility must be a habit, however it is understood. 4. Out of habit one is disposed to acting well or being active; habit moves potential to action, and since certain acts have been done out of habit of ignobility and malice and they are ignoble in themselves, and certain other deeds have been done out of habit of nobility and they are good and praiseworthy, it is well said that nobility is a habit that moves to good acts. 5. According to others, nobility is what makes someone have a good natural disposition for receiving virtuous habits; and if someone uses that good disposition well for acquiring virtuous habits, then he is called noble in nature and character.

6. There are three words meaning the same thing in this matter, that is as understood in themselves and properly, however they may differ, namely, *nobilitas, generositas,* and *altitudo generis.* 7. *Nobilitas* ["nobility," the ethical quality] in itself means a notable goodness of action; *generositas* [the extended aristocratic family], a notable multitude of the same family; *altitudo generis* ["eminence of birth"], great power and the quality that accompanies such greatness. 8. By the word *nobilitas* I understand these three things, [the ethical quality, the aristocratic family, and power], as occurs in popular usage.

Chapter 2

How Many Kinds of Nobility There Are

1. From what has been said in the description of nobility, we can show clearly that there are three kinds of nobility since it is a habit that, once acquired by directing potential into act, makes the act itself good. 2. It directs toward things that pertain to the potential of the soul, toward things that pertain to the potential of the body, or toward things that are attributed to fortune. 3. It is manifest to anyone that each man acts badly or well according to what is in him on the part of the soul, on the part of the body, or on the part of fortune. 4. Therefore there will be, generally speaking, three kinds of nobility, that is, nobility of soul,

species nobilitatis, scilicet nobilitas anime et corporis et fortune; et quia anima precellit corpus et fortunam, primo dicendum est de nobilitate anime.

Caput 3

De nobilitate anime

1. [A]nima humana tres habet operationes, unam scilicet propriam et duas communes. 2. Communes sunt quibus communicat plantis et bestiis universis; sentit enim homo et utitur alimento quod omnibus viventibus competit in hoc mundo. 3. Propria vero operatio est ratiocinari aut intelligere per medium rationis. 4. Ex bonitate vel malicia huius operationis dicitur homo nobilis sive vilis, quod ex communibus operationibus non contingit quia ex ipsis non laudatur vel vituperatur homo nisi forte in tantum in quantum deberet [eas subdere] rationi, si contingat eas esse rationi rebelles; sed vitup[er]atur vel laudatur secundum bonitatem vel maliciam operationis intellectus vel rationis, quare oportet nobilitatem anime illa operatione notare.

5. Hec autem operatio que ratiocinari vel intelligere dicitur duplex est. 6. Est enim una que dicitur intelligere vel cognoscere vel etiam inquirere veritatem omnium rerum secundum quod possunt per rationem cognosci, et hec pars dicitur speculativa per quandam metha[phora]m, quoniam sicut in speculo iudicamus speciem apparentem in eo, sic intellectus diiudicat fantasmata que de rebus adveniunt fantasie, in ipsis quod quid est et essentiam rerum querens aut in suas causas resolvens. 7. Ista operatio dirigitur per naturam et artem in notitiam omnium rerum quecumque sint, bone vel male, eo quod malarum rerum notitia valde est bona. 8. Alia vero pars est que dicitur activa vel practica que opus considerat et ea que requiruntur ad opus. 9. Providet enim et movet ad fieri que fieri possunt et debent, et prohibet que fieri non sunt digna.

10. Iste due operationes sunt nobiliores et meliores que sunt in homine ex parte anime, unde Philosophus decimo *Ethycorum* dicit, "Secundum intellectum operans et hunc curans est optime dispositus et deo amantissimus esse videtur," quia operatio sua similis est operationi divine. 11. Unde si operatio divina non tantum nobilis sed nobilitas ipsa est, de necessitate operationes erunt nobiliores que ei magis assimilantur, quare vere nobiles debent iudicari qui intellectualibus operationibus gaudent et vivunt. 12. Tales autem sunt philosophantes et sapientes qui "res intelligunt prout sunt," et quorum operationes bonitate prefulgent. 13. Preterea post mortem anima sola operatione intelligendi utitur; illa enim tamquam nobilior, non fuit servituti corporis obligata.

body, and fortune; and since the soul is more excellent than the body or fortune, we shall speak first of nobility of the soul.

Chapter 3

On Nobility of Soul

1. The human soul has three activities, one that is particular to it and two that are common. 2. The common ones are those by which it communicates with all plants and beasts; for man discerns and uses food that befits all creatures living in this world. 3. The activity particular to the soul is reasoning, or understanding by means of reason. 4. From the goodness or badness of this activity a man is called noble or ignoble, which does not happen from the common activities because a man is not praised or blamed for them, unless perhaps insofar as he should subject them to reason if they should happen to be rebellious against reason; but he is blamed or praised according to the goodness or badness of the activity of his intellect or reason, so we must study the nobility of the soul that is due to this activity.

5. This activity called reasoning or understanding has two parts. 6. One is called understanding or learning, or even seeking the truth of all things insofar as they can be known by reason, and this part is called "speculative" by a certain metaphor since just as we judge a reflection appearing in a mirror, so the intellect judges the phantoms that come from things of imagination, seeking the quiddity and essence of things in them or resolving them into their causes. 7. This activity is directed by nature and art for the cognizance of all things whatever they are, good or bad, since the cognizance of bad things is very good. 8. But there is another part called "active" or "practical" that considers action and whatever is necessary for action. 9. It looks ahead, causes what can and should be done to be done, and precludes things that are not worthy to be done.

10. These two activities that are in man on the part of the soul are the noblest and best, for as the Philosopher says in the tenth book of the *Ethics*, "He who acts according to the intellect and pays heed to it is best disposed and seems to be most beloved of God" since his activity is similar to divine activity. 11. Therefore if divine activity is not only noble but nobility itself, it must follow that activities will be nobler that more closely resemble it, so that truly they must be judged noble who rejoice in intellectual activities and live by them. 12. Such are philosophers and wise men who "understand things as they are" and whose activities shine with goodness. 13. Besides, after death the soul uses only the activity of understanding, for inasmuch as it was nobler it was not obliged to

14. Quare patet sufficienter quod illi erunt vere nobiles qui in hiis operibus erunt notati, et illi vere viles qui privabuntur eisdem.

15. Nobilitas igitur anime nichil aliud est quam sapientia in speculando et studiositas in agendo. 16. Est etiam hic advertendum quod iste due operationes ita sunt annexe quod una sine alia non perficitur; et causa huius est quia rectificatio operum adiuvat speculationem, et speculatio dirigit actionem. 17. Unde est sapiens perfecte qui studiosus est, quod patet per Platonem qui legitur discipulis suis, sicut testatur Galienus in libro de humana natura, dixisse: "Dum iuvenis es munda te ab omni mala re corporea, et postea cognosces omnem veritatem quia omnis mala operatio ex natura terre est que cogit corpus cum aliis elementis." 18. Hoc etiam sentit Boetius in libro *De consolatione* dicens:

Tu quoque si vis
lumine claro
cernere verum,
tramite recto
carpere callem:
gaudia pelle,
pelle timorem
spemque fugato
nec dolor assit.
Nubila mens est
hec ubi regnant
vinctaque frenis.

19. Cato etiam tangens unicam passionem dedit omnes intelligere, dicens, "Impedit ira animum ne possit cernere verum." 20. Et generaliter omnes philosophi intelligunt quod anima non est apta ad veritatis cognitionem nisi prius fuerit in quiete pacifica ab omnibus motibus animi passionum, secundum quod dicit Algazel in *Logica* sua, quod tunc est apta anima ut depingantur in ea forme universi "cum expiata fuerit a sordidis" (scilicet moribus) "et turpibus fantasiis." 21. Et causa huius est quia pars sensitiva in homine, que est proprium subiectum et principium passionum, debet intellectui deservire, passiones relinquens. 22. Unde si passiones insequitur et ad se trahit intellectum et in bestialem operationem declinat, tunc cessat operatio intellectus, quare nec acquiritur sapientia passionibus non domatis. 23. E contrario etiam intelligit Aristoteles tertio *Ethycorum* ubi dicit quod malus est ignorans ita quod

servitude of the body. 14. So it is clear enough that they will be truly noble who will be known for these acts, and they truly ignoble who will lack them.

15. Therefore nobility of soul is nothing else than wisdom in reflection and studiousness in action. 16. But notice here that these two activities are so closely related that one is not accomplished without the other, because harmonizing of acts aids reflection, and reflection directs action. 17. So he who is studious is perfectly wise, which is clear from Plato, who, as we read, said to his disciples, as Galen attests in his book on human nature, "While you are young cleanse yourself of every wicked bodily thing and afterward you will understand every truth, since every evil activity is of the nature of the earth, which, along with the other elements, controls the body." 18. Boethius too felt this in the book *On Consolation*, saying:

You too, if you want
In bright light
To see the truth,
On a straight way
To take your path,
Put off joys,
Put off fear,
Put hope to flight,
And feel no grief.
The mind is clouded
When these things reign,
And bound by restraints.

19. Cato too, touching on one passion, allowed us to understand them all, when he said, "Anger prevents the mind from discerning truth." 20. And in general all philosophers understand that a soul is not apt to understand truth unless it has first been in peaceful quiet, away from all the motions of the passions of the mind, as Algazel says in his *Logic*, that "when the soul has been cleansed of filth" (that is, of filthy morals) "and of sordid fantasies," it is ready to have depicted in it the forms of the universe. 21. And the cause of this is that the sensitive part in man, which is the proper subject and source of feelings, must leave feelings aside to serve the intellect. 22. So if it obeys feelings and draws the intellect after itself and declines into animal activity, then the activity of the intellect ceases, which is why wisdom is not acquired unless the feelings have been tamed. 23. In the third book of the *Ethics* Aristotle explains this by the contrary when he says that an evil man must be ignorant because evil actions

per ignorantiam contingit actionum malicia, et causa huius est quia defectus in actione non est nisi ex defectu alicuius vel aliquarum circumstanciarum que accionem informant; et defectus in actione circumstancie non est nisi ex defectu electionis in contemplacione ipsarum circumstantiarum, que nichil aliud est quam ignorantia in agendo. 24. Quare patet quod insipiens studiosus vel prudens non erit.

25. Licet ea que diximus veritatem contineant, ex hiis dubitare contingit quod postquam sapientia non potest haberi sine moribus, nec mores sine sapientia, dubium est a quibus incipiendum sit, utrum ab illis que faciunt scire vel ab eis que ad bene agere ordinantur. 26. Ad questionem hanc dicendum differenter primo quod oportet hominem esse bonum et bene in actibus moralibus connutritum antequam possit vel debeat dici sapiens, et causa huius est quia illa que apta nata sunt operationem moralem corrumpere in nobis et vicium facere prius stimulant nos ad opus, puta ad ea que ad virtutem vegetabilem et sensibilem ordinantur. 27. Unde Philosophus in septimo *De animalibus* dicit quod "Anima puerorum nichil differt ab anima bestiarum secundum tempus hoc," quare Philosophus [intelligit] quod primo bestialiter quodammodo vivimus antequam secundum intellectum. 28. Oportet igitur prius illam vitam regulare secundum rationem ut intellectus non impeditus valeat speculari, et in entibus querere veritatem et finaliter attingere sapientiam. 29. Ad hoc autem faciendum sufficit aliquam grossam cognitionem habere vel "premissionem operationum," qua mediante inclinemur ad bonum virtutis et, convenienter experti et exercitati, acquirimus habitum operationis illius. 30. Hec autem precognitio non est sapientia, nisi quis abusive existimationem appellet sapientiam et equivoce velit loqui et largo modo sumere sapientiam ad omnem precognitionem rerum. 31. Et tunc sine dubio oportet aliqualem sapientiam habere antequam sit studiosus.

32. Ex hiis satis apparet quid sit dicendum ad hoc quod dictum est, quod malus est ignorans. 33. Non enim est dubium quod malicia operationis ex ignorantia venit, sed ex hoc non sequitur quod bonitas eius veniat ex sapientia. 34. Sed sequitur bene quod veniat ex cognitione; non enim sapientia opponitur directe ignorantie, sed cognitio. 35. Et hec de nobilitate anime sint dicta.

occur through ignorance, and the cause of this is that a defect in action can only result from a defect of some circumstance or circumstances that inform action; and a defect of a circumstance in an action can only result from a defect of choice in the contemplation of those same circumstances, which is nothing other than ignorance in acting. 24. So it is obvious that an unknowing man will not be studious or prudent.

25. Although the things we have said contain truth, for these reasons it is possible to suspect that since wisdom cannot be gained without good character, nor good character without wisdom, it is uncertain from which one should begin, either the things that make us know or those that are ordered toward acting well. 26. To this question one may say differently, first, that a man must be good and well nourished in moral acts before he can or should be called wise, because [the instincts] that are born in us apt to corrupt moral action and to create vice first stimulate us to acts that are ordered for the vegetable and sensible virtues. 27. The Philosopher says, in the seventh book *On Animals,* "The soul of children differs not at all from the soul of animals, as is appropriate for this time in its development," for the Philosopher understands that at first we live in a certain sense like animals before we live according to the intellect. 28. We must learn to regulate that life according to reason so that the intellect will be able first to speculate unimpeded, then to seek truth in things, and finally to attain wisdom. 29. To do this it is enough to have a certain naive understanding or "anticipation of activities" that inclines us to the good of virtue and makes us, once we are appropriately experienced and exercised, acquire the habit of that activity. 30. But this precognition is not wisdom unless someone abusively calls opinion wisdom, and should wish to speak equivocally, taking wisdom in a broad sense for any precognition of things. 31. Without doubt, however, it is necessary to have some wisdom before one becomes studious.

32. It is clear enough, then, what to say about what has been stated, that a bad man is ignorant. 33. There is no doubt that badness of action comes from ignorance, but it does not follow that therefore goodness of action comes from wisdom. 34. Rather, it follows that it comes from experience, for not wisdom but experience is opposed directly to ignorance. 35. Let these things be said about nobility of soul.

Caput 4

De nobilitate corporis

1. [P]ost hanc de nobilitate corporis dicendum que duplex est, secundum quod corpus in duobus notatur: aut enim in se secundum speciem et propriam figuram, aut in respectu ad antecessores, scilicet parentes vel avos. 2. Secundum primam loquitur Porphyrius, dicens de Priamo quod eius species digna foret imperio. 3. Ille enim Priamus in bonis corporis plurimos excellebat, scilicet pulcritudine, fortitudine, promptitudine et similibus p[ertinen]tibus corpori. 4. Secundum etiam hanc nobilitatem olim Romani consueverunt milites facere et eligere ex aliis et statuere ad defensionem rei pupblice, sicut enim illi qui anime nobilitate prefulgent sunt fortes et potentes ad bene intelligendum veritatem in rebus et ad agendum operationes virtutis, ita isti sunt potentes a[d] bene defendendum et sustinendum guerrarum labores secundum quod sciunt utilitati rei pupblice pertinere. 5. Quare quicumque talis erat secundum corpus eligebatur in militem et instituebatur in hiis que ad artem pertinent militarem.

6. Altera vero nobilitas corporis que ab antecessoribus habet ortum est adhuc duplex, quia aut secundum veritatem aut secundum vulgarem opinionem tantum. 7. Si autem secundum veritatem, tunc est necessarium quod filius sit similis patri, et tunc sine mendacio potest dici quod est nobilis ad patris relationem, retinet enim formam eius. 8. Sed quando contingit quod filius erit patri contrarius, hoc est quod filius erit vilis vel malus qui patrem nobilem habebat, ignobilitat. 9. Dico quod talis est nobilis sola gentium opinione que de rerum veritate iudicare non possunt, quia talis secundum veritatem est cor[ru]ptor nobilitatis, et principium vilitatis existit. 10. Quod optime Salustius intellexit quando Marius miles strenuus sibi fuit presentatus ut eum confirmaret in senatorem. 11. Iste Marius erat miles optimus de se sed nobiles antecessores non habuerat, quare aliqui impediebant eum ne confirmaretur in senatorem, dicentes eum non fuisse nobilem genere. 12. Tunc Salustius respondens obicientibus dixit, "Nova nobilitas isti inest qua[m] melius est peperisse quam ab aliis habitam corrupisse," et statim confirmavit eum in senatorem, unde non tantum iudicabat eum nobilem sed nobilitatis principium.

13. Ulterius dedit intelligere Salustius quod si filii nobilium non assimilentur parentibus in nobilitate non solum erunt viles sed vilitatis principium et corruptores nobilitatis. 14. Et constat quod Salustius optime dixit, unde in hoc

Chapter 4

On Nobility of Body

1. After that we must speak of nobility of the body, which is twofold, according as the body is thought of in either of two ways: in itself, in terms of its beauty and its own appearance, or in respect to its ancestors, that is, its parents or grandparents. 2. Porphyry speaks in the first way when he says that Priam's beauty would have been worthy of an empire. 3. This Priam excelled many men in the good qualities of the body, in beauty, strength, quickness, and similar qualities pertaining to the body. 4. On the basis of this kind of nobility the Romans were accustomed in days past to make knights, to choose them from among others and put them in charge of the defense of the republic, for just as those who shine by nobility of soul are strong and powerful in understanding the truth in affairs and performing virtuous actions, so those noble in body are powerful in defending the republic and sustaining the toil of war because they know doing so serves the republic. 5. For this reason, whoever was noble in his body was chosen as a knight and trained in military skills.

6. But the other nobility of body that has its origin in ancestors is also of two kinds, either according to the truth or according to mere popular opinion. 7. If according to truth, then the son must be similar to the father, and it can be said without falsehood that he is noble in relation to his father since he retains his father's form. 8. But when it happens that the son is contrary to his father, that is, that the son who had a noble father is contemptible or evil, he becomes ignoble. 9. I say that such a man is noble only in the opinion of people who cannot judge the truth since such a man is in truth a corruptor of nobility and turns out to be a founder of ignobility. 10. Sallust understood this very well when Marius, a powerful knight, was presented to him to be confirmed as a senator. 11. This Marius was an excellent knight in himself but he had no noble ancestors, so some opposed his confirmation as senator, saying that he was not noble by birth. 12. In answer to the objectors Sallust said, "A new nobility is in him which it is better to have begotten than to have corrupted one received from others," and at once he confirmed him as a senator since he judged him not only noble but a founder of nobility.

13. Furthermore Sallust made us understand that if the sons of noblemen do not resemble their parents in nobility, they will be not only ignoble but founders of ignobility and corruptors of nobility. 14. And people agree that Sallust spoke very well, and the opinion of those who speak commonly and expressly contrary to good sense in this matter is truly astonishing, or I should rather

casu valde mirabilis, immo miserabilis, est opinio communiter loquentium et contra sensum expresse. 15. Quis enim esset ita mentis inops qui diceret filium turpem et deformem existentem esse pulcrum, quantumcumque pater pulcer fuisset, vel fatuum sapientem, quantumcumque pater sapiens? 16. Certe nullus, quamvis in hac falsa opinione vivant quamplures, unde videmus contingere frequenter quod tales viles filii destruunt et consumunt propter eorum vilitatem et maliciam omnia bona que parentum probitate et bonitate fuerunt acquisita, et faciunt sibi inimicos de quibus parentes amicos. 17. Quid igitur sint nobilitas corporis et qui corpore nobiles sive viles, nunc in tantum sit dictum.

Caput 5

De nobilitate fortune

1. [E]x hiis que dicta sunt conveniens est determinare de nobilitate fortune, preintelligendo tamen quid sit fortuna, distinguendo ipsam ab aliis que cum ipsa convenire videntur, ut directius habeatur circa que constent nobilitates ipsius. 2. Dicimus enim aliqua fieri a fortuna vel a casu aut a fato aut a providentia aut [a] predestinatione. 3. Unde Boetius quarto *De consolatione*, horum intendens differentiam assignare, incipit a providentia divina, dicens, "Omnium generatio rerum cunctusque mutabilium naturarum progressus et quicquid aliquo modo movetur causas, ordinem, formas ex divine ment[is] stabilitate sortitur." 4. De hiis incipiens [Boecius dicit quod si] res consideretur cuiuscumque motus seu cause vel ordinis sive forme si mente divina vel intellectu, providentia nuncupatur; hoc est, si res referantur ad Dei notitiam secundum esse vel fieri quodcumque, dicuntur esse vel fieri a divina providentia. 5. Ulterius si virtus providencie consideretur ut exsecutioni mandata secundum quod iam movet [res] ad esse vel fieri ut per motum habent explicari et per causas inferiores, magis dicitur esse fatum, a *for, faris* dictum per similitudinem, sicut sermo ordinatus ab intellectu ostendit quod precipit fieri que facienda sunt et significat operationis promotionem. 6. Ita fatum dicitur a providencia cecidisse et rebus mobilibus adhesisse, quod maxime poet[e] et astrologi circa motus notaverunt celestes; et realiter nichil aliud intelligunt pro universali natura. 7. Poete etiam considerando huiusmodi fatum sicut motum quendam, tres fatales finxerunt sorores quarum prima incipiebat motum, et secunda continuabat in usum, sed tertia terminabat, quod per unum versum insinuant: "Cloto colum baiulat, Lachesis trahit, Attropos occat." 8. Similiter astrologi stellas posuerunt in

say wretched. 15. Who could be so lacking in intelligence that he would call a wretched and deformed son handsome, regardless of how handsome the father was, or a foolish one wise, regardless of how wise his father was? 16. Surely no one, and yet many people continue in this false opinion, which is why we often see it happen that ignoble sons, because of their ignobility and badness, destroy and consume all the good that was gained by the honesty and goodness of their parents and make enemies of those whom their parents had made friends. 17. As for what nobility of body is and who are noble or ignoble in body, let this suffice.

Chapter 5

On Nobility of Fortune

1. After what has been said it is suitable to discuss nobility of fortune; first, however, we must understand what fortune is, distinguishing it from other things that resemble it the better to understand the characteristics of this kind of nobility. 2. We say some things happen by fortune, accident, fate, providence, or predestination. 3. So, intending to determine the differences among these in the fourth book *On Consolation*, Boethius begins from divine providence, saying, "The generation of all things, the whole process of mutable natures, and whatever is moved in any way take their causes, order, and forms from the stability of the divine mind." 4. Beginning from this axiom, Boethius says that if we consider the reality of any movement, cause, order, or form, whether it is due to divine mind or intellect, it is called "providence"; that is, if things are referred to the awareness of God in terms of their being or becoming, they are said to be or become by divine providence. 5. But if the virtue of providence is considered as ordered for execution according as it moves things to be or become, so that they have to be explained by movement and by lower causes, it is rather called "fate," which is so called from *for, faris* ("I speak, you speak") by a simile, as a word drawn up by the intellect shows that it orders to be done what must be done and gives the sign for the inception of action. 6. Thus fate is said to have befallen by providence and to have adhered to moveable things, as poets and astrologers have especially noted concerning celestial motions; and really they understand nothing else by universal nature. 7. Poets, indeed, considering fate of this kind as a certain motion, have imagined three fatal sisters, of whom the first would begin the motion, the second would keep it under way, and the third would end it, as they show with a verse: "Clotho carries the distaff, Lachesis draws out the thread, Atropos cuts it." 8. Similarly astrologers have set up the stars as the origins of all things that have to be explained in terms of movement under heaven—stars

principiis omnium rerum que per motum habent explicari sub celo, promotivas, continuativas, et terminativas. 9. Hoc etiam intelligunt naturales qui quadam peryodo mensurari dicunt omnia in celo proportionaliter accepto pro natura communi et intelligentie et corporis celestis. 10. Si autem ulterius hec eadem virtus consideretur ut magis descendens et referatur de uno mobili ad aliud secundum proportionem convenientem vel disconventientem, dicitur augurium vel presagium alicuius futuri ad actus humanos vel aliarum rerum torquendo, et semper accipitur in cognitis et aliis impressionibus altis et in avibus augurialibus et visionibus sompniorum et consimilium. 11. Ulterius si consideratur hec eadem vis ut facit res concurrere aliter quam proposite sint ab homine, et in aliis que a proposito non agunt, dicitur casus. 12. Fortuna autem dicitur proprie secundum quod facit aliter concurrere ea que fiunt a proposito quam fuerint secundum intellectum previsa, secundum quod latius secundo *Physicorum* docetur: generaliter tamen et in grosso gentes non faciunt differentiam; totum enim quicquid in negociis eorum contingit, dum tamen aliter quam previsum fuerit vel non previsum sit contingat, aut expediat aut impediat, si inexpectatum veniat dicitur fieri per fortunam. 13. Quod optime insinuat sua pictura; pingitur enim ceca vel cecis oculis volvens rotam, quia ipsa, quantum ad humanum intellectum, improvise venit et cito immutat res aliter quam sint provise. 14. Quare dicit Philosophus quod est causa per accidens in hiis que fiunt a proposito et que in minori parte contingant. 15. Et secundum hoc quod tales concursus sunt boni vel mali, dicitur ipsa bona vel mala et bene vel male fortunati quibus talia contingunt.

16. Ex hiis patet quid sit fortuna. 17. Et possumus convenienter accipere qualia sunt illa circa que contingit fortuna, quia oportet quod sint res mutabiles et cito provenientes sine provisione humana; que enim de levi non mutantur vel a provisione fiunt, secundum quod huiusmodi non dicimus fieri a fortuna. 18. Tales res sunt tres tantum: dominium, divicie, fama. 19. In istis enim proprie salvatur ratio fortuita, quia ista subito et sine provisione acquirit vel perdit homo, nec in hiis est intellectus humanus sufficiens ut eorum possessio fiat sibi firma. 20. Quare plures philosophy fuerunt qui ista spreverunt triplici ratione: primo quia, ut dictum est, possessio eorum non est firma; secundo quia dominium ut plurimum facit superbos, divicie intemperatos, fama vanigloriosos; amplius quia ipsi viderunt quod quelibet istarum rerum erat inter gentes propter defectum aliquem, non propter privationem nature, quia si omnes homines sapientes et amici fuissent et bonum alter alterius procurasset, nichil fuisset dominium, quia

that begin motion, continue it, or end it. 9. Natural philosophers understand this who say that all things are measured by a certain period in heaven, understood proportionally in accordance with the common nature of both intelligence and the celestial body. 10. But if this same force is considered rather as descending and is referred from one moveable thing to another according to an appropriate or inappropriate proportion, that is, if it is applied to acts of men or other things, it is called "augury" or "prediction of the future" and it is always received in deep thoughts and other perceptions, in birds of augury, and in visions of dreams and the like. 11. Furthermore, if this same force is considered as it makes things come about otherwise than as they are anticipated by man, and in other things that do not turn out as intended, it is called "chance." 12. Fortune is properly so called when it makes things that happen intentionally happen otherwise than as they were foreseen by intellect, according to what is taught more fully in the second book of the *Physics*: generally and roughly speaking people do not make the distinction, for whatever comes about in their affairs, when it happens otherwise than was foreseen or when it was unforeseen, whether it helps or hinders, if it comes about unexpectedly it is said to happen by fortune. 13. This is very well shown by the picture of Fortune, for it is painted as blind or as turning its wheel with blind eyes, since, as understood by human intellect, it comes unexpectedly and quickly changes things from what was expected. 14. So the Philosopher says that fortune is the accidental cause of those things that come about intentionally and that happen to a lesser degree intentionally. 15. Depending on whether such coincidences are good or bad, fortune itself is called good or bad and those to whom such things happen are called "lucky" or "unlucky."

16. From all this it is clear what fortune is. 17. We can understand what things fortune happens through since they must be changeable things and come forth quickly, without human foresight; we do not say that things that are not changed easily or that happen from foresight are caused by fortune. 18. There are only three such things: power, wealth, and fame. 19. To them, the concept of chance is properly reserved since man gains or loses them suddenly and without anticipation, and human intellect is not sufficient to make possession of them reliable. 20. Wherefore many philosophers have scorned these things for three reasons: first, because, as has been said, the possession of them is not reliable; second, because power often makes men proud, wealth makes them intemperate, and fame makes them vainglorious; and especially because these philosophers have seen that each of these things came among people because of some lack on their part, not because of deprivation of nature, for if all men were wise and friendly and each one sought the good of the other, power would

dominium statutum est ut ratio custodiatur contra stultos, et amicitia contra malos, et equitas contra perversos. 21. Similiter divicie non fuissent si avaricia et rapina non forent, quia quilibet cuilibet foret largus, quare in defectum alicuius non cumulasset nec etiam rapuisset; nec etiam fama fuisset, si lingua humana fuisset ratione frenata.

22. Hiis rationibus philosophi bona fortune spreverunt, tamen quia firmiter custodiri non possunt, tamen quia magis ad metum qu[am] ad virtutem faciunt homines declinare, tamen quia propter imperfectionem humanam contingunt. 23. Verumptamen quamvis illa bona in se considerata non sint magni valoris, multum tamen immutant qualitatem operationis humane. 24. Aliquam enim bonitatem habent in relatione generis humani, ut patebit inferius, et si non absolutam habent, tamen relativam. 25. Et circa talia homines quibus contingunt bonum possunt reddere opus suum vel malum, unde ulterius circa talia poterunt iudicari nobiles sive viles. 26. Unde secundum hoc erunt tres nobilitates fortune, sicilicet dominii, diviciarum, et fame.

Caput 6

De nobilitate dominiorum

1. [N]obilitas dominiorum in duobus consistit in perfectione, scilicet ut ratio inter homines conservetur et pax et amicitia inter ipsos. 2. Et est data auctoritas omnium uni soli ut ad utilitatem omnium sit pacis et rationis custodia, unde Philosophus primo *Polyticorum* dicit dominum esse naturaliter qui pre aliis viget intellectu, quare ipse est potens in aliis custodire qui de seipso prevalet intellectu. 3. Quare supreme competit domino et sibi et subditis [ut] intellectui et rationi studeat diligenter, ita quod sicut sol omnia illuminat, ita dominus ratione et intellectu subditos faciat relucere, stulticias et bestialitates reprimens, discordias et iniquitates castigans. 4. Quod optime dixit Plato, ut dicit Boetius primo *De consolatione*, dicens beatas fore res publicas si sapientes eas regerent, vel rectores earum sapientie studuissent. 5. Quando enim tales sunt domini et dominium suum taliter volunt deducere, optima vita vivunt et vere nobiles domini sunt, quocumque modo eis dominium contingat. 6. Et si contingat quod aliquis dominus voluerit nec rationi studere nec intellectui, nec pacem nec utilitatem suam nec subditorum servare, dico quod talis est vilis dominus et despectus, et quanto maius est dominium tanto maior est vilitas et despectus. 7. Et talis secundum veritatem non est dominus sed servus, nec nobilis sed

be nothing since power was established to protect reason against the foolish, friendship against the bad, and equity against the perverse. 21. Similarly there would be no wealth if there were no avarice and robbery, since everyone would be generous to everyone else and not seek to pile up anything or steal anything because he did not have enough of it; nor would there be fame if the human tongue were reined in by reason.

22. For these reasons philosophers have scorned the goods of fortune: because they cannot be kept reliably, or because they make men tend more toward fear than virtue, or because they arise out of human imperfection. 23. Nevertheless, although these good things are not of great value in themselves, they influence the quality of human actions greatly. 24. They have a certain goodness in relation to the human race, as will be clear below, and though they do not have absolute goodness, they do have relative goodness. 25. Because of such things, men to whom they befall make their acts good or bad, and furthermore, because of such things men will be judged noble or ignoble. 26. So we shall say that there are three nobilities of fortune, namely, those of power, wealth, and fame.

Chapter 6

On Nobility of Power

1. Nobility of power consists, in perfection, of two things, which are preserving reason among men and preserving peace and friendship among them. 2. Authority over all men is given to one alone to be the guardian of peace and reason for the benefit of all, which is why the Philosopher says in the first book of the *Politics* that he is naturally a lord who surpasses others in intellect. 3. It is most appropriate, then, for a lord to apply himself diligently to intellect and reason for the good of himself and his subjects, for just as the sun illumines all things, so the lord may make his subjects shine in reason and intellect, repressing folly and bestiality, chastising discords and iniquities. 4. Plato said this excellently, as Boethius reports in the first book *On Consolation*, saying that republics would be blessed if wise men ruled them or if their rulers applied themselves to wisdom. 5. When such men are lords and wish to employ their power in this way, they live an excellent life and are truly noble lords, however power may have befallen them. 6. But if a certain lord chooses to apply himself to neither reason nor intellect and not to preserve peace or utility for himself or his subjects, I say that such a man is an ignoble lord and despicable, and that the greater his power, the greater his ignobility and despicableness. 7. In truth such a man is not a lord but a slave, not noble but ignoble, wherefore many sinister

vilis, unde talibus dominis multa sinistra contingunt, occasione quorum eorum dominia sunt destructa. 8. Unde de talibus dominis loquens Oratius dicit, "Mox trahitur manibus regum fortuna retortis," quia propter eorum stultitiam talia sine ratione incipiunt et committunt in quibus eis contingit contrarium eorum que ipsis evenire credebant secundum eorum erroneam voluptatem. 9. Unde de talibus loquens Salomon dicit, "Ve terre cuius rex iuvenis est." 10. Et expressius pater eius David dicit, "Homo cum in honore esset," id est in dominio, "non [intellexit," id est non] cognovit qualiter agendum esset secundum honorem dominii sui; "comparatus est iumentis insipientibus et similis factus est illis."

11. Ex quibus patet quod nobilitas dominii nichil aliud est quam rationale regnum ex quo ratio et pax inter subditos conservantur. 12. De hac nobilitate loquitur Philosophus primo *Rethorice*, dicens quod "Nobilitas est genti et civitati sui iuris antiquos esse presides," quia sine dubio populares et cives sine aliqua nobilitate loqui nescirent. 13. De nobilitate dominii hec dicta sufficiant.

Caput 7

De nobilitate divitiarum

1. [Q]uamvis pro diviciis generaliter omnia mobilia aliquando intelligamus, proprie tamen intelligimus habundanciam pecunie congregatam ad possessionem alicuius pertinentem. 2. Quando igitur contingit quod aliquis secundum statum suum notabilem habet pecunie quantitatem dives communiter appellatur, quamvis secundum veritatem non sit, nisi sibi sufficiat et inde faciat quod recta ratio dictaret; non sit dives, quantamcumque magnam habeat pecunie quantitatem, quia divicie significant proprie sufficientiam quandam. 3. Unde postquam aliquis iudicat sibi non sufficere quod habet, statim iudicat non habere habundanciam, quare iudicat se non esse divitem; quare statim concupiscit et nititur cumulare et aliam ducere vitam quam recta ratio suaderet. 4. Unde Oratius in *Epistulis* suis dicit, "Imperat aut servit collecta pecunia cuique"; imperat enim avaris, servit autem hiis qui conantur vivere ratione recta, hoc est large, non prodige nec avare. 5. Hoc idem intelligit Boetius in libro *De consolatione* ubi dicit quod divicie in spargendo sive in distribuendo relucent, non in accumulando; quare subditur largos fore dilectos et avaros exosos, largi enim sibi et aliis benefactores existunt, avari autem nec sibi nec aliis sed nocivi.

things befall such lords that destroy their power. 8. Speaking of such lords [in tragic drama], Horace says, "Soon the fortune of kings with their hands bound is dragged in [to the play]," since in their foolishness they undertake and commit things without reason, and the opposite of what they thought would come about befalls them because of their misguided desire. 9. Speaking of such men, Solomon says, "Woe to the land whose king is a youth." 10. And more plainly his father David says, "Man, when he was in honor," that is, in power, "did not understand," that is, did not know how to act consonant with the honor of his power; "he hath been compared to senseless beasts, and made like to them."

11. It is clear, then, that nobility of power is nothing else than rational rule that preserves reason and peace among subjects. 12. Of this nobility the Philosopher speaks in the first book of the *Rhetoric*, saying, "Nobility is to be, by right, ancient guardians for the people and the city," since without doubt common people and citizens without any nobility would not know how to speak. 13. As for nobility of power, let what has been said suffice.

Chapter 7

On Nobility of Wealth

1. Although by wealth in general we sometimes understand all moveable things, properly we understand an abundance of money gathered together in the possession of one person. 2. Therefore when it happens that someone has a quantity of money that is notable for his state he is commonly called "rich," although in truth he is not, unless it is enough for him and consequently he does what right reason says; he is not rich, however great a quantity of money he has, for riches properly mean a certain sufficiency. 3. When someone judges that what he has is not enough for him, at the same time he judges that he does not have abundance, so he judges that he is not rich; therefore he desires wealth and tries to accumulate it, and to lead a life other than right reason calls for. 4. Horace says in his *Epistles*, "Money saved up either commands or serves everyone," for it commands the avaricious but serves those who try to live by right reason, which is to say generously, neither prodigally nor avariciously. 5. Boethius understands this in his book *On Consolation* when he says that riches shine in scattering them about or in distributing them, not in piling them up; he adds that generous people are beloved and greedy people hated, for generous people are helpful to themselves and others, while greedy people are not helpful but harmful to themselves and others.

6. Quare patet quod nobilitas diviciarum nichil aliud est quam usus rationabilis et secundum virtutem diviciarum ipsarum, et dominus et nobilis qui suis diviciis sic utitur, ut est dictum, quia operacio sua nobilis est et digna cognosci et similis operationi divine, que large et sine spe recompensationis suarum diviciarum distribuit. 7. Divites autem in hoc deficientes sunt viles et miseri in duobus. 8. Unum est defectus et animi paupertas que facit eos timere de defectu eorum quorum habent habundantiam ultra terminos rationis. 9. Aliud est quia ipsi nesciunt iudicare quantum eis debeat sufficere nec quomodo hiis que habent debent uti. 10. Sed quod apud sapientes mirabilius debet esse est quod tales miseri de quibus nunc loquor frequenter inveniuntur inter aliquos inter quos nullus reperiri deberet, licet inveniantur ubique in qualibet hominum manerie, quia ardentiores videmus ad accumulandum pecuniam quos sine herede legali oportet mori quam plures heredes habentes, et redditus maiores habere quam heredes habentes. 11. Ego autem credo quod illud vicium est in pluribus propter hoc quod quilibet dignum se iudicat ad possidendum amplius quam possideat, quare quod habet non sufficit, immo ex hoc ulterius incipit concupiscere plus et agregat ut statum suum possit ad altius promovere. 12. Et sic pauci sunt qui sciant certum terminum imponere voluntati; quare eorum tota vita peruritur ad habendum liquescens absque pace cordis in periculis agitata. 13. Unde Boetius dicit, "O preclara opum mortalium beatitudo, quam cum adeptus fueris securus esse desistis!" 14. Contingit autem quamplurimum periculum ex concupiscentia circa idem, quare Cato precepit filio suo dicens,

> Quod nimium est fugito, parvo gaudere memento;
> tuta mage puppis [est modico que flumine fertur].

15. Hoc idem dicit Oratius in *Epistulis* suis optime: "Serviet eternum qui parvo nesciat uti." 16. Omnes isti intelligunt quod nobilitas et libertas magna esset incertis imponere terminum voluntati et ad diviciarum superflua non vacare.

Caput 8

De nobilitate fame

1. [T]ercia species nobilitatis fortune est circa famam vel gloriam, que nichil aliud est quam laus currens communiter inter gentes, a qua, gratia sui operis, inter consortes iudicatur aliquis excellens. 2. Inter autem alia bona fortune est quod plus habet de for[m]a et minus de bonitate reali, quia paucissimi sunt qui

6. It is obvious, then, that nobility of wealth is nothing else than use of wealth that is rational and concordant with virtue, and lordly and noble [is he] who uses his wealth in this way, as has been said, since his action is noble, worthy to be known, and similar to the action of God, who distributes generously and without hope of repayment of his riches. 7. Rich people who are lacking in this respect are wretched and miserable in two ways. 8. One is a lack and poverty of spirit that makes them fearful beyond the limits of reason about loss of the things they have in abundance. 9. Another is that they cannot judge how much ought to be enough for them or how to use what they have. 10. But what should be more amazing to the wise is that such unhappy people of whom I now speak are frequently found among those among whom none of them ought to be found, although they may be found anywhere in any manner of men since we see that they who must die without legal heirs are more eager for piling up riches than many who have heirs, and they have larger incomes than those who have heirs. 11. I believe that this is a vice in many people who judge themselves worthy to possess more than they do and believe that what they have is not enough, so they begin to desire more and build up wealth in order to improve their status to a higher one. 12. There are few who know how to set a certain limit to the will, so all their life is burned up for getting what melts away, shaken by perils that leave them no peace of heart. 13. Boethius says, "O splendid blessing of mortal wealth; when you have gained it, you cease to be safe!" 14. Danger often befalls from greed for wealth, which is why Cato commanded his son, saying,

> Flee what is too great, remember to rejoice in little;
> Safer is the ship that sails a modest stream.

15. Horace says the same very well in his *Epistles*: "He will serve forever who does not know how to live on little." 16. All these authors understand that it is nobility and great liberty to "set a limit to the will" concerning uncertain things, and not to devote oneself to needless wealth.

Chapter 8

On Nobility of Fame

1. The third type of nobility of fortune involves fame or glory, which is nothing else than praise running commonly among the people, which causes someone to be judged excellent among those who share his fate because of what he has done. 2. Among the other goods of fortune this one has the most of appearance and the least of real goodness since there are very few who have a moderate

linguam habeant temperatam ad loquendum de aliis. 3. Ymmo, ut in pluribus loquitur unus de alio improvide et parva occasione ea vituperat que laudavit! 4. Verumptamen nobilitas ista quasi momentanea est in illo cui attribuitur, si talis sit ille qualis testatur fama communis. 5. Unde de tali loquens Oratius dicit, "Tu recte vivis si curas esse quod audis." 6. Hoc idem Cato filio suo dicebat: "Cum te aliquis laudat, iudex tuus esse memento," in hoc Cato intelligens quod filius esset talis secundum veritatem qualis bonitate fame predicaretur, ne alicuius adulatione vel inani gloria foret deceptus, quia isti vanigloriosi ad hoc non laborant quod eorum opera sint digna laudis et glorie, sed nituntur toto posse quia eorum opera appareant et quod appareant magne fame, unde laus supradicta moveatur, et lingua et aures diversorum. 7. Hoc sufficit eis; tamen quasi plures talium videmus facere opera largitatis specialiter illis qui plura loquuntur in diversis locis et de personis diversis, sed illis quibus deberent distribuere bona sua secundum ordinem largitatis nichil darent.

8. Alia quedam vanigloriosorum species reperitur satis vilis. 9. Sunt enim plures qui libenter mixtim in propriam laudem redundant cum turpibus et turpia cum laudibus, tamquam unum per alterum confirmantes. 10. Quod multum vituperavit Cato dicens,

Nec te collaudes, [nec te culpaveris ipsum;
hoc faciunt stulti quos gloria vexat inanis].

11. Hoc idem dicit Aristoteles Alexandro: "Laudare seipsum est vanitas, vituperare stultitie signum dabit." 12. Ex hiis satis patet quod nobilitas glorie nichil aliud est quam alicuius persone vera bonitatis fama que talia facit que digna sunt gloria.

Caput 9

De quibusdam dubitabilibus circa predictas species nobilitatis

1. [T]empus expostulat ut contra predicta de aliquibus dubitemus ut pateat melius veritas predictorum. 2. Primo igitur queritur utrum tot sint species nobilitatis quot superius sunt distincte. 3. Et videtur quod non, quia omnis [nobilitas ex bonitate] operationis accepta, apta cuilibet; huius operationis principium est anima; preterea videtur quod nulla sit nobilitas corporis, cum operationibus anime non possit nisi solum organice deservire. 4. Similiter potest ostendi de fortuna, quia operationes quibus nos nobiles iudicamur secundum

tongue in speaking about others. 3. No, how thoughtlessly one man speaks of another among many, and for little reason criticizes what he has praised! 4. Yet such nobility is as though momentary in the person to whom it is attributed, even if he is indeed as common reputation proclaims. 5. Speaking of such a person, Horace says, "You live rightly if you take care to be what you hear" [said about yourself]. 6. Cato said the same to his son: "When someone praises you, remember to be your own judge," meaning by this that his son should be in truth such as he would like to be called by the goodness of fame rather than be deceived by anyone's flattery or empty glory since these vainglorious people do not strive to make their deeds worthy of praise and glory but try with all their power to get their deeds seen and to be seen to be worthy of great fame, so that the aforesaid praise should be set in motion and the tongues and ears of various people. 7. This is enough for them; still we seem to see more such people doing generous acts especially to those who say many things in various places and about various people, but they give nothing to those to whom they should distribute their goods according to the course of generosity.

8. Another type of vainglorious people is found quite reprehensible. 9. Many overflow with their own praise mixed with shameful things about themselves and shameful things mixed with praise, as though strengthening one with the other. 10. Cato criticized this severely, saying,

> Neither praise yourself nor blame yourself;
> Fools do this, whom empty glory vexes.

11. Aristotle says the same to Alexander: "To praise yourself is vanity; to criticize yourself will give a sign of folly." 12. It is sufficiently clear, then, that nobility of glory is nothing else than true fame for goodness of some person who does things that are worthy of glory.

Chapter 9

On Certain Doubts about the Aforesaid Types of Nobility

1. Time demands that we proceed to express doubts about what has been said above, so that its truth will stand forth better. 2. First, therefore, it is asked whether there really are as many types of nobility as have been distinguished above. 3. It seems there are not, since all nobility accrues from goodness of action and is fitting to someone; the principle of this action is the soul; hence it seems that there is no nobility of the body, since the body cannot serve the actions of the soul except organically. 4. The same can be shown regarding

quod huiusmodi in libertate nostra consistunt, sed de rebus fortune ut sic nullatenus potest dici, secundum quod superius fuit dictum. 5. Quare videtur quod non nisi sola nobilitas anime sit.

6. Ad oppositum fuit superius satis dictum. 7. Ad questionem secundum predicta dicendum quod tres sunt species nobilita[t]is, licet una altera sit prior et nobilior, secundum quod in sequenti questione patebit, quoniam quamvis ita sit quod anima sit principium omnium formale, verumptamen corpus materiale et instrumentale [principium] plurium operationum consistit. 8. Unde secundum bonam vel malam ipsius dispositionem operationes in bonitate vel malicia disponuntur, unde anima viliter et nobiliter in operando procedit. 9. Ex quo patet ad rationem primam que nobilitatem corporis ammovebat.

10. Ad aliud dicendum quod quamvis ita sit quod fortune bona frequenter veniant non previsa et absque ratione humana contingant, tamen postquam con[ti]gerint oportet hominem circa ipsa secundum rationem facere quod est dignum, quia hoc potest facere et libere operari. 11. Licet enim talium bonorum sit fortuitus eventus, non tamen usus eorum debet esse fortuitus haberi. 12. Et circa huiusmodi usum bonum diximus hanc nobilitatem existere, non secundum quod talia bona improvisa diximus evenire. 13. Ex quo satis patet ad rationem.

Caput 10

Secunda questio

1. [S]ecundo queritur que species nobilitatis dignior vel melior debeat dici. 2. Videtur enim quod nobilitas dominii sit potior inter eas, quia, sicut dictum fuit superius, omnes nobilitates sunt cognite propter nobilitatem operacionis cognitam, quare nobilitas erit potissima cuius operatio in bonitate potissime cognoscitur; sed nobilitas dominii est huius, per se enim [patet] quod operationes unius nobilis domini meliores, communiores, et utiliores existunt quam operationes aliorum nobilium quorumcumque. 3. Ad res enim pupblicas primo et per se ordinantur maxime, quare videtur quod hec nobilitas nobilitates alias excellat. 4. Preterea composita secundum quod huiusmodi nobiliora sunt hiis ex quibus componuntur, ut elementata elementis; sed nobilitas dominii videtur esse composita ex anime nobilitate et fortune, quare videtur melior.

5. Oppositum fuit declaratum superius et sufficienter probatum. 6. Ad questionem intelligendum, secundum quod iam superius fuit tactum, quod non dicitur

fortune, as actions for which we are judged noble are in our power, but this can by no means be said about affairs of fortune, according to what was said above. 5. So it appears that the only nobility is that of soul.

6. Enough has been said above to show the opposite. 7. In response to the question, it should be said, according to what has been said before, that there are three types of nobility, even though one is prior to another and nobler than it is, as will become clear in the following question, since, although it is true that the soul is the formal principle of all things, nevertheless the body constitutes the material and instrumental principle of many actions. 8. For this reason, actions are inclined toward good or bad according to their good or bad disposition, so that the soul proceeds in action reprehensibly or nobly. 9. It is clear, then, as to the first argument that banished nobility of the body.

10. Regarding the second, it should be said that although it is true that goods of fortune frequently come unexpectedly and befall without human reason, yet after they befall a man must do with them what is worthy according to reason, because he can do this and freely cause it to happen. 11. Although the coming of such good things is fortuitous, the use of them should not be considered fortuitous. 12. We have said that this nobility arises from the good use [to which such things are put]; we have not said [it arises] because such good things happen unexpectedly. 13. It is clear enough, then, as to this argument.

Chapter 10

Second Question

1. Second, it is asked which type of nobility should be called more worthy or better. 2. It seems that nobility of power is the most powerful among them since, as has been said above, all nobilities are recognized for nobility of action, so that the nobility will be most powerful whose action is recognized as most powerful in goodness; and nobility of power is of this kind, for it is clear in itself that the actions of a noble lord are better, more broadly efficacious, and more useful than the actions of other nobles whosoever. 3. First and intrinsically, the actions of a noble lord are particularly directed toward public affairs, so it is apparent that this nobility excels other nobilities. 4. Besides, combinations by this logic are nobler than the things of which they are combined, as compounds are nobler than elements; and nobility of power seems to be compounded of nobility of soul and fortune, so it seems better.

5. The opposite was declared above and sufficiently proved. 6. On this question it is to be understood, according to what has already been touched on above,

dominus nobilis a suo dominio nisi pro tanto quod ipse sapiens est et studiosus in omnibus secundum virtutes que pertinent ad dominium; alias dominium in vilitatem convertitur. 7. Unde nobilitas anime forma et perfectio est omnium aliarum; hec enim perficit et dirigit alias, vivificat et illuminat, sine qua relique mortue et tenebrose vilescunt. 8. Ex quo patet quid sit dicendum ad primum in oppositum, quia quamvis ita sit quod operationes nobilis et boni domini sint meliores et rem pupblicam magis respicientes, hoc non habent [in] quantum dependent a domino, sed in quantum sunt virtute et sapientia informat[e], quia cum dominus est sapiens et virtuosus secundum rationem debet regere ea que fortuite contingunt, unde fortuita in hoc materiam prebent solum.

9. Ad rationem secundam dicendum quod minor est falsa que accipit nobilitatem dominii tamquam ex duabus nobilitatibus compositam, quod non est verum. 10. Sicut enim diximus, in rebus dominii nulla est nobilitas nisi inicium quantum virtute et sapientia informatur; et ideo non concludit, quare patet quod nobilitas dominii est nobilitatis effectus anime. 11. Et si forsan velit quis ulterius querere quare communiter homines de sola hac nobilitate loquuntur, dicendum quod vulgaris sententia ut plurimum est imperfecta. 12. Unde Philosophus hoc intelligens dixit, "Loquendum est ut plures, sed sapiendum est ut pauci," quare in dictis communibus firmiter non est standum nisi dictis sapientum concordarent.

Caput 11

Questio tercia

1. [T]ercio queritur utrum omnes homines sint nobiles per naturam, et videtur quod sic. 2. Omnes enim qui sunt eiusdem speciei in natura sunt eiusdem operationis et forme; sed omnes homines sunt eiusdem speciei et operationis, quare omnes erunt eiusdem nobilitatis, ut videtur. 3. Maior patet de se, et minor etiam: omnes habent animam rationalem cuius operatio nobilis est, ut patuit ex predictis.

4. Hoc idem patet aliter ex dicto communi: "Omnes" enim "qui sunt eiusdem patris et matris sunt eiusdem nobilitatis," sed omnes homines sunt huiusmodi, quare, et cetera. 5. Quare videtur quod omnes homines sint nobiles vel viles. 6. Cuius oppositum superius est ostensum, et patet ad sensum. 7. Videmus enim plures ita viles et miseros, et eorum nequitiam, quod propter eorum nequitiam oportet eos expelli a communi, et exterminantur ab aliis propter malitiam

that a lord is not called noble because of his power but insofar as he is wise and studious in all things according to the virtues that pertain to power since otherwise power turns into ignobility. 7. Therefore nobility of soul is the form and perfection of all the others, for it perfects and directs the others, gives them life and light, and without it the rest grow ignoble, dead, and dark. 8. So it is clear what should be said to the first objection since, although it is true that the actions of a noble and good lord are better and more important for public life, this is not true inasmuch as they depend on the lord but inasmuch as they are informed by virtue and wisdom since when a lord is wise and virtuous he must rule according to reason the things that befall by chance, so fortuitous events in this connection offer only material [for noble action, not nobility itself].

9. On the second argument it should be said that the minor premise is false that takes nobility of power as compounded of two nobilities, which is not true. 10. As we have said, in affairs of power there is no nobility except insofar as its beginning is informed by virtue and wisdom; therefore [the syllogism] does not conclude, for it is obvious that nobility of power is an effect of nobility of soul. 11. If someone should wish to ask why men commonly speak of only this nobility, it should be said that vulgar opinion is usually imperfect. 12. Understanding this, the Philosopher said, "Speak like the many but know like the few," for one should not stand firmly on common sayings unless they agree with the words of the wise.

Chapter 11

Third Question

1. Third, it is asked whether all men are noble by nature, and it appears that they are. 2. All who are of the same species in nature have the same action and form; and all men are of the same species and action, so they will all have the same nobility, as is apparent. 3. The major premise is obvious in itself, and the minor too: all men have a rational soul whose action is noble, as has been apparent from what has been said.

4. The same is obvious in another way from a common saying: "All who have the same father and mother have the same nobility," and all men are such, so that, and so on. 5. So it is apparent that all men are noble or ignoble. 6. The opposite of this has been shown above and is obvious to sense. 7. We see that many people are so ignoble and wicked that they must be expelled from the community, and they are exterminated by others because of the badness of their actions, because their actions corrupt the common good and infect the honesty

operationum suarum, quia eorum operationes bonum commune corrumpunt et aliorum inficiunt honestatem. 8. Unde Philosophus in primo *Politicorum* dicit quod "Talium iniusticia sevissima gerit arma." 9. Et sicut optimum est animalium homo vivens secundum legem et rationem, separatus a lege et iusticia pessimum est omnium. 10. Sic etiam videmus aliquos quorum doctrina, bonitas, et honestas sunt lumen et regula inter alios quorum studium ad bona omnia se extendit, unde aperte videmus quod operationes aliquorum hominum plus differunt quam operationes multorum secundum speciem differentium, puta leonis et vulpis. 11. Unde quia nobilitas et vilitas formam accipit ex operationum qualitate, oportet quod sapientes et probi secundum quamlibet speciem nobilitatis nobiles iudicentur, stulti autem et improbi debent ignobiles iudicari.

12. Ad rationes vero, ad primam dico quod ea que sunt eiusdem speciei, si habent formam in materia, non oportet quod habeant operationem eiusdem nobilitatis vel malitie. 13. Contingit enim talibus quod ex bona vel mala dispositione in materia, sint bene vel male in suis operationibus expedita. 14. Unde homines [male] dispositi secundum corpus bene disponuntur in mente, ut vult Philosophus in libro *De anima*; dicit enim "Molles carne aptos mente." 15. Et si forte aliquis instaret quod anima rationalis a corpore non dependet secundum quod huiusmodi, dico quod falsum est; licet enim anima non dependeat vel indigeat forte corpore ut subiecto, indiget tamen ut obiecto. 16. Sed videtur vehementius contra hanc solutionem esse quod Philosophus dicit in *Phisonomia* sua: dicit enim quod diverse sunt dispositiones in corpore per diversas virtutes ipsius anime, quare non videtur quod ex natura ipsius materie vel corporis sit accipienda causa nobilitatis in operatione vel nobilitatis impedimentum. 17. Unde dicunt aliqui quod licet omnes homines sint eiusdem forme secundum speciem, non tamen secundum n[atura]m; immo in anima vel forma uniuscuiusque est aliqua proprietas, vel alique proprietates sunt ita in uno quod non sunt in altero. 18. Secundum hoc ponunt causam principalem in anima, et si queratur ab eis unde habet anima hoc, dicunt quod acquiritur hoc in sui creatione a motoribus celestibus, confirmantes hoc per Ptholomeum et Haly, quod sicut sunt elementa in corporibus, ita stelle in animabus (id est motores stellarum animabus), per quas virtutes explicantur ea que a Deo principaliter procreantur. 19. Sed quia hec solucio metas naturales transcendit, hic magis naturaliter est loquendum. 20. Dico ergo quod omnes homines habent animam eiusdem speciei, ut dictum est, et causa magis accipienda est ipsius vilitatis a parte corporis quam anime, quia motores celestes secundum quod huiusmodi

of others. 8. So the Philosopher says in the first book of the *Politics* that "The injustice of such people bears most cruel arms." 9. Just as man living according to law and reason is the best of animals, separated from law and justice he is the worst of them all. 10. We see some men whose teaching, goodness, and honesty are a light and a rule among others whose study extends to all good things, so we see clearly that the actions of some men differ from those of others more than the actions of many creatures that differ in species, as for example the lion or the fox. 11. So, since nobility and ignobility receive their form from the quality of actions, wise and honest men must be judged noble according to some type of nobility, but foolish and dishonest men must be judged ignoble.

12. As for the arguments, on the first I say that even though things that have the same species have the same material form, it is not necessary that they have action of the same nobility or wickedness. 13. It happens that such things may be well or badly directed in their actions because of good or bad disposition in matter. 14. Some men who are badly disposed in body are well disposed in mind, as the Philosopher claims in the book *On the Soul*, for he says, "Those who are soft in flesh are apt in mind." 15. And if perchance someone insists that rational soul does not depend on body, as it would by this logic, I say this is false, for although soul may not depend upon body or need it as a subject, it does need it as an object. 16. But what the Philosopher says in his *Physiognomy* seems to be vehemently against this solution [that soul needs body as an object], for he says that there are diverse dispositions in body for diverse virtues of the same soul, so it is not apparent that the cause of nobility in action or any impediment to nobility is to be received from the nature of the same matter or body. 17. Some say that although all men have the same form according to species, they do not according to nature; rather, in the soul or form of each one there is some property or properties that are such in one as they are not in another. 18. By this reasoning they put the principal cause in the soul, and if they are asked where soul gets this, they say that it is acquired when soul is created by the heavenly movers, which they confirm by quoting Ptolemy and Hali, who say that just as elements are to bodies, so are stars to souls (that is, movers of the stars to souls), and these powers explain the things that are directly procreated by God. 19. But since this solution transcends natural bounds, here we must [depart from it and] speak instead in natural terms. 20. I say, then, that all men have soul of the same species, as has been said, and the cause of ignobility is to be understood rather on the part of the body than of the soul, since the heavenly movers, according to this logic, remain altogether uniform, so that they must cause uniform souls; but since heaven cannot remain uniform in the formation

omnino uniformiter se habent, quare uniformes causantur anime; sed quia celum uniformiter non potest se habere in formatione omnium corporum, oportet quod difformiter informetur. 21. Unde [Philosophus quarto] *De animalibus* dicit quod virtus informativa proportionaliter operatur coordinationi astrorum. 22. Anima igitur, que naturalem habet inclinationem ad corpus et ipso in suis operationibus utitur tamquam organo vel obiecto necessario, inducitur ad agendum per ipsum secundum aptitudinem corporis ipsius; et istam talem inclinationem significant astronomi per stellas, et naturales vel phisionomi per membrorum figuras. 23. Aliter non est intelligendum quod Philosophus dicit in *Physonomia* et Ptholomeus in *Centilogio.*

24. Ad rationem secundam dicendum breviter quod quamvis omnes homines essent eiusdem patris et matris, non tamen oportet quod sint eiusdem nobilitatis. 25. Eadem enim mater non disponit uniformiter materiam filiorum, immo numquam, quare filii dissimiles in pluribus sunt reperti. 26. Unde quibus ita contingit quod corpus bene dispositum et temperatum et bene formatum existit animam habent expeditam, nec malicia complexionis torquentur; immo naturaliter tendunt ad ea que sunt rationis et intellectus tamquam ad operationem propriam inclinat[i]. 27. Unde tales dicuntur boni [primo *Ethicorum*] per se, et primo *Politicorum* dicuntur domini per naturam. 28. Alii vero quorum corpora dura, rudia, et inepta formantur habent multum animam impeditam, et de facili ad rudem sensualitatem declinant, et, deficientes ab operatione humana, in operationes bestiales labuntur et sunt viles. 29. [Unde primo *Ethicorum* dicuntur tales viri inutiles,] et servi iudicantur naturaliter. 30. Qui autem medio modo se habent indigent doctrina, et possunt fieri boni per alium, licet non per se perfecte. 31. Ex dictis igitur patet quomodo omnes homines nobiles debent iudicari.

Caput 12

Questio quarta

1. [Q]uarto queritur utrum mulier sit ita nobilis sicut vir, et videtur quod non, quia cuius operationes sunt meliores et nobiliores, eius nobilitas est maior et melior; sed operationes viri sunt huiusmodi, quare, et cetera. 2. Operationes enim viri sunt communes, mulieris vero domestice et private; qu[are] mulier, ut videtur, non erit ita nobilis. 3. Hoc idem probatur aliter, quia in natura omne perfectius est nobilius; sed vir est muliere perfectior, ergo nobilior.

of all bodies, they must be informed in various forms. 21. In the fourth book *On Animals* the Philosopher says that the informative virtue works in proportion to the coordination of the stars. 22. Therefore soul, which has a natural inclination to body and uses it in its actions as an organ or necessary object, is induced to acting through it according to the aptitude of the body; and astronomers signify just such inclination through the stars and natural philosophers or physiognomists by the shapes of parts of the body. 23. In no other way must we understand what the Philosopher says in the *Physiognomy* and Ptolemy in the *Centiloquio*.

24. On the second argument one should briefly say that although all men have the same father and mother, it is nevertheless not necessary that they should have the same nobility. 25. For the same mother does not dispose the matter of her children uniformly, indeed never, so that in many cases children [of the same mother] are found to be dissimilar. 26. Those whose body happens to be well disposed, temperate, and well formed have an unencumbered soul, and are not distorted by malice of complexion; rather, they naturally tend toward things of reason and intellect, insofar as they are inclined to proper action. 27. In the first book of the *Ethics* such people are called good in themselves, and in the first book of the *Politics* they are called lords by nature. 28. But others whose bodies are formed hard, rude, and inept have an encumbered soul, and decline easily into rude sensuality; falling away from human action, they subside into bestial actions and become ignoble. 29. In the first book of the *Ethics* such men are called useless, and they are naturally judged slaves. 30. Those who hold themselves in a middle way need teaching and can become good through someone else but not perfectly good by their own efforts. 31. From what has been said it is clear how all men must be judged noble.

Chapter 12

Fourth Question

1. Fourth, it is asked whether woman is as noble as man, and it seems not, since if someone's actions are better and nobler, that person's nobility is greater and better; and the actions of man are of this kind, so that, and so on. 2. The activities of man are public but those of woman domestic and private, so it is apparent that woman will not be as noble. 3. The same thing can be proved another way, since in nature every more perfect thing is nobler; and man is more perfect than woman, therefore nobler.

4. In oppositum est quod apparet frequenter; videmus enim operationes multarum mulierum meliores quam operationes multorum virorum. 5. Preterea mulieres sunt eiusdem speciei cum viris, quare eiusdem nobilitatis videntur. 6. Ad questionem dicendum breviter, accipiendo illud quod Philosophus dicit octavo *Ethycorum*: quod opera viri et mulieris confestim natura distincta sunt, ita quod privata et domestica et familiariter ordinata pertinent mulieri, sed opera exteriora que maiorem providentiam et forciorem laborem requirunt pertinent viro; et sic ad bonum commune dirigitur operatio utriusque. 7. Si igitur ita sit quod uterque operationes suas recta regulet ratione, dico quod equaliter erunt nobiles secundum proportionem, licet non simpliciter et absolute. 8. Quantum enim cadit sexus mulieris a perfeccione nature virilis, tantum operatio ab operatione et nobilitas a nobilitate discedit.

9. Ex hiis facile est respondere ad rationes. 10. Prime enim bene concludunt quod simpliciter et absolute mulier non est ita nobilis, et hoc verum est, sed proportionaliter loquendo non est verum. 11. Ad rationes alterius partis, dicendum ad primam quod non queritur questio de viris imperfectis, quia vir in eo quod vir numquam habet deteriores operationes quam mulier in eo quod mulier.

Caput 13

Questio quinta

1. [C]onsequenter queritur utrum aliquis puer sit nobilis. 2. Videtur quod non, quia ut dicit Philosophus in libro *De animalibus*, vita puerorum ut est dicere a vita bestiarum non differt, quia eorum operationes non regulantur ratione nec intellectu; unde nobilitas, que sequitur rationem, non videtur quod possit esse in pueris.

3. Oppositum patet per vulgare proverbium dicens quod in vitulo bene apparet si debeat esse taurus. 4. Hoc est dictu[m] quod in pueris sunt operationes presignantes nobilitatem virilem. 5. Ad istam questionem dicendum quod pueri secundum actum non possunt esse nobiles; sunt enim adhuc sub esse imperfecto, et in motu ad perfectionem. 6. Unde quamvis possunt esse dispositi ad nobiles actiones universaliter, quousque tamen perficiantur secundum ea que sunt corporis et anime, ad formam nobilitatis perfecte venire non possunt. 7. Sunt in potentia et in fieri nobiles, sicut sunt in potentia et in fieri viri. 8. Ex hiis satis patet quid sit dicendum ad rationes.

4. To the contrary, as often happens, we see that the activities of many women are better than the activities of many men. 5. Moreover, women are of the same species as men, so that they seem to have the same nobility. 6. On this question we should speak briefly, accepting what the Philosopher says in the eighth book of the *Ethics*: that the acts of man and woman are distinct in nature from the start, so that acts that are private, domestic, and directed toward the family pertain to woman, but public acts that require greater foresight and stronger effort pertain to man; and thus the action of each is directed toward the common good. 7. Therefore if each one regulates his or her actions by right reason, I say that they will be equally noble in proportion, although not simply and absolutely. 8. As much as the sex of woman falls short of the perfection of man's nature, so much [woman's] action diverges from [men's] action and nobility from nobility.

9. It is easy, then, to answer the arguments. 10. The first ones prove that woman is not as noble [as man] simply and absolutely, and this is true, but speaking proportionally it is not true. 11. As for the arguments on the other side, one should say to the first that the question is not asked about imperfect men, since a man just because he is a man never has worse actions than a woman just because she is a woman.

Chapter 13

Fifth Question

1. Next it is asked whether any boy may be noble. 2. It appears not, since, as the Philosopher says in the book *On Animals*, the life of boys scarcely differs from the life of animals, since their actions are not regulated by reason or intellect; so it does not seem that nobility, which follows reason, could be found in boys.

3. The contrary is seen in a vernacular proverb saying that one can tell in a calf whether it will become a bull. 4. This is said because there are actions in boys foretelling manly nobility. 5. On this question one should say that boys cannot be noble in act, for they are still in a state of imperfect being and in motion toward perfection. 6. Although they can be altogether disposed to noble actions, still until they reach perfection regarding things of the body and soul, they cannot come perfectly to the form of nobility. 7. They are noble in potential and in process, just as they are men in potential and in process. 8. It is clear enough, then, what should be said about the arguments.

Caput 14

Questio [sexta]

1. [S]exto queritur utrum viles per naturam possunt fieri nobiles per doctrinam vel nutrituram. 2. Videtur quod non, sicut enim dixit poeta, "Quod natura negat nemo feliciter audet." 3. Si igitur natura negat nobilitatem in aliquo, videtur quod sibi per doctrinam concedi non possit. 4. Preterea opera nature et artis opera sunt intellectus, sed intellectus, principaliter naturam dirigens, dirigit et regulat omnia; intellectus autem dirigens est humanus, solum artificialia secundum quod huiusmodi dirigens. 5. Tunc arguo sic: sicut intellectus divinus ad humanum, ita effectus divinus ad humanum; sine comparatione est magis perfectus et infallibilis quam humanus. 6. Ubi ergo natura vel intellectus divinus deficit, nullo modo videtur quod natura humana sufficere possit.

7. Oppositum videmus, quod per doctrinam bonam multi meliorantur in actionibus suis. 8. Ad primam [rac]ionem dicendum quod Philosophus dicit primo *Ethycorum* quod etiam superius fuit dictum, scilicet quod quidam sunt boni per se, ita quod eorum natura semper directa est ad bene agere et ad bene scire; et tales sunt nobiles per seipsos, et sunt rectores et magistri. 9. Alii sunt in quibus non invenitur perfecta natura, immo invenitur impedita in aliquibus propter aliqualem intemperiem corporalem, quare alterius auxilio indigent; verumptamen defectus non est ita fortis nec firmus quin sit possibile quod alterius beneficio corrigatur, unde tales emendantur convenienti doctrina et fiunt nobiles beneficio nutriture. 10. Tertius est gradus hominum in quibus natura ita defecta est quod iuvari non potest, et tales per se nec per alios nobilitari possunt. 11. Unde dicit Philosophus quod ad mores tales sunt inutiles. 12. Ex hiis est facile ad questionem respondere et ad rationes.

13. Ad questionem igitur dicendum quod aliqui sunt viles si sibi dimittantur qui tamen per alios boni fiunt, et aliqui qui non possunt corrigi, ut est dictum. 14. Ad rationes dico quod in illis in quibus perfecte negat natura, in illis numquam perficiet nutritura; sed in illis in quibus imperfecte natura perficit et aliquid imperfectum relinquit, ars bene perficit auxiliante natura, quod optime dicit Philosophus septimo *Politicorum*: "Omnis doctrina et omnis [disciplina] quod nature deficit vult supplere." 15. Et est intelligendum in illis in quibus natura tantum dedit quod in maiori parte a perfectione non distant, et tunc aliquis iuvando naturam ducit rem in melius. 16. In hoc tamen natura omnium

Chapter 14

Sixth Question

1. Sixth, it is asked whether those who are ignoble by nature can become noble by teaching or training. 2. It seems not, for as a poet said, "What nature denies no man successfully dares." 3. If nature denies nobility to someone, it appears that teaching cannot give it to him. 4. Moreover, works of nature and art are works of intellect, and intellect, principally directing nature, directs and rules all things; and the directing intellect is human, which by this logic directs only artificial things. 5. Then I argue thus: just as divine intellect is to human, so divine effect is to human; it is incomparably more perfect and infallible than human. 6. When nature or divine intellect is lacking, in no way does it seem that human nature could be sufficient.

7. To the contrary, we see that many people are improved in their actions by good teaching. 8. On the first argument one should say what the Philosopher says in the first book of the *Ethics* that was just said above: certain people are good in themselves, so that their nature is always directed to doing good and to knowing good, and such people are noble in themselves and are leaders and teachers. 9. In others nature is not found perfect; rather, it is found undeveloped in some people because of a certain bodily intemperance, so that they need help from someone else; but their defect is not so strong or so firm that it is impossible for someone's help to correct it, so that such people can be set right by suitable teaching and become noble by benefit of training. 10. In a third grade of men nature is so defective that it cannot be helped; such people cannot be made noble by themselves or by others. 11. The Philosopher says such men are useless for good conduct. 12. It is easy, then, to answer the question and the arguments.

13. Therefore one should say on the question that some people are ignoble, if they are left to themselves, who may yet become good through others; but some cannot be corrected, as has been said. 14. On the arguments I say that training will never make perfect those whom nature perfectly refuses; but with the help of nature, art indeed makes perfect those whom nature, leaving something imperfect, makes perfect imperfectly, as the Philosopher says excellently in the seventh book of the *Politics*: "All teaching and all discipline want to supply what is lacking in nature." 15. This is to be understood of those to whom nature granted that for the most part they are not far from perfection, and then someone improves the situation by helping nature. 16. In this way nature is the

operatrix est, et artifex est minister, ut dixit Galienus in *Tegni*. 17. Ex hiis solvitur vis rationis secunde.

Caput 15

Septima questio

1. [S]eptimo queritur cui filius in nobilitate debeat assimilari, utrum patri vel matri. 2. Videtur enim quod patri, quia ut dicit Philosophus in libro *De animalibus*, pater dat formam, hoc est virtutem informantem propinquam, et mater dat materiam corporalem, quare videtur quod filius debeat assimilari patri et non matri.

3. Oppositum patet in pluribus qui mores et operationes secuntur matris et non patris. 4. Hanc questionem generalius positam soluit Philosophus in libro *De animalibus*, capitulo [quarto], de similitudine generatorum, dicens quod in generatione multi sunt motus et ex parte patris et ex [par]te matris generales et particulares. 5. Hoc est, virtus generativa sortis non tantum movet secundum quod est sortis sed secundum quod est rei per se existentis vel subsistentis, id est substantie et corporee substantie animate, sensibilis et rationalis, vel sic composite [vel] complexionate, et secundum quod masculus et femella generant. 6. Nunc autem est ita quod motus viri contrariantur aliqualiter motibus mulieris, et quando concurrunt ad generationem virtus informativa oportet quod fortiores sequatur, debiliores enim solvuntur. 7. Ex quo contingit quando paterni motus omnes maternos vincunt, tunc filius omnino assimilatur patri, et quando e contrario omnino assimilatur matri. 8. Quare ad questionem dicendum quod utrique potest assimilari vel alteri secundum quod in temperie generationis contingit. 9. Unde ad rationem dicere oportet quod pater virtutem prebet informativam, et nisi impediatur, ut dictum est, similem filium faciet patri; sed si motus matris prevaleant informabitur secundum illos, et assimilabitur matri secundum quod huiusmodi. 10. Ex quo patet ad rationem in oppositum.

Caput 16

Questio octava

1. [O]ctavo queritur quare homines non loquantur nisi de una specie nobilitatis, cum sit superius determinatum eas esse quinque species. 2. De hoc breviter sine

operator of all things, and the artist is the servant, as Galen said in the *Tegni*. 17. These considerations weaken the force of the second argument.

Chapter 15

Seventh Question

1. Seventh, it is asked whom a child will resemble in nobility, the father or the mother. 2. It seems the father since, as the Philosopher says in the book *On Animals*, the father gives form, that is, the close formative virtue, and the mother gives bodily material, so that it seems that the child must resemble the father and not the mother.

3. The opposite appears in many people who follow the morals and actions of their mother and not their father. 4. The Philosopher solved this question as put more generally in the book *On Animals*, fourth chapter, on the resemblance to parents, saying that in generation there are many general and particular motions, both on the part of the father and on the part of the mother. 5. The virtue generative of fate does not move only insofar as it is of fate but also insofar as it is of a thing being or subsisting, that is, of substance and of animate corporal substance, sensible and rational, either thus compounded or made complex, and according to what the male and female generate. 6. But it is true, now, that the motions of the man are resisted somewhat by the motions of the woman; when they come together for generation the formative virtue must follow the stronger [motions], since the weaker ones are overcome. 7. The result is that when the father's motions overcome all those of the mother, the child thoroughly resembles the father, and when [it happens] to the contrary, the child thoroughly resembles the mother. 8. One should say on the question, then, that the child can resemble either one parent or the other, according to what happens in the mingling of generation. 9. On the argument one must say that the father provides the formative virtue, and unless it is impeded, as has been said, it will make a child like the father; but if the motions of the mother prevail, the child will be formed according to them, and by this logic will resemble the mother. 10. It is clear, then, as to the argument to the opposite effect.

Chapter 16

Eighth Question

1. Eighth, it is asked why men speak of only one type of nobility, although it has been shown above that there are five types. 2. One should say of this briefly

argumentis dicendum quod commune iudicium gentium licet presumptionem vel probabilitatem aliquam faciat, tamen de levi decipiuntur eo quod pauci sunt qui subtiliter et provide sciant iudicare de rebus; immo communiter alter alterius sequitur dicta, realitatem supponens. 3. Unde Philosophus in *Topicis* dicit, "Loquendum est ut plures, senciendum est ut pauci"; id est, ut sapientes tenent tenenda est veritas de rebus, non ut populares locuntur, sed in locutionibus loquamur communiter et ut plures. 4. Difficile enim est cum popularibus disputare qui ad detrahendum de eodem loquendo opposita minimo moventur motu. 5. Unde in proposito non est eis credendum sicut nec pluribus aliis, accipiunt enim pro nobilitate dominium tantum, ut Philosophus dicit primo *Rethorice*. 6. Unde ipse dicit quod "Genti et civitati est nobilitas sui iuris antiquos esse presides"; et non dixit "sapientibus," sed "genti et civitati."

Caput 17

Questio nona

1. [N]ono queritur utrum rex sit nobilior comite, vel imperator rege, quia hoc videtur tenere communitas et domini inter seipsos. 2. Cuius oppositum potest contingere, ut patet per predicta superius. 3. Ad questionem istam dicendum quod homines si fuerint equaliter dispositi ad bene regendum magnum vel parvum dominium, equaliter sunt nobiles, sive magnum sive parvum habere contingat dominium. 4. Sed bene contingit quod aliqui sibi sunt boni rectores in parvis et quidam alii in magnis, qui transmutati male se haberent; et tales sunt proportionaliter nobiles et non equaliter. 5. Alii sunt qui, licet in parvo dominio sint boni, adhuc bene et melius se haberent in maiori; et isti sunt nobiles sicut reges, dato quod essent simplices milites. 6. Ex hiis et predictis patet ad questionem et rationem.

Caput 18

Questio [decima]

1. [U]ltimo queritur utrum nobilitas inveniatur in aliis rebus sicut in avibus, equis, et canibus, quia hoc etiam tenere videtur communis opinio. 2. Dicendum absque maiori disputatione quod nobilitas in aliis animalibus ab homine notatur dupliciter, scilicet generaliter et absolute, aut particulariter et in relatione ad aliquid. 3. Primo modo dicitur animal nobile vel generosum, ut Philosophus dicit

without arguments that although the common judgment of people may create some presumption or probability [of truth], yet they are easily deceived since there are few who know how to judge things subtly and far-sightedly; rather, one commonly follows the words of another, supposing [that they correspond to] reality. 3. The Philosopher says in the *Topics*, "Speak like the many but think like the few"; that is, we should hold the truth about things as the wise hold it, not as the people say, but we should speak in words commonly and like the many. 4. It is difficult to dispute with common people, who are moved by the least impulse for departing from what is given, for the sake of saying the opposite. 5. On this subject they should not be believed, nor on many others, for they take power alone as nobility, as the Philosopher says in the first book of the *Rhetoric*. 6. He himself says, "Nobility is to be, by right, ancient guardians for the people and the city"; and he did not say "for the wise," but "for the people and the city."

Chapter 17

Ninth Question

1. Ninth, it is asked whether a king is nobler than a count, or an emperor than a king, since common opinion seems to hold this as do lords among themselves. 2. The opposite of this can happen, as is obvious from what has been said above. 3. On this question one should say that if men are equally disposed to rule well either a great domain or a small one, they are equally noble, whether it befalls them to have a great domain or a small one. 4. But it does happen that some are good leaders in small [domains] and others in great ones who would conduct themselves poorly if they changed places; such men are noble proportionally, not equally. 5. Others, although they are good in a small domain, would conduct themselves as well or better in a greater one, so they are as noble as kings even though it is given to them to be simple knights. 6. From these considerations and what was said before it is clear as to the question and the argument.

Chapter 18

Tenth Question

1. Finally, it is asked whether nobility is found in other things such as birds, horses, and dogs since common opinion seems to hold this too. 2. One should say without greater debate that nobility in animals other than man is noted in two ways, that is, generally and absolutely, or in particular and in relation to something. 3. In the first way an animal may be called noble or high-born, as the

in primo *De animalibus*, quod perfecte facit quod pertinet ad opus suum. 4. Unde individua alicuius generis animalium que ita operantur quod non dimittunt opus proprium sui generis dicuntur generosa animalia vel nobilia in relatione ad hominem, sicut aves quedam et quecumque fuerint illa. 5. Secundo modo dicuntur generosa animalia vel nobilia in relatione ad hominem, sicut aves quedam et canes et que ordinantur ad aliquam recreationem eorum qui tedio sunt affecti per longum et continuum laborem qui ad utilitatem rei pupblice ordinatur; et talis est labor nobilium dominorum, sicut enim dicit Cato, "Curis quandoque interponenda sunt gaudia." 6. Unde nobiles viri possunt quandoque rationabiliter talibus uti, et usus eorum sic factus nobilis potest dici. 7. Sed si aliquis nimis delectatur in talibus, ita quod ex hiis opera que ad suam pertinent nobilitatem frequenter postponat, dico talem usum ad [vi]litatem et bestialem fatuitatem converti. 8. In altioribus enim, ut fuit dictum, debent oper[a] nobilium frequentari. 9. De hiis que pertinent ad primum librum sit determinatum in tantum.

Pars 2

0. Prologus

Incipit pars secunda.

1. [P]ars huius libelli secunda tangit breves et tutas lecturas quibus quilibet sive nobilis sive vilis cognoscetur perfecte. 2. Erunt enim decem capitula quibus harum ostendentur proverbia et sententie quinque specierum nobilitatis dictarum et quinque de oppositis earumdem.

Caput 1

De proverbiis sapientum

1. [S]ecundum quod Philosophus disputat et sufficienter dat intelligere prohemio *Metaphisice*, "Sapiens est qui scit omnia difficillima per certitudinem et causam, seipsum dirigens et aliis persuadens." 2. Hermes in libro *De quindecim stellis* dicit quod "Sapiens est qui res cognoscit prout sunt et ratione probari possunt." 3. Plato dicit in libello de materia prima, "Sapiens est qui non operatur preterquam utilia et honesta." 4. Alfraganus dicit in quibusdam secretis suis quod "Sol solus in celo, sapiens solus in mundo," quia ille solus tempora distinguit, nebulas dissipat, viventia confortat, omnia illuminat; hic homines ordinat, vicia corrigit,

Philosopher says in the first book *On Animals*, that does perfectly what pertains to its work. 4. So that individuals of some race of animals who act in such a way that they do not refuse the work proper to their race are called high-born or noble animals in relation to man, such as certain birds or whatever else they may be. 5. In the second way animals are called high-born or noble in relation to man, like certain birds and dogs and those [animals] that are directed to recreation of those who are wearied by long and continuous labor that is directed toward the utility of the public good; and such is the labor of noble lords, for as Cato says, "Sometimes joys should be put between cares." 6. So noble men can sometimes make rational use of such animals, and the use they make of them can be called noble. 7. But if someone takes too great delight in such [animals], so that because of them he frequently postpones the work that pertains to his nobility, I say such usage changes into ignobility and bestial fatuousness. 8. Among people of higher station, as has been said, the acts of noblemen must be carried out habitually. 9. Let this suffice for the things that pertain to the first book.

Part 2

0. Prologue

Here begins the second part.

1. The second part of this little book touches on concise and prudent readings by which anyone will be perfectly recognized as noble or ignoble. 2. There will be ten chapters in which will be shown proverbs and sentences about these five types of nobility and about their five opposites.

Chapter 1

On Proverbs of the Wise

1. As the Philosopher argues and sufficiently explains in the introduction to the *Metaphysics*, "A wise man is one who knows all very difficult things through certainty and cause, directing himself and persuading others." 2. Hermes says in the book *Of Fifteen Stars*, "A wise man is one who understands things as they are and can be proved to be by reason." 3. Plato says in his little book on first matter, "A wise man is one who does none but useful and honest deeds." 4. Alfraganus says, in certain secret writings of his, "The sun is alone in the sky, the wise man alone in the world," since only the former distinguishes the seasons, dissipates clouds, comforts the living, and lights all things; the latter governs

virtutes inserit, et animas ignorantium informat. 5. Sapiens principaliter diligit Deum quia fons bonorum omnium, et sui amore diligit omne bonum. 6. Sapiens sobrie bonis utitur, et mala si contigerint intrepidus sustinet. 7. Sapiens omnes diligit, neminem despicit, sed in paucis omnino confidit et omnino de nullo diffidit. 8. Sapiens est qui de malis et bonis elicit bona. 9. Sapiens terram respicit et celum considerat. 10. Sapiens se et alios cognoscit, et est exemplar noticie et operationis perfecte. 11. Ex hiis suprema patet nobilitas et quia sapiens nobilis est.

Caput 2

De proverbiis [insipientum]

1. [P]tholomeus dicit in proverbiis *Almagesti* quod "Insipiens est qui sui ipsius quantitatem ignorat" (supple non corporis sed anime virtutem). 2. Salomo vero dicit quod "Stultus est qui prius respondet quam audiat, et confusione dignus est." 3. Willanus dicit quod "Stultus est qui ponit pedes ante oculos," eo quod stulti improvide operantur. 4. Similiter, "Stultus est qui de factis penitet"; hoc est dictum quod quilibet deberet ita provide operari ne haberet occasionem penitendi. 5. Stultus nec Deum nec divina cognoscit, et si forte sentit, postponit. 6. Demostenes dicit quod stultus universalibus volvitur: primo in oculis per superhabundantiam, secundo in lingua mendaciis et sermonibus inhonestis, tertio in manibus per turpia facta, quarto in corde malitia voluntatis et consideracione maligna, quinto in pedibus propter velocitatem cursus ad malum. 7. Hoc idem intelligit Salomon in Parabolis ubi dicit, "Septem sunt que odit Deus." 8. Stultus est qui alios turbat. 9. Stultus est qui [ubique suam stulticiam ostendit. 10. Stultus] parum scit et multum putat et post factum et ante. 11. Et quamvis inter stultum, insipientem, et ignarum et malum, aliqua sit differentia, ad presens tamen accipimus pro eodem.

Caput 3

De proverbiis nobilitatis secundum corpus

1. [D]e nobilibus secundum corpus, plurium ordo philosophorum multa dixerunt, inter quos Fulco Marsiliensis dicit, "Si corpus bene formetur et eidem cor bene proportionetur sive in viro sive in muliere, nobilitatem ostendit." 2. Et hoc dat intelligere Philosophus per totam *Phisonomiam* suam, iudicando

men, corrects vices, implants virtues, and informs the souls of the ignorant. 5. Most importantly, the wise man loves God since he is the font of all good things and for love of him loves every good thing. 6. The wise man makes sober use of good things and bears bad things, if they befall, without fear. 7. The wise man loves everyone, despises no one, but trusts few completely and distrusts none completely. 8. The wise man is one who draws good things from among bad and good. 9. The wise man beholds the earth and considers heaven. 10. The wise man knows himself and others and is an example of perfect knowledge and action. 11. It is clear, then, that nobility is supreme, and that the wise man is noble.

Chapter 2

On Proverbs of the Unwise

1. Ptolemy says in the proverbs of the *Almagest*, "He is a fool who ignores his own quantity" (understand not the virtue of his body but of his soul). 2. Solomon says, "A fool is a man who answers before he hears, and he is worthy of confusion." 3. The peasant says, "A fool is a man who puts his feet before his eyes," because fools act without forethought. 4. Similarly, "A fool is he who repents his deeds"; this is said because anyone should act with forethought so that he will have no occasion to repent. 5. A fool knows neither God nor divine things, and if perchance he becomes aware of them, he puts them off. 6. Demosthenes says that a fool is rolled along by all things: first by his eyes with overabundance, second by his tongue with lies and dishonest words, third by his hands with foul deeds, fourth by his heart with malice of will and malignant reflection, and fifth by his feet with the speed of his race to evil. 7. Solomon means the same when he says in Proverbs, "There are seven things that God hates." 8. A fool is one who disturbs others. 9. A fool is one who shows his folly everywhere. 10. A fool knows little and thinks much both after the deed and before. 11. Although there is some difference between a fool, an unwise man, an ignorant man, and a bad man, for the present we nevertheless take them as the same.

Chapter 3

On Proverbs of Nobility in the Body

1. As for those who are noble in the body, a troop of many philosophers has said many things, among whom Folquet de Marseille says, "If the body is well formed and the heart is well proportioned to it, in either a man or a woman, it shows nobility." 2. The Philosopher makes this understood throughout his

ex parte forme corporis membrorum mores hominum naturaliter perfectos. 3. Unde proverbialiter dicitur, “Est v[ult]us testis quales intrinsecus estis.” 4. [“Distortum voltum sequitur distortio morum.”] 5. Petrus Vitalis dicit quod “Pulcritudo corporis est magnum precium,” nisi intrinsecus paciatur defectum. 6. Unde Arnoldus dicit quod “Pulcritudo corporis sine cordis pulcritudine et absque nobilitate est vilitas et flos transiens sine fructu.” 7. Gaufridus Rodel dixit, “Multi laudant magnitudinem cum fortitudine, et ego laudo si racio gerat frenum.” 8. Odantagalus dicit quod “Promptitudo corporis vel levitas dominium habet pedum, sed laus erit si pedes absque stultitia moveantur.” 9. Omnes generaliter virtutes corporee perfecte corpus nobilitant si recta ratione in suis operibus regulentur.

Caput 4

De proverbiis corporum vilium

1. [A]ntequam proverbia vilium corporum proponantur, sciendum generaliter quod vilitas propter aliquam contingentem occasionem in complexione vel compositione corporis denotatur, unde figura corporis vel membri non est situata vel plasmata secundum quod speciei deceret plasmari. 2. Unde contingit defectus in operationibus que nature debentur corporali. 3. Sed est advertendum quod hec vilitas est duplex: uno modo reperitur corpus habere defectum in operationibus, cuius defectus incorrigibilis est per naturam, de quo etiam dolent habentes, et corrigerent libenter si possibile foret eis. 4. Et talis vilitas corporis non efficit hominem vilem, quia non est in potestate sua correctio talis defectus. 5. Unde ceci vel claudi a nativitate vitup[er]ari non debent. 6. Alio modo contingit hominibus talis defectus propter maliciam propriam, sed contingit in illis in quibus manus vel pedes vel huiusmodi abscinduntur bonitate iusticie observata in eis. 7. Unde tales vilissimi iudicantur, sicut proprie nature contrarium operantes. 8. Similiter etiam sunt viles qui maliciam complexionis secuntur que posset subici iudicio rationis. 9. Unde proverbia huius capituli intelligenda sunt de illis qui in operationibus corporalibus deficiunt que posse[n]t corrigi ratione.

10. Menbra autem corporis que maiorem vilitatem ostendunt sunt illa: oculus, manus, pes, os, nasus, auris, ut patet in physonomiis philosophorum, et hoc rationabiliter dixerunt quia deterior defectus est qui in membris dignioris operationis contingit. 11. Unde Philosophus in libro *Topicorum* dicit quod

Physiognomy, judging the morality of men, naturally perfect, by part of the form of the members of their bodies. 3. So it is said proverbially, "The face is witness to what you are inside." 4. "Twisted morals follow a twisted face." 5. Peire Vidal says, "Beauty of body is a great merit," unless it suffers an inner flaw. 6. Arnaut [de Mareuil] says, "Beauty of body without beauty of heart and without nobility is ignobility, and a flower passing away without fruit." 7. Jaufre Rudel said, "Many praise generosity with nobility, but I give praise if reason holds the rein." 8. Odantagalus says, "Swiftness or lightness of body has power of the feet, but there will be praise if the feet move without folly." 9. In general all perfect bodily virtues ennoble the body if they are ruled by right reason in their actions.

Chapter 4

On Proverbs of Ignoble Bodies

1. Before the proverbs of ignoble bodies are put forth, it should be known in general that ignobility because of some contingent occasion is denoted in complexion or composition of the body, so that the shape of the body or a limb is not situated or formed as it is fitting to be formed for the species. 2. For this reason there arises a fault in actions that are due to bodily nature. 3. But it should be noticed that this ignobility is of two kinds: in one kind a body is found to have a flaw in actions that is incorrigible by nature, which even those who have it regret and which they would gladly correct if it were possible for them. 4. Such ignobility of body does not make a man ignoble since the correction of such a defect is not in his power. 5. For this reason people who are blind or lame from birth should not be reproached for it. 6. In another way such a flaw befalls men because of their own wickedness, as happens to those whose hands or feet, or what have you, are cut off by the goodness of justice carried out upon them. 7. Such people are judged most ignoble, as acting contrary to their own nature. 8. Others are similarly ignoble who follow wickedness of complexion that could be subjected to the judgment of reason. 9. For this reason the proverbs of this chapter should be understood as concerning those who are deficient in bodily actions that could have been corrected by reason.

10. The parts of the body that show the greatest ignobility are these: the eye, the hand, the foot, the mouth, the nose, and the ear, as is clear in the physiognomies of the philosophers, and they have said so reasonably since the worst flaw is one that befalls in the members [capable] of worthiest action. 11. The Philosopher says in the book of *Topics* that the eye is to the body as the intellect

oculus est in corpore [sicut] intellectus in anima, hoc est proportionaliter: sicut intellectus excellit omnes vires anime, ita virtus oculorum virtutes omnium membrorum. 12. Unde sicut mala dispositio oculi multum vilificat corpus habent[i]s, nisi malicia fuerit in actibus ratione correcta. 13. [Unde versus:

Inconstans animus, oculus vagus, instabilis pes
sunt hominis signa de quo mihi nulla boni spes.]

14. Plinius etiam dicit in physonomia sua quod grossus oculus, rubens et inversus, rammosus et expositus, inverecundum vel luxuriosum ostendit; et si cum hoc os grande fuerit, et labia grossa et carnosa, et brevis nasus sursum versus, significat glutonem et maledicum; et si cum hiis habuerit tybia[s] et cavillas pedum grossas et [u]ncas ad posterius, in incessu ad utrumque latus vacillans tamquam in pedibus paciens, talis habebit corpus supreme male figuratum et adhuc vilius. 15. Si cum hoc habuerit manus grossas et duras brevium digitorum, qualis fuit in Hanonia Bradefer, tale corpus vilissimum existit et secundum animam mali moris. 16. Et est adhuc quedam vilitas corporis que causatur magis ex complexione cordis; reperiuntur enim aliqui optime formati et complexionati in exterioribus membris, et in tempore necessitatis nullum habent vigorem; et tales dicuntur communiter pulcri et mali. 17. De istis dicit Montaneolus quod "Pulcri corpore sine cordis vigore sunt ymagines sine vita," quod optime dictum est, utrobique enim apparet quod non existerit. 18. Et de vilibus corpore sint hec dicta.

Caput 5

De proverbiis dominorum

1. [C]onsequenter aliqua dominorum proverbia tangamus. 2. Sed prius advertendum quod proverbia vel breves sententie circa dominos dicta tria maxime respiciunt, scilicet eorum docilitatem in consiliis, et eorum iusticiam in correctionibus et penitenciis, et largitatem in eorum beneficiis tribuendis. 3. De isto Aristoteles ad Alexandrum scripsit ei probos viros habere in suis consiliis eo quod proborum consilia sunt sententie summe disputate. 4. Cato vero docuit filium suum largius in hac parte, dicens,

Utile consilium dominus ne despice servi;
nullius sensum, si prodest, spreveris umquam.

to the soul, that is, proportionally: just as the intellect excels all the other forces of the soul, so the virtue of the eyes [excels] the virtues of all the other members. 12. So likewise a bad disposition of the eye makes the body of one who has it greatly flawed, unless its badness is corrected in actions by reason. 13. Hence the verses:

An inconstant mind, a roving eye, and a wandering foot
Are signs of a man in whom I have no hope of good.

14. Pliny says too, in his physiognomy, that a large eye, reddish and enigmatic, shifty and bulging, shows an immodest or lecherous person; and if along with this the mouth is big, the lips thick and fleshy, and the nose short and pointing upward, it means a glutton and a foul-mouthed person; and if along with these he has tibias and ankles that are thick and bent toward the back, and he walks shifting from side to side as though suffering in his feet, such a man will have a body supremely badly shaped and still more ignoble. 15. If along with this he has big, hard hands with short fingers, as did Bradefer in Hainault, such a body is most ignoble and shows a soul of bad morality. 16. And there is yet a certain ignobility of body that is caused rather by the complexion of the heart; for some people are found very well shaped and complexioned in their exterior members, but in time of need they have no strength; such people are commonly called "beautiful and bad." 17. Montanhagol says of them, "The beautiful in body without strength of heart are images without life," which is very well said, for such a person seems to be alive in neither [body nor heart]. 18. About the ignoble in body let these things be said.

Chapter 5

On Proverbs of Lords

1. Next let us touch upon a few proverbs about lords. 2. But first it should be noticed that proverbs or short sentences about lords concern three topics especially, that is, their willingness to accept advice in councils, their justice in [administering] corrections and punishments, and their generosity in granting benefices. 3. On this subject Aristotle wrote to Alexander, telling him to have honest men in his councils because the counsels of honest men are judgments excellently debated. 4. But Cato taught his son more extensively on this subject, saying,

As a lord, do not despise useful advice from a slave;
Never scorn anyone's opinion if it is helpful.

5. Quantum ad secundum, summe precipit vitare avariciam, avari enim principes nullo modo sunt iusti. 6. Unde [Aristoteles]:

> cum semper obtinuit viciorum mater in aula
> pestis avaricie, que sola incarcerat omnes,
> verumptamen, spreto moderamine iuris,
> curritur in facinus nec leges curia curat.

7. Quantum ad tertium dixit, "Non opus est vallo quem dextera dapsilis ambit." 8. Unde proverbialiter de dominis dicitur quod "Avari fortibus non tuentur, nec largi in planicie sunt devicti." 9. Et hec sufficiant in hoc loco.

Caput 6

De proverbiis servorum

1. [N]unc dicamus de servitute vel servo, et quia decet bonum servientem quod sit amicus domino et humilis et eciam curialis, fidelis, et providus, proverbia que ad hoc capitulum pertinent semper recipiunt aliquam proprietatem dictorum vel oppositas servientium malorum. 2. Unde dicit [rusticus] quod "Amor servientis cordi domini requies non suspecta est." 3. Item dicit quod "Servus fidelis multorum custodum est clavis." 4. Item dicit quod "Servus irascibilis extitit cordi domini honus grave." 5. Et Seneca dicit quod "Servus piger est propheta." 6. De curialitate servi Petrus Vitalis dicit quod "Prudentia servi et valor est magnus si dominus fuerit silvester et iracundus, quod ab ipso sine infamia separetur." 7. Hec et similia pertinent ad hanc partem.

Caput 7

De proverbiis divitum

1. [N]unc divitum proverbia tangamus. 2. Plurium philosophorum est sententia quod dives est cui suum cor sufficit; alii dicunt quod dives est qui sufficit suo cordi. 3. Idem tamen intelligunt, quia ex cordis iudicio sufficiencia venit rerum que facit hominem divitem, ut patuit satis supra. 4. Unde Dyogenes dicebat quod ipse erat ditior et quod vita et fortuna sua plus valebant quam regis Persarum quia cordi Dyogenis nichil deficiebat, regi autem nichil sufficiebat. 5. Ptholomeus in proverbiis *Almagesti* intendit quod dives est qui habet dominium intellectus. 6. Cato dicit quod "Dives avarus habet nummos, sed non

5. As for the second topic [the lord's justice], [Cato] commands especially to avoid avarice, for greedy princes are in no way just. 6. So Aristotle:

> Since the plague of avarice, the mother of vices at court,
> Has always had power, alone, to jail anyone,
> Indeed, with scorn for the moderation of law,
> The court rushes into crime and shows no care for laws.

7. As for the third topic, [which is generosity], he said, "He has no need for a rampart whom a wealthy right hand protects." 8. It is said proverbially about lords, "The miserly are not protected by the strong, nor are the generous conquered in an open field." 9. Let these suffice in this place.

Chapter 6

On Proverbs of Servants

1. Now let us speak about servitude or the servant; and since it befits a good servant to be a friend to his lord, humble, even courtly, faithful, and prudent, the proverbs that pertain to this chapter always involve some quality of these terms or the opposite [qualities] of bad servants. 2. The peasant says, "The love of a servant is rest, not uneasy, for the heart of his lord." 3. Also he says, "A faithful servant is the key of many chests." 4. Also he says, "An angry servant has become a heavy burden to the heart of his lord." 5. And Seneca says, "A lazy servant is a prophet." 6. Regarding the courtliness of a servant Peire Vidal says, "The prudence and courage of a servant are great if his lord is crude and wrathful, and he manages to leave him without scandal." 7. These and similar sayings pertain to this part.

Chapter 7

On Proverbs of the Rich

1. Now let us touch upon proverbs of the rich. 2. Many philosophers hold that a rich man is one for whom his heart is enough; others say that a rich man is one who is enough for his heart. 3. They mean the same thing since a sufficiency of things comes from the judgment of the heart that makes a man rich, as has been made sufficiently clear above. 4. Diogenes used to say that he was richer than the king of the Persians and that his life and fortune were worth more [than the king's] since nothing was lacking to the heart of Diogenes but nothing was enough for the king. 5. Ptolemy maintains, in the proverbs of the *Almagest*, that a rich man is one who has power of intellect. 6. Cato says, "A rich miser has coins

habet corpus." 7. Boetius dicit quod "Dives plures habet amicos sed de nullo est certus." 8. [Dyonisius dicit in libro *De divinis nominibus* quod dives est qui bona et pulchra habet. 9. Rusticus dicit quod "Dives est cui suum sufficit," et hoc optime dictum est; "suum" intelligatur de suo fortuito vel naturaliter. 10. Et] hec et similia in hoc loco possunt scribi, sed hec sufficiant propter opus.

Caput 8

De proverbiis pauperum

1. [H]iis habitis est de paupe[re] subiungendum. 2. Invenitur in hystoriis Grecorum quod Alexander quesivit ab Aristotele quid sibi de paupertate videretur; respondens Philosophus ait, "De paupertate non plus sentio nisi quod pauperibus subvenire non possum." 3. In quo subtiliter respondit, quia sive large sive stricte sumatur paupertas, verum respondit; pauper enim est qui alium iuvare non potest de suis mobilibus sive corporali vigore sive sciencie et consilii bonitate. 4. Et hoc intendit rusticus qui dicit quod "Pauper est cui suum non sufficit," quia paupertas large non est nisi defectus alicuius trium predictorum et maxime intellectus. 5. Dyogenes multum laudavit paupertatem div[i]ciarum propter tria, quia scilicet subtiliat ingenium, salvat sanitatem, et facit statum securum: [primum] facit providendo, secundum facit per temperanciam, tertium quia nullus invidet pauperi nec videt quod rapiat paupertati. 6. Unde Boetius dicit, "O preclara [opum] mortalium beatitudo [quam cum adeptus fueris securus esse desistis]." 7. "Et cantabat vacuus coram latrone viator." 8. Cato consuluit filio,

> Infantem nudum [dum te natura creavit,
> paupertatis onus pacienter ferre memento].

9. Et precipit, "[Dilige] denarium, [sed parce dilige formam]"; hoc est ad usum, non ad cumulum, quia cumulator diligit formam, sed largus denarium. 10. Sine dubio sapientes non fecerunt vim de diviciis, et rationes superius fuerunt dicte; immo in solo intellectu posuerunt divicias, quia istas perdere non poterant, et alie fortuite secuntur istas—unde Salomon: "Venerunt mihi omni[a] bona pariter cum illa"—quare pro vera paupertate non intellexerunt aliud quam defectum sapiencie et intellectus. 11. Et Oratius dicit quod "Non est pauper cui sufficit rerum usus," qui plane et satis subtiliter verum dixit.

but does not have himself." 7. Boethius says, "A rich man has many friends but is sure about none of them." 8. Dionysius says in the book *On Divine Names* that he is rich who has good and beautiful things. 9. The peasant says, "He is rich to whom his own is enough," and this is very well said; understand "his own" as his either by chance or naturally. 10. And these and similar sayings can be written in this place, but let these suffice for this work.

Chapter 8

On Proverbs of the Poor

1. Since we have had these, we must add proverbs about the poor man. 2. It is found in the histories of the Greeks that Alexander asked Aristotle what he thought about poverty; the Philosopher answered, "About poverty I think nothing more than that I cannot help the poor." 3. He answered subtly, since he spoke truth whether poverty is taken in the broad sense or strictly, for a poor man is one who cannot help another with his possessions, bodily strength, or goodness of knowledge and counsel. 4. The peasant understands this who says, "A poor man is one to whom his own is not enough," since poverty in the broad sense is nothing but a lack of one of the three things just mentioned, and especially of intellect. 5. Diogenes greatly praised poverty for three reasons, that is, since it sharpens wit, preserves health, and makes one's state secure; it does the first by looking ahead, the second by temperance, the third since no one envies the poor man or sees anything to steal from poverty. 6. So Boethius says, "O splendid blessing of mortal wealth; when you have gained it, you cease to be safe!" 7. "And the empty-handed traveler sang in the bandit's face." 8. Cato advised his son,

> Since nature created you a naked child,
> Remember to bear patiently the burden of poverty.

9. And he ordered, "Love money, but love sparingly its beauty"; that is, [love it] for use, not for piling up, since he who piles it up loves its beauty, but the generous man loves the money. 10. No doubt wise men have set no great importance on wealth, and the reasons have been said above; they have considered wealth only in the intellect, since they could not lose it, and other kinds that depend on chance come after [wealth of intellect]—as Solomon said, "All good things have come to me along with it" [that is, with the spirit of wisdom]—so they understood true poverty as nothing else than a lack of wisdom and intellect. 11. Horace says, "He is not poor to whom the use of things is enough," and he spoke the truth plainly and quite subtly.

Caput 9

De proverbiis gloriosorum

1. [N]unc de gloriosis dicamus. 2. Socrates dicit, quod Valerius narrat septimo *Hystoriarum*, quod "Illi veniunt ad gloriam qui tales sunt in operibus quales hominibus cupiunt apparere." 3. Hoc idem dicit Tullius in libro *De officiis*, quod "Brevior via ad gloriam est quod talis sit homo in se qualis cupit esse inter gentes." 4. Oratius dicit, "Tu recte vivis, si veram" (supple: non vanam) "gloriam curas, esse quod audis," id est, quod vis audiri. 5. Quamvis fama vel gloria bona sit, parum appreciatur inter sapientes eo quod inter gentes vix secundum rationem potest haberi, quia pa[u]cissimi sunt qui de bonis hominibus recte iudicent, aut quia nesciunt eos esse tales, aut si sciant livoris occasione tacebunt. 6. Adhuc est fama magna vi laboris ad tuendum, et magni tumoris et vacuitatis, quare parum valet.

Caput 10

De proverbiis [vanigloriosorum]

1. Ultimo est de vanigloriosis dicendum. 2. Opus talium est seipsos laudare aut vituperare gratia consequende laudis. 3. Unde Cato precipit filio,

> Nec te collaudes [nec te culpaveris ipse;
> hoc faciunt stulti quos gloria vexat inanis].

4. Et tales sunt generaliter omnes qui aliis bene vivere precipiunt, secundum Senecam, et ipsi ad hoc laborare non curant. 5. Quare [Plato] dicit quod similes sunt naute loquaci de gubernacione navis qui postea navem tempestati dimittit; unde ipse dicit quod homo debet facere et non loqui, quia gloria bonorum virorum non est in propria lingua, sed eorum gloria inter bonos.

6. Tales et similes sententias sapientes dixerunt quibus quilibet cognoscitur nobilis sive vilis, quod a principio huc diximus describendum; sufficiat igitur quod dictum est. 7. Laudetur altissimus qui nobis hec concessit scribere licet pauca, a quo fluit omnis nobilitas et in quem omnis actio nobilis terminatur.

Chapter 9

On Proverbs of the Famous

1. Now let us speak of famous people. 2. Socrates says, as Valerius relates in the seventh book of his *Histories*, "They come to fame who are the same in their actions as they wish to appear to men." 3. Cicero says the same in his book *On Duties*: "The shorter way to fame is for a man to be the same in himself as he wishes to be among people." 4. Horace says, "You live rightly if you care for your true" (understand "not empty") "fame, to be what you hear," that is, what you want to be heard. 5. Even though fame or glory is good, it is not valued highly among the wise because it can scarcely be kept according to reason among people, since there are very few who judge rightly about good men, either because they do not know that they are good or, if they do know, because they remain silent out of jealousy. 6. Fame must be protected with a great effort of toil, great swelling, and emptiness, so it is worth little.

Chapter 10

On Proverbs of the Vainglorious

1. Finally we must speak of vainglorious men. 2. The work of such men is to praise or blame themselves for the sake of gaining praise. 3. Cato orders his son,

> Neither praise yourself nor blame yourself;
> Fools do this, whom empty glory vexes.

4. Such people are generally all who tell others to live well, according to Seneca, and do not trouble to work at it themselves. 5. [Plato] says they are like a sailor who chatters about steering a ship and then sends the ship into a storm; so he himself [Seneca] says that a man must act and not speak since [as Cato says above] the glory of good men is not in their own speech; rather, their glory is among the good.

6. Wise men have said these and similar sentences by which each one may be recognized as noble or ignoble, which we said at the beginning we would describe; so let what has been said suffice. 7. Praised be the Highest, who granted us to write these things, albeit few, from whom flows all nobility and in whom every noble action has its end.

Explicit libellus *De nobilitate animi*.

[*Versus*
H[e]c lectura petit quisnam sit lector et unde,
        Ne careat titulis ut peregrin[a] suis.
Hic est Wille[l]mus medicine sorte magister;
        Regis Arrogonie de dicione fuit.]

Here ends the little book *On Nobility of Mind.*

Verses

This reading asks who the reader is and where he is from,
Lest it lack its titles like a stranger.
He is Willelmus, by profession a master of medicine;
He was from the domain of the king of Aragon.

Notes on the Text

1.0.1 *Noti*, "having knowledge (of a fact)" (*OLD*); here the *noti* have knowledge of the good.

1.0.4 Color differentiates a visual impression; the basis of all colors is white, according to Aristotle in *Metaphysica* (see "Sources and Analogues").

1.1.7 *Generositas* here refers explicitly to the extended aristocratic family, *multitudinem unius generis*, "a multitude of the same family," a kin group that possesses nobility of stock rather than the moral quality itself (as the *OLD* defines the word). Cf. Augustine, *De moribus ecclesiae*, *PL* 32, col. 1323: *An vero generositas solet significare aliud quam parentes?* "But does *generositas* mean anything but relatives?" Compare Du Cange, 4, col. 54, s.v. *generositas*: "familia, genus."

1.3. Title The margin of P_2 reads *De nobilitate anime* but *B* substitutes *animi*, followed by A. Thomas and Colker. (The chapter has no title in P_1KRS.) *Anime* is correct, as is clear from what precedes in 1.2.2–4 and what follows in 1.3.1, 1.3.4, 1.3.10, 1.3.15, etc.

1.3.6 Guillelmus suggests a metaphor based on the alliteration in *speculativa, speculo*, and *speciem*.

1.3.16 *Rectificatio*, "harmonizing," that is, by the effect of *habitus*, "habit," in P_1P_2RS; *rectitudo*, "righteousness," in *BK* and Colker.

1.5.6 *Poeti* in P_1, *poete* in P_2BKRS and Colker. Compare *poete* 1.5.7. *Universali* in P_1P_2BKRS; Colker reads *vili* in P_1B. For the abbreviation *v'li*, see Cappelli, 393.

1.5.20 *Philosophy*: The unusual graphy is found in P_1; *philosophi* in *BS*, *philosophorum* in P_2KR.

1.7.14 In the *Disticha Catonis* the second line reads, "Tuta mage est puppis, modico quae flumine fertur" (Safer is the ship that sails a modest stream), with elision of *mage* and *est* to make the required long syllable. Manuscripts of *De nobilitate animi* separate *mage* and *est* in order to avoid elision, as medieval poets typically did. Most render the line unmetrically: "tuta magĕ puppis et cetera" in P_1P_2R, "tuta magis puppĭs est" in *BS*. *K* makes correct meter while avoiding elision: "tuta magis puppis modico que flumine fertur."

1.7.16 *In certis* P_1, *in incertis B*, *incertis S*. Guillelmus plays on his own version of Horace, "certum terminum imponere voluntati" (1.7.13; see "Sources and Analogues"), by reversing *certum*, said of a self-imposed limitation, and making it into *incertis*, referring to unreliable wealth.

1.8.2 *For[m]a*: *Fortuna* in P_1P_2KRS, *forma* in *B* and Colker. *De forma* contrasts with *de bonitate reali.*

1.8.6 *Laus supradicta* in P_1; *laus sophistica*, "sophistical praise," in P_2BKRS (Colker reads *sophistica* in P_1). This praise is "abovesaid" at the beginning of the chapter: "laus currens communiter inter gentes" (1.8.1). The thought is developed here: "unde laus supradicta moveatur, et lingua et aures diversorum."

1.9.10 *Contingerint* in P_1P_2, *contigerint* in *BKRS* and Colker. The correct form is *contigerint*; it recurs at 2.1.6 in P_1P_2RS (but *contingerit* in *B*, *contingant* in *K*). *Contingerint* is a future perfect based, contrary to classical conjugation, on the present stem *conting-* instead of perfect *contig-*. Erroneous *contingerint* 1.9.10 (P_1P_2) and *contingerit* 2.1.6 (*B*) are balanced by correct *contigerint* 1.9.10 (*BKRS*), 2.1.6 (P_1P_2RS). We attribute the errors to the scribes.

1.10.2 *Communiores*, "more broadly efficacious": cf. *communis*, "Of, belonging to, or affecting the whole community or state" (*OLD*).

1.11.16 Contrary to his usual vigorous Aristotelianism, here Guillelmus appears to take gingerly exception to the teaching that he attributes to the Philosopher. (*De physiognomia* is today considered anonymous.)

1.11.18 "Ea que a Deo principaliter procreantur" (The things that are directly procreated by God) are the elements.

1.11.23 "Philosophus dicit in *Physonomia* et Ptholomeus in *Centilogio*": as above, at 1.11.16 and 1.11.18 respectively.

1.12.2 *Communes*, "public," in contrast to *domestice et private.*

1.12.6 *Exteriora*, "public."

1.12.8 This can be understood to mean that women collectively fall short of the perfection of men, or more specifically, in a medical perspective, that the sexual organ (*sexus*) of women falls short of men's.

1.14.8 "Superius fuit dictum": at 1.11.27a.

1.14.17 The "second argument" is stated in 1.14.4–6.

1.15.7 *Paterni motus*: In *B* these words end line 33 of folio 319v; below this line there is a marginal note on Quintilian that amplifies the arguments in 1.15. The note is clearly an addendum, since other folios have 33 lines of text. For the note see "Sources and Analogues."

2.4.14 *Plinius* (Plinius P_1P_2BR, Iplinius *K*, Plnnus *S*): A. Thomas (170n) and Colker (75) emend to *Philosophus*, referring to physiognomical writings including Pseudo-Aristotle, *Physiognomica*. However, these passages do not match the text in detail; indeed, the passage adduced from Pseudo-Aristotle does not refer to the eyes, mouth, nose, tibia, ankle, or hand, as does Guillelmus. We do not emend; for the source in Pliny, see "Sources and Analogues." *Ramosus*, "branching, ramified" (*OLD*); used by the physician Gilles de Corbeil (d. 1224) to describe a deceptive pulse that seems now fast, now slow (Du Cange 7, col. 12); hence, as used here of the eyes, "shifty."

2.4.15 *Bradefer*: M. Thomas (76 n. 1) called attention to Baudouin I, Count of Flanders (d. 879), known as *Bras de fer*. The name was also borne by a former provost (*quondam praepositus*) of Chauni, in the arrondissement of Laon (Aisne), who appeared in legal documents about 1269. See *Recueil des Historiens des Gaules et de la France*, vol. 24, part 2 (Paris, 1904), 716 e, f, j, l. (The department of Aisne borders that of Nord, which was formed of Hainaut.) This man may or may not have been the same as Odardus Bradefer, who appeared in the same proceedings (ibid., 717 f.).

2.5.5 "Quantum ad secundum": that is, "eorum iusticiam in correctionibus et penitentiis" (2.5.2), lords' "justice in [administering] corrections and punishments."

2.5.7 "Quantum ad tertium": that is, "largitatem in eorum beneficiis tribuendis" (2.5.2), "their generosity in granting benefices."

2.7.6 *Corpus*, "his own body, himself," is used here like Occitan *cors*, which meant "body" and also "self." *BC* substitute *ipsum*.

2.8.4 The *tria predicta* are *mobilia*, "possessions," *corporalis vigor*, "bodily strength," and *scientie et consilii bonitas*, "goodness of knowledge and counsel."

2.8.10 *Illa* refers to wisdom, *sapientia*, as in Wisdom 7.7–11; see "Sources and Analogues."

Rejected Readings in P_1

LISTED HERE are passages where we reject a reading in the body of P_1. Not listed here are paratextual elements such as titles and marginalia, the initial letters of the first words in chapters, which are often omitted in P_1, or passages where we adopt a correction present in P_1. For fuller information, see "Variants."

1.0.12 nobilitate: notabilitate.

1.1.4 [et illa . . . **1.1.5** et moribus]: in se vilia et despecta sunt, dictum est quod nobilitas est habitus, et cetera.

1.2.2 [aut in . . . potentiam corporis] *lacking*. **1.2.3** b[e]ne: bone.

1.3.4 vitup[er]atur: vitupatur. [eas subdere]: esse subditus. **1.3.6** metha[phora]m: metha'em. **1.3.27** [intelligit] *lacking*. **1.3.30** appellet: appellent.

1.4.3 p[ertinen]tibus: partibus. **1.4.9** cor[ru]ptor: corumptor. **1.4.12** [quam]: in qua.

1.5.2 [a] *lacking*. **1.5.3** ment[is]: mente. **1.5.6** poet[e]: poeti. **1.5.22** qu[am]: quod.

1.6.3 [ut] *lacking*. **1.6.10** [intellexit id est non] *lacking*.

1.7.11 et: et et P_1. **1.7.14** [est modico que flumine fertur]: et cetera. **1.7.16** incertis: in certis.

1.8.2 for[m]a: fortuna. **1.8.10** [nec te . . . vexat inanis]: et cetera.

1.9.3 [nobilitas ex bonitate]: bonitas ex nobilitate. **1.9.7** nobilita[t]is: [t] *illegible in* P_1. [principium] *lacking*.

1.10.2 [patet] *lacking*. **1.10.8** [in] *lacking*. informat[e]: informata.

1.11.14 [male]: bene. **1.11.17** [naturam]: numerum. **1.11.21** [Philosophus] *lacking*. [quarto]: quindecimo. **1.11.25** disponit: disponiter. **1.11.26** inclinat[i]: inclinatam. **1.11.29** [Unde primo . . . viri inutiles] *lacking*.

1.12.2 qu[are]: quia.

1.13.4 dictu[m]: dictu.

1.14.8 [rac]ionem: questionem. **1.14.14** [disciplina] *lacking.*

1.15.4 [quarto]: primo. [par]te: par *destroyed by hole.* **1.15.5** vel sic vel sic. [vel]: quod. **1.15.6** sequatur: sequantur.

1.16.2 provide: providere.

1.18.7 [vi]litatem: utilitatem. **1.18.8** oper[a]: operi.

2.2.9 [ubique suam stulticiam ostendit. **2.2.10** Stultus] *lacking.*

2.3.3 v[ul]tus: virtus. **2.3.4** *lacking.*

2.4.1 situata: scituata. **2.4.3** corrigerent: corrigerentur. **2.4.5** vitup[er]ari: vitupari. **2.4.9** posse[n]t: posset. **2.4.11** [sicut]: sed. **2.4.12** habent[i]s: habentes. **2.4.13** *lacking.* **2.4.14** tybia[s]: tybia. [u]ncas: oncas.

2.5.6 [Aristoteles]: Alexander.

2.6.2 [rusticus] *lacking.*

2.8.1 paupe[re]: paupe. **2.8.5** div[i]ciarum: diuciarum. [primum] *illegible.* **2.8.6** [opum] *lacking.* [quam cum . . . esse desistis]: et cetera. **2.8.8** [dum te . . . ferre memento]: et cetera. **2.8.9** [Dilige] *lacking.* [sed parce dilige formam]: et cetera. **2.8.10** omni[a]: omnium.

2.9.5 pa[u]cissimi: pacissimi.

2.10.3 [nec te . . . vexat inanis]: et cetera. **2.10.5** [Plato] *lacking.* **2.10.8** *lacking.*

Variants

Sigla

P_1 Paris, Bibliothèque nationale de France, lat. 16089, f. 238rA.1–242rA.45.
P_2 Paris, Bibliothèque nationale de France, nouv. acq. lat. 3074, f. 7r.13–18r.31.
B Bruges, Bibliothèque municipale, 424, f. 312r.1–322v.32.
K Cologne, Historisches Archiv der Stadt, HAStK 7002 70, olim GB 2o 70, f. 193rA.1–201rA.25.
R Rein (earlier Reun), Austria, Stiftsbibliothek, 205, f. 231v.15–246r.27.
S Salzburg, Stiftsbibliothek Sankt Peter, a.V.14, f. 181vD.20–189vC.25.
Thomas (A.): edits 1.0; the titles of 1.1–8; topic sentences of 1.9–18; 2.0; beginnings and endings of 2.1–11; and selected passages concerning troubadours in 2.3, 2.4, and 2.6.
Colker: edits integral text from P_1 and *B*; uses the orthography of P_1 but frequently adopts readings in *B*.

Title of work De nobilitate animi *K (in top margin of K 194r, 195r, 196r, 197r and v, 198r and v, 199v;* Animi *in top margin of K 200v), Colker, and in a faint later hand in R;* De nobilitate *in margin of* P_2*;* Tractatus de nobilitate anime *[sic] in upper margin of S 182r;* Liber de nobilitate animi *Thomas (A.); lacking in* P_1*B.*

Part 1

1.0. Prologue *P_1 238rA.1; P_2 7r.13; B 312r.1; K 193rA.1; R 231v.15; S 181vD.20.*
Incipit Incipit libellus de nobilitate P_2; Incipit liber de nobilitate animi *B Colker;* Incipit quidam Tractatus de nobilitate animi *K; lacking in* P_1*RS.*
Marginalia in P_1 *asterism at 1.0.6.* ***In*** P_2 Nobilitas nichil aliud est quam bene operans *1.0.2;* Quod multi fallunt[ur] in cognitione nobilitatis *1.0.8; text at 1.0.10 (see below).*
1.0.1 [E]x: X *capital letter intended to follow an ornamental initial that was not inserted, as in most chapters in* P_1*;* Ex *B with guide letter* e. et eius *BS,* et ex eius *corrected from* et ad eius *R.* operibus movemur boni (movemur *expunctuated)* P_2. boni *lacking in S.* noti boni *K.* notabiles: nobiles *B.* iudicamus *S.*

1.0.2 Dico autem *K*. nobilis enim ... bene operans: bona enim operatio indicat nobilem *B*. enim: autem *K*. aliud est: ad esse *R*.

1.0.3 sui: suum *B*. notabilis: nobilem *K*. faciet: facit *BR*. nobilem *lacking in K*, nobilem iudicari *B*, notabilem *S*.

1.0.4 nobilitas: notabilitas *S*. videtur esse: videtur P_2, est *B*, esse videtur *K*. bona operatio P_2BKR. est bone: est ipsius bone *K*. operandum bene P_2. sicut enim nichil *R*.

1.0.5 operationem: ipsam operationem P_2KR. procedat *R*.

1.0.6 sit nobilis *B*. bene et notabiliter P_2KR. nobilitatem: notabilitatem *B*.

1.0.7 Nunc: Quoniam *S*. est ita *K*. plura *R*. plures notitia *K*.

1.0.8 Quidem *Thomas (A.)*. eam credunt *K*. cognoscere et habere *B*. eam nec *R*. nec habent eam P_2. etiam qui *B*. habeant: habent *B*. tamen eam non *K*. credunt eam *BS*. non cognoscunt: non cognoscant *B*. et cognoscunt ... **1.0.10** Ut igitur: et cognoscunt et hii sunt vere nobiles; alii sunt qui eam cognoscunt, non tamen ea utuntur ut deberent; et hii veri litterati male operantes. Ut igitur *B Thomas (A.) (165n)*. deberent: dicunt *K*.

1.0.9 sunt nobiles P_2R. notabiliter *lacking in K*.

1.0.10 igitur: ergo *KR*. et hii qui sunt *K*. hunc *in margin, corrected from* h'c *in* P_2. librum *K*, ilibellum (*first* i *expunctuated*) *S*. posse meo *S*. instruere *S*. ostenditur *S*. quot: quod *R*. sunt *S*. secundum sententiam: intencionem *S*. qui ad noticiam veritatis laboraverunt *K*.

1.0.12 ostenditur *S*. quid: quit *R*. ipsa: ea *KR*. quas de nobilitate fieri *K*. nobilitate: notabilitate P_1.

1.0.13 plura *lacking in B*. p. et: seu *B*. sententie succincte quibus *B* (et sermones *lacking in B*). voluerit: velit *S*.

1.0.14 libellus *B*. liber iste P_2R. Anime *S*. potior: potencior *K*. in *lacking in S*. processu *K*, persecutione *R*. libri *lacking in BK*.

Chapter 1 *P_1 238rA.36; P_2 7v.7; B 312r.28; K 193rB.10; R 232r.15; S 182rA.26.*
Title *BK Colker, in margin of P_2*; Quid s *cut off in margin of R; lacking in P_1S.*
Marginalia in P_1 *asterisms at 1.1.1, 1.1.7.*

1.1.1 [N]obilitas: Obilitas P_1R, Nobilitas *B with guide letter* n *partially cut off*. movet: mos *S*. opera faciendum: operandum *K*. recognoscuntur *S*. pertinent *K*.

1.1.2 est: sit *K*. quia in cum in (*first* in *expunctuated*) *S*. et: vel *B*. corpore sit non sit *K*. nobilitas non est: et nobilitas non sit *K*. nec: vel *BKS*. quia per ... vel passionem *lacking in S*. vel: aut *K*.

1.1.3 igitur: ergo *KRS*. quecumque P_2.

1.1.4 dispositus ad operandum *B*. bene *lacking in K*. vel operari *lacking in K*, vel bene operari *R*. facta sunt: sunt facta *B*, facta *S*. vilitatis: utilitatis *K*. [et illa

... **1.1.5** et moribus] *B* (aliquis b.: *Colker reads* quis *in B*); in se vilia et despecta sunt, dictum est quod nobilitas est habitus, et cetera *P_1S Colker;* que in se sunt vilia et despecta dictum est quod nobilitas est et cetera *P_2;* in se sunt vilia et despecta, dictum est quod nobilitas est habitus movens ad operandum in bonitate communiter *K;* per se sunt vilia et despecta, dictum est quod nobilitas est habitus etiam movens ad opera in bonitate communiter *R.*

1.1.6 Nota secundum naturam sunt autem *KR* (eorum naturam *R*). propositum: oppositum *S.* et *lacking in B.* quoquomodo: quodam modo *BR Colker.* differant *corrected from* differanter *P_1.* differant quoquomodo *K.* nobilitas in *S.* generositas: gentilitas *K.* et altitudo *BKR.*

1.1.7 enim *lacking in S.* proprie *lacking in K.* significat proprie *P_2.* notabilem: nobilem *R.* operis *lacking in B.* operis bonitatem: bonitatem generacionis *K.* generositas: operacionis gentilitas *K.* altitudo: altitudinem *P_2.* vero generis significat *K.*

1.1.8 illa: ista *KRS.* sicud *R.* et *lacking in B.*

Chapter 2 *P_1 238rB.4; P_2 7v.22; B 312v.16; K 193rB.38; R 232v.2; S 182rB.10.*

Title *KR* (sunt *R*)*;* De speciebus nobilitatis *B Thomas (A.) Colker; lacking in P_1P_2S.*

1.2.1 [E]x: X *P_1 with guide letter* e, Ex *B with guide letter* e. Ex hiis que dicta sunt *P_2.* in *above line in P_2.* in descriptione nobilitatis dictum est *K.* o. quod: quot *R.* sunt *inserted above line in P_1.* species nobilitatis *KR.* habitus qui cum acquisitus dirigens: habitus qui est acquisitus dirigens *KR,* habitus qui est dirigens *P_2,* habitus cum acquisitus est dirigit *B,* habitus qui cum acquisitus dirigit *Colker.* in bonum opus et ipsum reddit *B.* opus ipsum reddit *K.*

1.2.2 pertinet *S.* [aut in hiis que pertinent ad potentiam corporis] *S,* aut in hiis que corpori aut *K,* aut ad potenciam corporis aut *B Colker, lacking in P_1P_2R.* fortune potentiam tribuunt *K.* attribuuntur *P_2.*

1.2.3 est enim *lacking in K.* manifestum cuilibet: notum *B,* cuilibet manifestum *S.* quod: quos *R.* bene aut male *K.* b[e]ne: bone *P_1.* secundum: sed *K.* sibi inest: sibimet *S.* aut ex parte anime aut *lacking in P_2.*

1.2.4 igitur: ergo *K,* autem *R.* loquendo *lacking in K.* scilicet nobilitas *lacking in K.* anime corporis *BK.* primo: prius *K.* de nobilitate anime est dicendum *K.* anime: animi *B. After* animi: Nota Quidam distingunt nobilitatem in nobilitatem nature secundum quod habet bonas dispositiones naturales, in nobilitatem morum, et nobilitatem generis *B.*

Chapter 3 *P_1 238rB.12; P_2 7v.29; B 312v.26; K 193vC.12; R 232v.12; S 182rB.24.*

Title De nobilitate anime *in margin of P_2,* d. n. animi *B Thomas (A.) Colker, lacking in P_1KRS. After* **1.3.1** habet, *blank space left for rubricator to insert chapter title in K.*

Marginalia* in P_1** *asterisms at 1.3.6, 1.3.17, 1.3.18, 1.3.19, 1.3.20, 1.3.21, 1.3.27; text at 1.3.23 (see below).* ***In* P_2** Nota *1.3.15*, Dubium Nota *1.3.25*, Solutio *1.3.26*; *asterisms at 1.3.15, 1.3.23; text at 1.3.6, 1.3.11, 1.3.16, 1.3.17 (see below).* ***In B *text at 1.3.20, 1.3.26 (see below).*

1.3.1 [A]nima: Nima P_1 *with guide letter* a; Pnima *B* [sic] *with guide letter* a (*Colker reads* Prima); nima *R*. habet tres P_2. scilicet *lacking in K*. communes *lacking in S*. *After* communes: unam scilicet propriam *expunctuated in* P_2.

1.3.2 communicat cum *B*. quod omnibus viventibus competit in hoc mundo: primum sibi commune est cum bestiis, secundum commune est sibi cum omnibus viventibus *B*. competit: aptum *Colker*.

1.3.3 vero: enim *BK*. vero ratio operatio (ratio *expunctuated*) *S*. operatio hominis *B*. aut intelligere per medium rationis *lacking in S*. rationis omnibus (omnibus *expunctuated*) P_2.

1.3.4 vel malicia: et malicia *B*. quod com ex (com *expunctuated*) *S*. non laudatur aut vituperatur homo ex ipsis *K*. nec vituperatur *R*. vitup[er]atur: vitupatur P_1. in tantum in quantum: in quantum homo *B*, in tantum quantum *KS*. deberet *corrected to* debent P_2, debent *K*. [eas subdere]: esse subditus P_1S, esse naturaliter subditus P_2KR (subdite *K*), eas subdere *B Colker*. eas: eos *KS*. rationi esse *B Colker*. sed vituperatur vel: sed vituperatur et P_2, vituperantur et laudatur homo *K*, sed laudatur et vituperatur homo *R*. rationis vel operationis intellectus *K*. quare: quia *K*. anime *lacking in* P_2. illa: istius *K*, ista *R*. operationes *K*. notare illa operatione *B*.

1.3.5 intelligere vel ratiocinari *K*.

1.3.6 Est *in margin of* P_2. cognoscere: cogitare *B Colker* (*cf.* cognosci *later*). hec: hic *R*. metha[phora]m: metha'em P_1, metaphoram *K*, metaforam *R*, metha^{am} *S*. esse apparentem speciem (esse *crossed out*) *K*. fantasie adveniunt *B*. quid est: quidem *R*, quid s est (s *expunctuated*) *S*. et essentiam rerum: essentiam rerum eorum *K*. resolvens: resolvans *R*.

1.3.7 et artem *lacking in K*. *Between* rerum *and* quecumque: Noticia est valde bona alia vero pars que dicitur *crossed out in R*. sunt *BR*. est *lacking in* P_2K. est valde *R*. bona est *B*.

1.3.8 pars q. d. a. v. p. est *R*. activam (m *expunctuated*) P_2. practica vel activa *B*.

1.3.9 debet P_2, dn debent (dn *expunctuated*) *S*. non sunt: non possunt P_2.

1.3.10 meliores et nobiliores P_2K. sunt in: fiunt in *B Colker*. decimo: in decimo *K*, quarto *R*. dicit intellectum curans et secundum hunc bene operans est optime *S*. Secundum: Homo secundum *K*. hunc: huic P_2. optime est *K*. sua operatio P_2. similis est: est similis *K*, simul et *R*. est operationi: et operationi *R*.

1.3.11 Unde operatio divina cum non sit nobilis sed nobilitas ipsa de *B*. nobilis est sed ipsa nobilitas *K*. debent *in margin of* P_2.

1.3.12 intelligunt res *S*. operaciones: opiniones *B*. prefulgent bonitate *K*.

1.3.13 Preterea: Et preterea *R*. anima post mortem *K*. sola anima *B Colker*. utitur: notatur *S*. tamquam servituti nobilior (servituti *expunctuated*) P_1. fuit: servit *B*. obligata: alligata *K*.

1.3.14 erunt: errant erunt (errant *crossed out*) *K*. operacionibus P_2*BKRS*.

1.3.15 igitur: ergo *R*. aliud *lacking in K*. sapientia in agendo speculando (agendo *crossed out*) *S*. *After* agendo: Et vilitas anime nichil aliud est quam intelligendo insipientiam et maliciam in agendo *K*.

1.3.16 hic *lacking in* P_2, hoc *KS*. huius causa *R*. rectificatio: rectitudo *BK Colker*. operum: operacionum P_2*KR*.

1.3.17 Unde non est *K*. qui non *K*. est studiosus *BK*. quod patet: nec qui caret aliqua sapientia studiosus est previum patet *KR* (est previum: et primum quidam *R*). legitur discipulis suis: in legibus suis discipulo suo *K*. suis discipulis *R*. suis dixisse sicut *B*. natura dum *B*. De natura humana P_2. dixisse *lacking in K*. mundate te (*first* te *expunctuated*) *S*. corporea (*faint*) P_1, corporea P_2*KS*, corpore *B Colker (reads* corpore *in* P_1*)*, p (= *per?*) corporea *R*. postea: poste *R*. veritatem omnem P_2. cum aliis *in margin of* P_2. elementis: materiale cum qualitatibus *K*.

1.3.18 hoc etiam: hoc idem P_2*K*, hic idem *R*. in de con de consolatione *K*. verum: veritatem *S*. carpere: carpe *Colker*. spem: spiritus *R*. nubula *KS*, nubilia *R*. est vinctaque frenis hec ubi regnant *K*. victaque P_2.

1.3.19 tangens etiam *B*. omnes: alias *R*. dicens *lacking in BS*. verum *corrected from* vere P_2.

1.3.20 Et generaliter *lacking in K*. philosophi: isti *K*. intelligunt et generaliter omnes philosophi *K*. quiete pacifica: pace et quieta *K*. motibus *lacking in K*, mortibus *R*. passionum animi *B*. passionibus *K*. Agazel *BK*. Logica *corrected in margin from* Mathematica *in B*, sua logica P_2, sua loyca *R*, loca sua *S*. apta est *K*. anima apta P_2. anima est apta *R*. impingantur *K*. forme: fortune *R*. universi esse P_2*KR*. cum: quando *K*. sordibus *B*. scilicet *lacking in K*. *After* fantasiis: quare patet quod non erit sapiens neque studiosus *K*.

1.3.21 proprie P_2*KR*. subiectum: som' (= *solum?*) P_2. et principium: seu principium P_2*KR*, vel principium *B*. relinquens passiones P_2. relinquendo *K*, reliquas *B*.

1.3.22 in: ad *K*. inclinat *K*. non: nec P_2.

1.3.23 E contrario: Quare eodem modo *K*. E contrario ... **1.3.24** non erit *lacking in B*. Aristotiles *Colker*. tertio: in tertio P_2. per: p *R*. contingit: convenitt (sic*)* *R*. que accionem informant ... circumstantiarum que *in margin of* P_1. accionum *R*. que nichil: quod nichil *KR Colker*.

1.3.24 insipiens: sapiens *KR*. non erit vel prudens *K*.

1.3.25 que: quod *R.* hiis tamen *K.* contingit: convenit *R.* quod *lacking in B,* quod q (*second* q *expunctuated*) *S.* sit: est sit *R.* sit incipiendum *K.* i. que: qui *B.* eis: illis *BK.* e. que: qui *K.*

1.3.26 questionem breviter dicitur primo *B.* dicendum videtur quod primo oportet P_2R, dicendum est breviter *K.* differenter: dr' P_1S (= *differenter; for the abbreviation see Cappelli, 108–109; Colker reads* de *expunctuated in* P_1). quod primo *K.* actionibus P_2KR. connutritum: assuetum *B.* antequam *twice, second lined out in* P_2. est quare quia (quare *crossed out*) *S.* nata *lacking in* P_2K. operationem: actionem *K.* in *lacking in R.* stimulant nos: stimulabant *B.* ad opus: nature *added in margin of B.* virtu (*new line*) tutem *S.* et: vel P_2R, seu *K.* sensibilem: sensitivam *K.*

1.3.27 in *lacking in BK,* in libro P_2R. *De Animalibus: lacking in R.* quod *lacking in B.* differt nichil P_2K, differens *R.* ab anima: ut est dicere anima *K.* ab anima bestiarum: a bestiarum anima P_2R, ad bestiarum animam *K,* ab anima l bestiarum (l *expunctuated*) *S.* secundum s tempus (*second* s *expunctuated*) *S.* quare: autem *B.* Philosophus [intelligit] quod: Philosophus quod P_1 *Colker,* Philosophus dicit eo *B,* vult philosophus quod *S.* quodammodo bestialiter *BK.* vivamus P_2KR.

1.3.28 igitur: ergo *R.* ut cognitus intellectus *K.*

1.3.29 habere cognitionem *K.* operationum: operum *K.* inclinamur P_2R. virtutis et: virtutis ut *K.* exercitati experti (exercitati *crossed out*) *R.* illius operacionis *K.*

1.3.30 Hec *above line in R.* appellet: appellent P_1P_2R. et *lacking in K.* equivoce: equitate P_2. vellet *K.* et largo: vel largo P_2K.

1.3.31 aliqualem: aliquam *B.* habere aliqualem sapientiam P_2KR.

1.3.32 Ex hiis (Ex hoc P_2K) ... **1.3.34** ex cognitione: Licet malitia operationis ex ignorantia procedat quia omnis malus ignorans non tamen bonitas operationis venit ex sapientia sed bene venit ex cognitione *B.* apparet: patet *K.* sit *lacking in KR.* ad quod *S.* omnis malus *K.*

1.3.33 est enim *R.* est *lacking in R.* ex *lacking in R.* hoc: hic *R.* veniat: venit *S.*

1.3.34 bene sequitur *K.* ex cognitione: ex eius cognitione *R.* directe opponitur *B Colker.* sed cognitio: sed cognitioni *B.*

1.3.35 hec: hic *R.* animi *B,* anima *R.* sint dicta *lacking in B,* dicta sint *K.*

Chapter 4 *P_1 238vC.44; P_2 9r.10; B 314r.8; K 194rB.36; R 234r.18; S 183rA.36.*

Title *BK Thomas (A.) Colker, in margin of P_2 (cut off); lacking in P_1RS.*

Marginalia in P_1 *asterisms at 1.4.1, 1.4.4, 1.4.12, 1.4.13.* ***In P_2*** Nota *1.4.12; text at 1.4.4, 1.4.9 (see below).* ***In B*** *text at 1.4.4 (see below).*

1.4.1 [P]ost: Ost P_1 *with guide letter* p; Dost P_2; Ost *R*. hanc: hanc autem *KR*, hoc autem P_2, nobilitatem animi *B*. corporis nobilitate P_2KR. figuram propriam P_2KR. avos: quos P_2.

1.4.2 primam acceptionem *B*. de Priamo dicens P_2. dicens quod species Priami *B*. foret: est *B*.

1.4.3 Ille: Iste P_2KR. enim *lacking in* P_2. corporis: operibus P_2. excellebat: antecellebat *R*. pulcritudine et fortitudine *S*. fortitudine et *K*. p[ertinen]tibus: partibus P_1, attenentibus *B*. corpore pertinentibus *K*. *Between* pertinentibus *and* corpori: secundum etiam milites exercitati f (*three letters illegible*) us *lined out in* P_2. corporis *BS*.

1.4.4 etiam *lacking in B*. hanc etiam *K*. Romani olim *K*. anime nobilitate: nobilitate animi (animi *in margin*) *B*. intelligendum *corrected from* pugnandum *R*. veritatem *in margin of* P_2. virtutes *R*. ita *lacking in R*. a[d]: d *smeared in* P_1.

1.4.5 Quare *lacking in B*. quicuque P_2. instruebatur *S*.

1.4.6 Et altera P_2. opinionem vulgarem P_2KR.

1.4.7 autem sit *K*. necessarium est P_2KR. sit *lacking in S*. similis sit *B*. quod talis est P_2KR. retinetur enim forma P_2. formam: fortunam *R*. eius *lacking in R*.

1.4.8 quando *lacking in B*. contingit: convenit *R*. erit patri: est patri *K*. hoc: id *K*, hic *R*. erit vilis vel malus: sit malus et vilis *K*. vel malus *lacking in B*. habebat: habuerat P_2R, habebit *B*, *lacking in K*. ignorabilitat P_2, ignorat *K*.

1.4.9 Et dico P_2. dico quod *lacking in B*. talis et est *B*. nobilis est P_2. opinione *in margin, corrected from* operatione (?) P_2. que: qui *K*. rerum: rere P_2. possunt: potest *BK*. secundum veritatem *lacking in B*. cor[ru]ptor: corumptor P_1S *Colker*. corruptor est *K*. nobilitatis vere *B*.

1.4.10 Quod optime Salustius intellexit *lacking in* P_2. Marinus *KS*. strennuus miles *K*. strenuus *lacking in B*. fuit presentatus sibi P_2R.

1.4.11 Marinus *S*. optimus miles *R*. sed tamen *B*. eum impediebant *B*.

1.4.12 respondens: respondit *R*. dicit *B*. Nova inest isti nobilitas *B*. isti inest: mihi est *K*. [quam]: in qua P_1BKS *Colker*, in quo P_2R. est *lacking in B*. habitam *lacking in S*. corrumpisses *S*. eum: ipsum *K*. iudicavit P_2K, eum iudicavit *B*.

1.4.13 Unde ulterius P_2KR. assimilarentur *KS*. non solum: quod non solum *K*. vilititatis P_2.

1.4.14 Et *lacking in B*. mirabilis est P_2R. est mirabilis *K*. imo *Colker*. expresse *corrected from* expressum *in* P_2.

1.4.15 existentem *lacking in B*. p. quantumcumque: quamquam *B*. fuisset: extitisset *K*. fatuum filium esse *B*. s. quantumcumque: quamquam *B*. sapiens fuisset *B*.

1.4.16 nullus dicerent P_2, nullus deberet *K*, nullus diceret *R*. quamplures: plures *R*. frequenter quod communem opinionem deberet corrigere hoc est quod tales *K*. destruuntur *S*. propter eorum vilitatem et maliciam: propter vilitatem et eorum stulticiam *K*. bonitate et probitate *KR*. fuerant *K*. inimicos *twice, the first crossed out in R*. amicos fecerunt P_2*KR*.

1.4.17 igitur: ergo *KR*. sint: sit P_2*BKRS*. qui: qus *R*. nobiles sint *K*. nunc dictum sit in tantum *K*. dictum sit P_2*R*.

Chapter 5 *P_1 238vD.40; P_2 9v.17; B 314v.15; K 194vD.24; R 235v.3; S 183vC.26.*

Title *BK Thomas (A.) Colker, in margin of P_2; lacking in P_1RS.*

Marginalia in P_1 *asterisms at 1.5.3, 1.5.6, 1.5.7, 1.5.11, 1.5.17, 1.5.19, 1.5.20; text at 1.5.5 (see below).* ***In P_2*** *asterism at 1.5.25; text at 1.5.7, 1.5.12, 1.5.16, 1.5.18 (see below).* ***In B*** *text at 1.5.3 (see below).* ***In R*** -enit *(?) in margin 1.5.20.*

1.5.1 [E]x: X P_1 *with guide letter* e, Ex *B with guide letter* e, x *R*. preintelligendo: preaccipiendo *K*, premittendo *Colker*. quid: quit *R*. ipsam fortunam *S*. que: quid *K*.

1.5.2 aliquando *K*. aut a casu *K*. [a] *lacking in P_1P_2 Colker.*

1.5.3 quarto *lacking in B*, in quarto *K*. de quarto Consolacione *R*. intendens: videns *B*. intendens dare horum differentiam incipit *K*. Omnia genera (*repeated in margin*) *B*, Cum generacio *K*. re *expunctuated before* rerum P_1. cuttusque P_2. progressus: processus *B*. quidquid *K*, quicquit *R*. modo: motu *B*. movetur causas: monstrans *K*. formam *R*. a divine *K*. ment[is]: mente P_1. sortitur stabilitate *S*.

1.5.4 Et de P_2*KR*. Boecius dicit quod si: *illegible in P_1*, Boecius dicit si *B*. considerentur *K*. seu cause: cause *B*, sui cause *K*, sive causa *R*. vel ordinis sive: seu ordinis seu P_2, sui ordinis sui *K*, sive ordinis sive *R*. forme a mente P_2*K*, forme fuerit in se a mente (in *expunctuated*) *B*, fortune a mente *R*. intellectu *lacking in S*. hoc est si res: hoc est quod si res P_2*R*, huius res si *B*, id est si res *K*. si res referantur ad Dei notitiam secundum esse P_1P_2*KR* (si *lacking in S;* quod si *R;* referatum *K;* secundum: vel *K*), *illegible except for* notit *in B*. quodcumque dicuntur: quod habebant dicuntur *B*. quodcumque dicuntur esse vel fieri a *lacking in K*. providentia divina *B*.

1.5.5 si: tamen si *K*. consideretur *in margin of P_1, lacking in B*, provideretur *R*. mandatis P_2. [res] *conjecture by Colker.* ut *lacking in K*. habent: hunc *K*. et per: et *expunctuated in P_2*. magis: manifestari *B*, magis tamen *K*. fatum esse P_2*R*. similem *K*. sicud *R*. ordinatus: ordinandus *R*. ab intellectu: ad intelligendum *K*. quod: et P_2*BKRS Colker*. fieri etiam que *R*. operis P_2*KR*. promocione *R*.

1.5.6 Ita: Item *B Colker*. fatum *corrected from* faltum *expunctuated in P_2*. poet[e]: poeti P_1. celestia *B*, celestes et naturales P_2, celestes et naturales et qui realiter *K*, celestes et naturales qui realiter *R*. natura consideradum *B*.

1.5.7 etiam: enim *K*. considerando: considero *R*. huius P_2*BR*. sicut: tamquam *K*, circa *R*. quendam considerantes *B*. fixerunt *S*. finxerunt tres fatas sorores

K. secunda: alia P_2*KR*. sed: et *BK*. *After* terminabat: lachesis trahit artropres occat similiter astrologi *crossed out in R*. quod ipsi *K*. colum *corrected from* collum *B*, colon *K*. Artropres *R*. occat *in margin, corrected from* accat *in* P_2.

1.5.8 posuerunt: ponunt *K*. et continuativas P_2*KR*.

1.5.9 dicunt: ostendunt *K*. accepto: accepta *B Colker*. intelligentie: intellective *K*, intelligencie corporis *R*. celestis est utriusque *K*.

1.5.10 et *lacking in B*. dicitur: dicit *S*. prosagium *K*. ad actus: ad *above line in B*. retorquendo *BK*. et aliis: et in aliis P_2*KR*. avibus *corrected from* avis P_2. augurialibus *lacking in B*. in visionibus P_2*K*. in sompniorum visionibus *R*. similium *K*.

1.5.11 Ulterius autem *K*. consideretur P_2*R*. hic *R*. ut: secundum quod P_2*KR*. sint: sunt *B*, *lacking in S*. ab homine ... dicitur casus *lacking in R*. et in: vel *K*. non agunt: non *above line in B*. dicit *S*.

1.5.12 autem *lacking in K*. aliter facit P_2*KR*. concurrere: currere *S*. fuerint: fuerunt *BS*, sint P_2*K*. i. previsa: provisa P_2*BRS*, provise *K*. docetur: dicitur *KR*. differentiam inter ista *K*. quicquid: inquit *R*. provisum fuerit P_2*BKR*. provisum sit P_2*BKR*. aut impediat: aut re...at *in margin of* P_2. eveniat *K*.

1.5.13 vel cecis oculis *lacking in K*. mo rotam (mo *crossed out*) *S*. immutat: mutat *K*. sint provise: fuit provisum *B*, sicut provise *R*.

1.5.14 Philosophus dicit *K*. est causa: sint cause *K*. que: qui *R*. parte con- *illegible in B*. contingunt P_2*BKRS*.

1.5.15 et hoc secundum quod P_2, secundum hic *R*. ipsa *lacking in S*.

1.5.16 hiis satis P_2*K*, hiis autem *R*. quid sit fortuna: aliquid est fortuna *corrected in margin to* quid [*blank space*] fortuna P_2, quid est *R*.

1.5.17 convenienter: communiter *B*. accipere: sumere *BK*. sint *K*. cito mutabiles et cito venientes *K*. provenientes: venientes *KR*. sine: et sine *B*. sine promissione P_2. non de levi P_2. non *lacking in KR*. a visione *S*. huiusmodi: huius P_2*BRS*.

1.5.18 Tales autem *K*. tres tantum: que tantum P_2, tres tamen *B*, tantum tres scilicet *K*. divicie dominium P_2. fama: et fama P_2. *After* fama: nuncupantur *in margin of* P_2.

1.5.19 istis: hiis P_2. proprie *lacking in* P_2. ista: illa *B*, *lacking in K*. et sine provisione: sine ratione *B*. acquiritur *B*. vel perdit *lacking in K*. homo ista nec in istis *K*. est in hiis *R*. sibi fiat possessio *K*. fiat sibi: sibi fiat P_2*KR*, fuerit *B*.

1.5.20 philosophy (ph'y P_1): philosophorum P_2*KR*, philosophi *BS*. qui omnia ista P_2*R*, qui omnino *K*. ista tria *K*. prima *K*. quia *lacking in B*. possessio: processio vel possessio *B*. amplius autem P_2*KR*. quod: quia P_2. quilibet *R*. erant *K*. non: nec *K*. privationem: perfectionem *K*. homines *lacking in K*. sapientis *R*. et alter alterius bonum P_2. fuisset omnium quia inter sapientes et amicos non est dominium *K*. contra stultos et amicitia: inter amicos et iustitia *B*. amitia *S*. equitates P_2*R*.

1.5.21 fuissent *corrected from* fuisset P_2. foret: fuisset *K*. largius P_2, larga *R*. alicuius non: alterius nec *K*. cumulassent P_2R. etiam *lacking in K*. rapuissent *R*. fama mala (mala *expunctuated*) *B*. si: in *R*. humana: mala non *K*. ratione frenata *lacking in K*, ratione frenata ratione *S*.

1.5.22 spreverunt bona fortune *R*. tamen q. f., tamen q. m., tamen q. p.: tum, tum, tum *Colker*. qu[am]: quod P_1.

1.5.23 illa: ista P_2BKR. sunt *B*. magni *lacking in K*. multi maxime tamen *K*. mutant P_2KR. humane operationis *S*.

1.5.24 Aliqua *B*. non absolutam habent, tamen: non habent absolutam habent tamen *K*.

1.5.25 Et: quod *K*. unde ulterius ... sive viles *lacking in B*. poterunt iudicari: iudicari poterunt P_2R, iudicari possunt *K*.

1.5.26 tres erunt *K*.

Chapter 6 *P_1 239rB.17; P_2 10v.18; B 315v.20; K 195vC.19; R 236r.23; S 184rB.23.*

Title *B Thomas (A.) Colker, in margin of P_2;* De nobilitate domini *K; lacking in P_1RS.*

Marginalia in P_1 Versus *1.6.8; asterisms at 1.6.3, 1.6.4, 1.6.9, 1.6.11.* ***In P_2*** Nota *1.6.4; text at 1.6.2, 1.6.6, 1.6.10 (see below).* ***In B*** *text at 1.6.3 (see below).*

1.6.1 [N]obilitas: Obilitas P_1 *with guide letter* n; Nobilitas *B with guide letter* n; Obilitas *R*; Nobilitas autem *K*. in perfectione *lacking in S*, perfectione *K*. *First* et *corrected from* ut *crossed out in R*.

1.6.2 sit et pacis et rationis P_2K, sit et pacis rationis *R*. dicit esse dominum *KR*. dominum *Colker*. aliis sensu et intellectu viget *K*. *After* intellectu P_2 *or* viget *K*: servus qui deficit naturaliter intellectu P_2K (servum *K*). quare: quia *KS*. seipso: ipso *in margin of* P_2.

1.6.3 et sibi: ut sibi P_2KRS. suis subditis rationem custodiat et intellectum at diligenter *K*. [ut] *Colker, lacking in P_1P_2KRS, obscured by smear in B (Colker seems to read* ut *in B)*. intellectu *R*. quod: ut *B*. sol *above line in P_1, in margin of B*. omnia subdita P_2R, omnia sibi subdita *K*. ita dominos dominus subditos suos intellectu et ratione *K*. subditos ratione et intellectu P_2R. relucere: illucere *B*, elucere *K*. reprimans *R*. reprimens stulticias et bestialitates *K*.

1.6.4 dixit: dicit *B*. dicit: allegat *B Colker*. primo: in libro P_2, in *K*, libro *R*. dicens *lacking in BS*. fore: esse *K*, fore et *S*. si eas sapientes P_2, si eas studiosi sapienter *R*. ea *S*. sapientia P_2. studuissent *corrected from* studuisse *in* P_2.

1.6.5 taliter suum dominium P_2KR. taliter: regulariter *B*. volunt *lacking in K*. vere *lacking in S*.

1.6.6 Et: Quod *K*. Et si contingat *in margin of P_2, lacking in S*. contingat quod *lacking in K*. voluerit: noluerit *BK*. nec rationem studere nec pacem *K*. racione *R*. seu intellectui P_2, sive intellectui *R*. suam nec *lacking in B*. subditorum suorum *K*. est vilis: vilis *S*. et quanto ... et despectus *lacking in S*. eius dominium *K*. tanta *R*. maior *corrected from* magis *in B*. eius vilitas P_2*KR*.

1.6.7 non *in margin of* P_2. unde: un *R*. contingunt et periculosa P_2, contingunt et pericula *KR*. eorum quorum *K*.

1.6.8 Unde talibus *K*, Unde mdo talibus *R*. manibus: dominis P_2, navibus *R*. resortis *K*. talias *B*. incipiunt sine ratione *S*. et: vel *B*. eis: eius *R*. contingit eis *B*. ipsi *K*. crediderunt *K*.

1.6.9 Unde *lacking in* P_2*KR*. iuvenis: puer *BK Colker Ecclesiastes*.

1.6.10 dicit *lacking in R*. id est in dominio *lacking in BR*. in d.: in *lacking in* P_2*K*. dominio *in margin, corrected from* domino P_2. non [intellexit id est non] cognovit: non cognovit P_1*S*, non intellexit *Colker*. c. est *lacking in B*. illis: eis *K*.

1.6.11 optime patet P_2*KR*. regnum: regimen dominorum P_2, regimen dicitur *R*. inter subditos: in subditis *K*. conservatur P_2*RS Colker*, servatur *B*, conservetur *K*.

1.6.12 hac *lacking in B*. dicens: dicit *K*. quod *lacking in B*. iuris: mat' (= *materne?*) *K*. q. sine: absque *B Colker*. sine aliqua: de alia P_2*KR*.

1.6.13 dicta hec *S*.

Chapter 7 *P_1 239rB.49; P_2 11r.114; B 316r.17; K 195vD.32; R 236v.30; S 184vC.29.*

Title *BK, in margin of* P_2 *cut off, Thomas (A.) Colker; lacking in* P_1*RS*.

Marginalia in P_1 Versus *1.7.5*, Versus *1.7.15*; *asterisms at 1.7.5, 1.7.10, 1.7.13*; *text at 1.7.11 (see below)*. ***In*** P_2 Contradictio *1.7.2*; *text at 1.7.2 (see below)*. ***In R*** Contra divites avaros *1.7.10*.

1.7.1 [Q]uamvis: Uamvis P_1 *with guide letter* q; uamvis *R*. diviciis *corrected from* dividii *R*. diviciis intelligamus omnia mobilia generaliter aliquando *K*. intelligunter *B*. habunadanciam (*second* a *expunctuated*) *S*. aggregatam *K*. possessionem peccunie (peccunie *lined out and expunctuated*) P_2.

1.7.2 igitur: ergo *KR*. contingit: convenit *R*. suum *lacking in B*. habet *lacking in R*. quamvis *in margin of R*, licet P_2*K*. et inde faciat *lacking in S*. faciat secundum *K*. recta *lacking in K*. dictaret: declaret P_2, dictat *KS*. non sit dives: et sic dives *B*, *lacking in K*. sit: fit P_2*R*. habet *R*. quantitatem quia: quantitatem si sibi non sufficiat non est dives quia *B*. divicie *corrected from* pecunie P_2. proprie significant P_2*BK*, proprie signant *R*. sufficientiam: habundantiam *BKR*. quandam *lacking in K*, quandam et sufficienciam *R*, quanda sufficientiam *S*.

1.7.3 aliquis: quis P_2*R*. non iudicat sibi *B*. iudicat se non *K*. quare s.: quia *K*. concupiscit *corrected from* concupisset *in* P_1. accumulare *K*. quam quam *K*. suadet *B*, dictat *K*.

1.7.4 collecta: occulta *K*. cuiquam *S*. enim *lacking in K*. avaris et *K*. autem *lacking in K*. recta sive directa *R*. hoc: id *K*, sed *R*.

1.7.5 intelligit *lacking in B.* libro *lacking in K.* ubi dicit quod: dicit *B.* divicie in spargendo: spargendo *R.* in spargendo sive *lacking in K.* spargendo *corrected from* spargengo *S.* in distribuendo: distribuendo P_2*R.* lucent *B.* et non *K.* recumulando *B.* subditor *R.* sibi *corrected from* sib *in* P_2. nocivi: nocui *R.*

1.7.6 Quare: Unde *K.* quod *inserted above line in* P_2, quid sit *K.* nichil enim *K.* est *lacking in BK.* ipsarum diviciarum P_2. et dominus: et < est > dominus *Colker.* nobilis est *S.* sic *lacking in R.* dictum est *BS.* sua operacio P_2. divine bonitatis P_2. que: qui *B.* large sine *K.* distribuit bonitates *KR* (bonitatis *R*).

1.7.7 autem *lacking in K.*

1.7.8 que: qui *B.* timerere (*second* re *erased*) P_2. eorum: illorum *B.*

1.7.9 debeat: debet P_2*K.* debent: deberent P_2, debeant *BR Colker.*

1.7.10 aput *R.* debet esse mirabilius *K.* esse debet *R.* esse: esse quam divitos avaros *R.* est *lacking in B.* frequencius P_2*KR.* inter quos: ubi *B.* nullus: alius *K.* inveniatur *K.* ubicumque *B Colker*, uterque *K.* videmus eos *R.* cumulandum *B.* accumulandas pecunias *K.* oporteret *B.* quamplures heredes: quamplures *S.* habentes heredes *KR.* et plures redditus magnos habentes quam non habentes *K.*

1.7.11 autem verissime P_2*KR.* illud: id *R.* hoc: hic *R.* quod q.: quod communiter P_2*K*, quod convenienter *R.* cuilibet *R.* se iudicat dignum *B.* quare quod habet ... concupiscere plus et *in margin of* P_1, *lacking in B.* sufficit *lacking in R.* immo: sed *K.* et: et et P_1. quod agregat *B.* suum altius possit promovere *K.*

1.7.12 sciunt *BK.* quare: quia *K.* cordis pace *B Colker.* et in P_2*KR.* periculo P_2*K.*

1.7.13 dicit Boecius *S.*

1.7.14 autem periculum quia plurimum est concupiscentia *K.* autem periculum quam plurimum *R.* quamplurimum pli (pli *expunctuated*) P_1. concupiscentia multorum *B.* precipit *R.* magis *BKS.* [est modico que flumine fertur] *KRS* (est *lacking in K*), et cetera P_1P_2 *Colker,* est et cetera *B.*

1.7.15 Oracius optime in suis epistulis *K.* serviat *R*, servit *S.* in eternum *S.* parvo: puer *R.* *Between* parvo *and* nesciat, *the first stroke of* v *expunctuated in* P_1. nesciat: nesciet *B Colker Horace.*

1.7.16 isti: enim *K.* magna *lacking in S.* esset: est *B.* incertis: in certis P_1, in incertis *B*, certum P_2, in paucis certum *KR.* terminum imponere P_2*BKR.*

Chapter 8 *P_1 239vC.41; P_2 11v.22; B 316v.25; K 196rB.20; R 237v.21; S 185rA.16.*

Title *K;* De nobilitate fame *in margin of* P_2; De nobilitate fame seu glorie *B Thomas (A.) Colker; lacking in* P_1*RS.*

Marginalia in P_1 Versus *1.8.5*, Versus *1.8.6; asterisms at 1.8.6, 1.8.11, 1.8.12.* ***In B*** *text at 1.8.1 (see below).* ***In R*** De laude et vituperio *1.8.10*, Aristoteles *1.8.11.*

1.8.1 [T]ercia: Ercia P_1 *with guide letter* t; Tercia *B with guide letter* t; Ercia *R.* nobilitatis *in margin of B.* fortune *lacking in B.* que: quod *K.* communiter currens *B Colker*. a qua: de aliquo qui *K*. aliquis iudicatur P_2R. aliquis *lacking in K*.

1.8.2 bona *lacking in K*. fortune illud *K*. est *lacking in S*. est hoc quod *B*. for[m]a: fortuna P_1P_2KRS. quia: quam *B*. habent *BS*. aliis: vero *S*.

1.8.3 Ymmo *lacking in S*, Ymo *Colker*. alio: altero *K*. ea: eadem die P_2KR. que: quam *K*, quo *R*.

1.8.4 ista: illa P_2B. quasi *lacking in K*. in *lacking in K*. ille: illi *K*. qualem P_2KR.

1.8.6 Cato *lacking in* P_2. dicebat: dicebat et ulterius quod ipsemet esset iudex sui ipsius consulebat P_2KR. aliquis: quis *K*. memento plus alii de te quam tu tibi credere noli *KR* (aliis *R*). intelligens Catho *K*. in veritate *K*. foret deceptus: deciperetur *K*. isti sunt vanigloriosi qui *K*. quod: ut *K*. opera eorum P_2. sint: non sint *R*. toto posse nituntur P_2. quia: quod P_2BKRS. et quod appareant *lacking in BS*. q. appareant: habeantur *K*. magne fame *corrected from* magna fama *in* P_2. supradicta: sophistica P_2BKRS *Colker (who reads* sophistica *in* P_1*)*. et lingua: ad linguas *B Colker*, et lingue *K*.

1.8.7 tamen: tantum *B*. quasi plures: quamplures *BS*, quia plures *K*. videmus qui nituntur *K*. facere *lacking in B*. specialiter illis: specialiter in illis *K*, exercere erga illos *B*. loquantur *B*. in diversis locis personis (locis *expunctuated*) *B*, in locis et personis diversis *K*. de *lacking in K*. tribuere *B*. deberent secundum ordinem largitatis distribuere bona P_2KR.

1.8.8 species vanigloriosorum *R*. reperitur: invenitur *K*.

1.8.9 Sunt: Sicut *S*. Sunt enim plures *lacking in B*. mixtim aliqua P_2R, mixtim aliqua que *K*. turpibus: turpiloquio *B Colker*. cum laudibus: collaudantibus *K*. laudibus dicunt *B*.

1.8.10 dicens: dicit enim *K*. [nec te ... vexat inanis] P_2KR (ipsum: ipse *KR*), nec te vituperes ipse *B*, et cetera P_1S *Colker*.

1.8.11 Hoc *lacking in K*. Aristotiles *Colker*. se vituperare P_2KR. stultitie est signum *K*.

1.8.12 patet satis P_2R. alicuius *lacking in B*. sint P_2. gloria et eorum sermo laudabilis verus currit *KR* (currit: ostendit *R*).

Chapter 9 *P_1 239vD.19; P_2 12r.18; B 317r.18; K 196vC.28; R 238a.25; S 185rB.18.*

Title *K;* Utrum tot sint species nobilitatis quot superius sunt distincte *in margin of* P_2*;* Dubium est de numero specierum nobilitatis *B Colker*; Primo queritur utrum tot sint species nobilitatis quot sunt superius distincte *Thomas (A.); lacking in* P_1RS.

1.9.1 [T]empus: Empus P_1 *with guide letter* t; Empus *R*. contra: circa *K*. de aliquibus: aliqua *K*. ut predictorum veritas planius elucescat *K*. patet *R*. predictorum veritas P_2R.

1.9.2 igitur *lacking in P_2R*, ergo *K*. queratur *K*. sint tot *K*. sunt *R*. quot: quod *R*. sunt superius *B*. distincte: expresse *K*.

1.9.3 quia cum *K*. [nobilitas ex bonitate] *P_2BKR Colker* (ex: a *K*), bonitas ex nobilitate *P_1S*. nobilitas ex bonitate operationis sit *K*. apta cuilibet huius operationis: est sed cuiuslibet talis operationis *B*, et *K*. est anima: cuiuslibet operacionis sit unum scilicet anima ergo et cetera *K*. preterea: igitur *B*. corporis nobilitas *P_2*. cum: quia *K*. operationibus anime: corpus *B*, operacionibus *K*. possit: potest *K*, possint *R*. organice anime deservire *B*. deserviri ergo et cetera *K*.

1.9.4 ex quibus *R*. nos *lacking in B*. huiusmodi: huius *BRS*. nostra libertate *K*. nullatenus ut sic *K*. secundum *lacking in B*. superius iam (iam *faint*) *B*.

1.9.5 sit nisi sola nobilitas anime *P_2KR*.

1.9.6 Ad oppositum: Oppositum *K*. satis superius *B*. satis: satis potius *S*.

1.9.7 quot *R*. nobilita[t]is: [t] *illegible in P_1*. licet una altera sit: sed una altera est *B*. licet una l altera (*l = vel, missing a stroke?*) *S*. una prior altera et nobilior sit *R*. prior sit *K*. prior et nobilior sit *P_2*. prior altera et *R*. questione sequenti *KR*. quoniam quamvis: quamvis autem *B*. formale omnium *K*. verumptamen: operacionum tamen *K*. corpus est principium *K*. et: ut *R*. in d strumentale (d *expunctuated*) *P_2*. [principium]: *transposed as just above in K, lacking in P_1BS Colker*. operationum plurium *P_2*. consistit: existit *B Colker, lacking in K*.

1.9.8 bonam vel: bonam et *K*. dispositionem ipsius *P_2*. operationes vel in (vel *expunctuated*) *P_2*. malica *R*.

1.9.10 aliud: secundam *K*. bona fortune *K*. venient *P_2*, eveniant *K*, moveniant (mo *expunctuated*) *S*. provisa *P_2KR*. absque: ab *K*. contingant *lacking in K*. contingerint: contigerint *BKRS Colker*. secundum quod (quod *expunctuated*) *B*. quia hic *R*. operarie *S*.

1.9.11 eventus fortuitus *K*. eorum usus *P_2R*. eorum: eorumdem *B*. esse *lacking in P_2BKRS*. haberi fortuitus *K*.

1.9.12 huius usum *BKS*, usum huius *R*. existere *lacking in B*.

1.9.13 ad aliam *K*.

Chapter 10 *P_1 239vD.45; P_2 12v.7; B 317v.8; K 196vD.27; R 238v.21; S 185vC.15.*

Title *K;* Secundo *P_2;* Que nobilitas sit melior *B Colker;* [Que]stio *in margin of R; lacking in P_1S;* Secundo queritur que species nobilitatis nobilior vel melior debeat dici *Thomas (A.)*.

1.10.1 [S]ecundo: ecundo *P_1B with guide letter* s; Ecundo *R*. que species nobilior et dignior debent dici **1.10.2** Videtur enim *transposed to end of 1.9.13 in R*. species melior vel dignior debeat *P_2*. dignior: nobilior *B Thomas (A.)*. debet *K*.

1.10.2 enim *lacking in BK*. sicud *R*. fuit: est *K*. propter: per *K*, propter o (o *crossed out*) *R*. cognitam quare: quia *K*. nobilitas erit: nobilitas eius erit *K*. erit potissima cuius: potissima erit eius cuius *R*. cuius: eius cuiusmodi *K*. operationes *K*. potissime in bonitate *S*. bonitate: bono *K*. cognoscuntur *K*. huiusmodi *K*. [patet]: *lacking in* P_1*S*, patet enim *B Colker*. unius *lacking in K*. meliores: nobiliores P_2*KR*. communiores: convenientiores *K*. existunt: dicuntur *B*. nobilium *lacking in K*.

1.10.3 publicas enim *R*. primo et per se ordinantur: maxime ordinantur *K*. maximo *S*. quare videtur ... alias excellat: ergo et cetera *K*.

1.10.4 et preterea *R*. huius P_2*BRS*. elementata elementis *corrected from* elementa elementatis P_1. esse composita: componi P_2, composita *R*. nobilitate anime *K*. quare videtur melior: ergo et cetera *K*. videtur esse melior *B*.

1.10.5 declaratum: determinatum *K*, *lacking in R*. et sufficienter: insufficienter *R*.

1.10.6 questionem: questionem illam P_2, questionem istam *KR*, questionem est *B*. intelligendum: intelligendam *K*, dicendum *S*. superius fuit *lacking in K*. tactum est *K*, dictum et tactum *R*. dicitur nobilis a suo dominio dominus aliquis P_2, dicitur nobilis secundum quod a suo dominio dominus aliquis *R*, dominus non dicitur *K*. a: in *K*. pro tanto quod: quia *K*. in omnibus: inter omnes *K*. que: quod *R*. ad dominia *B*. vilitate *R*. convertetur *K*.

1.10.7 nobilitas: voluntas *K*. aliarum: aliter *R*. vivificat *lacking in K*. illuminat et vivificat *S*. tenobrose *R*.

1.10.8 quid: quod *R*. sit *lacking in K*, sicut *R*. in oppositum *lacking in* P_2. domini *lacking in S*. sint: sicut P_2. meliores: nobiliores *K*. hoc habent non habent (*first* habent *crossed out*) *S*. habent: sunt *R*. [in] *lacking in* P_1. domino: dominio *B Colker*. sapientie *R*. informat[e]: informata P_1P_2*KRS*. cum: enim *K*. virtuosus scit *K*. debet *lacking in K*. fortuite: fortune *K*. fortuita: fortuna *K*. solum materiam *K*. materiam: manet *R*. prebet *KS*.

1.10.9 nobilitatibus: nobilibus P_2.

1.10.10 Sicud *R*. inicium quantum: in quantum *BK*, inicium in quantum *S*, in tantum quantum *Colker*. effectus nobilitatis *K*.

1.10.11 quis *lacking in* P_2. quis velit *K*. ulterius *corrected from* ultius *in S*. hac sola P_2*KS*. hac nobilitate sola *R*. loquuntur nobilitate *K*. loquuntur: loquantur P_2*B Colker*. sententia est ut in pluribus imperfecta P_2*KR* (ut *lacking in K*).

1.10.12 hoc: hic *R*. dicit *K*. est: esse *K*. sed sapiendum est: sapiendum P_2, sed pau sapiendum (pau *expunctuated*) *B*, senciendum vero *K*, senciendum *R*. communibus: quibus P_2. firmiter *lacking in B*. concordaverint *K*.

Chapter 11 *P_1 240rA.27; P_2 13r.3; B 318r.5; K 197rA.38; R 239r.25; S 185vD.25.*

Title *K*; Utrum omnes [homi]nes si[nt] nobiles [per] naturam P_2; An omnes sint nobiles per naturam *B Colker*; Tercio queritur utrum homines sint nobiles per naturam *Thomas (A.)*; *lacking in* P_1*S*.

Marginalia in P_1 *asterisms at 1.11.8, 1.11.10, 1.11.18, 1.11.21, 1.11.22.* ***In P_2*** *text at 1.11.11, 1.11.16, 1.11.17, 1.11.22, 1.11.29 (see below).* ***In R*** Nota ben[e] et consid[era] *1.11.1 in right margin, cut off in photograph; in left margin, a hand points upward.*

1.11.1 [T]ercio: Ercio P_1 *with guide letter* t; Ercio *R*. sic quia *K*.

1.11.2 enim *lacking in K*. forme: fortune P_2. omnes erunt: omnes homines erunt (erunt *corrected from* sunt *crossed out*) *R*, erunt omnes *B*. eiusdem nobilitatis erunt *K*. nobilitatem P_2.

1.11.3 Maior patet de se et minor etiam omnes: Minor patet quia omnes *B*. habent omnes P_2KR. rationabilem *S*. est *lacking in B*. patuit: patet *B*. ex: in P_2KR.

1.11.4 patet: probatur *B Colker*. ex dicto communi *lacking in B*. enim *lacking in BK*. qui sunt filii eiusdem *K*, qui eiusdem *S*. eiusdem sunt *K*. eiusdem nobilitatis sunt *S*. huiusmodi: eiusdem patris et matris *K*, huius *BS*. quare et cetera: igitur et cetera P_2, ergo et cetera *KR*, igitur quia de Adam et Eva descenderunt igitur et cetera (*first* igitur *expunctuated*) *B*.

1.11.5 Quare videtur ... viles **1.11.6** Cuius *lacking in* P_2BK. vel: et *R*.

1.11.6 oppositum huius superius satis est (superius *corrected from* superioris) P_2. ostensum est *KS*.

1.11.7 plures enim *K*. et eorum nequitiam *lacking in BK*, et eorum maliciam P_2R. p. eorum nequitiam: ipsorum maliciam *K*. ab aliis exterminantur *K*. corrupunt P_2.

1.11.8 in *lacking in K*. quod *lacking in B*. quod talium ... arma **1.11.9** Et *lacking in K*.

1.11.9 Et sicut: sicut enim perfectum *K*. sicut: sic *R*. animalium est P_2RS. animalium homo est *K*. homo *lacking in* P_2. vivens secundum legem et rationem *lacking in K*. rationem: rationem sic P_2S, iusticiam sic *R*. separatus: sic et separatum *K*, sic separatus *S*. est *lacking in K*. omnium sevissima est enim iniusticia habens arma *K*.

1.11.10 studia *S*. omnia bona P_2R. omnia: opera *B*. extendunt *S*. multorum aliorum *K*. multorum differentium secundum speciem puta *B*. secundum: sed *S*.

1.11.11 accipiunt P_2KR. autem: aute *R*. debent *in margin, corrected from* debet P_2.

1.11.12 rationem *S*. vero: vero dicendum P_2R, *lacking in B*, dicendum *K*. primum P_2. habeant *K*. quod habent *R*, quod habeat *S*. operationes *BK*. nobilitatis: bonitatis P_2KR.

1.11.13 Contingit: convenit *R*. enim: siquidem in *B*, in *K*. talibus: in talibus P_2BK, in talibus *corrected from* ex talibus *R*. mala vel bona P_2KR. sint: sit P_2R, fit *K*. male: male forma P_2R, male formata *K*. expediti *B*.

1.11.14 Unde: Hinc *B*. [male]: bene P_1*BKRS Colker*, bene *corrected from* non *in* P_2. in mente *lacking in B*. ut vult ... aptos mente *lacking in* P_2. Philosophus vult *B*, vult Aristoteles *K*. in libro: libro *B*. Anima secundo *K*. enim ibidem *B*. carnes *R*. mente dicimus *BKRS*.

1.11.15 dependent secundum *R*. huius *BRS*. corpore forte *R*. tamen: tantum *R*.

1.11.16 Philosophus *lacking in K*. dicit Philosophus *B Colker*. dicit Aristoteles in libro suo de *K*. sua phisonomia P_2*R*. sua *lacking in K*. quod *lacking in B*. dispositiones in corpore sunt diverse *B*. per: propter *K*. virtutes: naturas *BK*. ipsius *lacking in* P_2*KR*. ipsius anime materie (anime *expunctuated*) P_1. materie *in margin, corrected from* m'rie *in body of* P_2. vel corporis ... **1.11.17** eiusdem forme *lacking in S*. causa ipsius nobilitatis *B*. nobilitatis vel vilitatis in operatione *K*. impedimentum *lacking in K*.

1.11.17 quod *lacking in B*. sint: sunt *R*. n[atura]m: numerum P_1*KR*; numerum *in margin, corrected from* n'rum *in* P_2. immo *lacking in B*. aliqua *lacking in B*. vel alique proprietates sunt *lacking in K*. ita *lacking in B*, ut *S*. quod: que *B*. sunt *lacking in K*.

1.11.18 hoc: hic *R*. in anima principalem P_2. in anima: in homine anima *K*. et *lacking in B*. hoc habet anima *B*. habeat *K*. quod hoc acquirit P_2*R*. acquirit *K*. a. hoc *lacking in S*. sua *S*. celestibus *lacking in K*. confirmanti hic *R*. elementa sunt *S*. elementa corporibus ita sunt stelle animabus P_2*KR* (sunt *lacking in KR*). id est *lacking in B*. stellarum sunt *B*. quas: quorum P_2*KR*. virtutes earum *B*. principaliter a deo P_2*K*. procreantur principaliter *R*. *After* procreantur: Species tamen cuiuslibet hominis diversas proprietates acquirit secundum quod motores in sui creatione diversivius de se habent ad ipsam *K*.

1.11.20 ergo: igitur P_2. homines *lacking in S*. ut dictum est *lacking in B*; ut dictum *R*. causa vilitatis est magis accipienda a parte *K*. accipiendum ipsius *R*. a: ex P_2*B*. huius *RS*, huiusmodi et *K*. causantur: creantur *K*. se non potest habere *K*.

1.11.21 [Philosophus]: *lacking in* P_1*BS*, Aristoteles *K*. [quarto]: quindecimo P_1P_2*BKRS*, in quinto *Colker*. dicit Philosophus *B Colker*. quod *lacking in B*. informativa totaliter (totaliter *crossed out*) *S*. proportionaliter: principaliter *R*. coordinationi: ordinacioni P_2.

1.11.22 Anima igitur: Anima ergo *K*, Ergo anima ergo (*first* ergo *crossed out*) *R*. naturaliter *K*. inclinacionem *corrected from* inquisicionem *expunctuated in* P_2. inclinationem habet *R*. ipso: ipse P_2, corpore *B*. operibus *in margin, corrected from* partibus P_2. per *in margin of* P_2. aptitudinem: applicationem P_2*B*. ipsius corporis *KR*. inclinationem anime *K*. significant: assignant P_2. astronomi: astrologi P_2. vel: sive *R*. phisonomici *B*, physoniones *K*, phisonomia *R*, phisionomi *S*. figuras membrorum *B*.

1.11.23 Philosophus: Aristoteles *K*. dicit Philosophus *S*. dicit in: dicit *R*. in de *K*. in Physonomia *lacking in S*. et: nec alibi nec P_2R, nec alibi *K*. Centilogia *K*.

1.11.24 dicendum breviter quod: breviter dicendum *B*. breviter *lacking in K*, videtur *R*. quod *lacking in B*. omnes *lacking in KR*. sint: sunt *R*.

1.11.25 Eadem: Idem P_2. disponit: disponiter P_1. materiam uniformiter P_2KR. quare *lacking in K*. dissimiles: consimiles ut *K*. sunt sunt *S*.

1.11.26 quibus: quilibet P_2. bene *lacking in B*. formatum: fortunatum *S*. animam etiam *K*. malicia compositionis vel *K*. torquantur P_2, torquetur *BK*. tendit *KR*. inclinat[i] *Colker*, inclinatam P_1P_2BKRS.

1.11.27 tales: tali *B*. primo Ethicorum *K*.

1.11.28 rudia dura *K*. formantur: sunt *K*. animam multum *K*. i. et *lacking in K*. sensualitatem: besti *(new line)* alem alitatem (alem *crossed out) R*.

1.11.29 [Unde primo *Ethicorum* dicuntur tales viri inutiles] P_2KR.

1.11.30 licet: sed *K*. per se *in margin of* P_2. perfecti *R*.

1.11.31 igitur: ergo *KR*, *lacking in S*. quomodo: quod non *K*. debent nobiles P_2KR. sig' iudicari (sig' *crossed out) R*.

Chapter 12 *P_1 240rB.49; P_2 14r.2; B 319r.1; K 197vD.26; R 240v.14; S 186vC.5.*

Title *K;* Questio P_2; De nobilitate mulieris in comparatione ad virum *B Colker;* Nota valde quartum *in margin of R;* Quarto queritur utrum mulier nobilis sicut vir *Thomas (A.); lacking in P_1S.*

Marginalia in P_1 *asterism at 1.12.6.*

1.12.1 [Q]uarto: Uarto P_1 *with guide letter* q; Quarto *BS with guide letter* q; Uarto *R*. viri P_2. et *lacking in* P_2R. videtur *above line in* P_2. quia *lacking in B*. melior vel nobilior *B*, nobiliores et meliores *KR*. operationes sunt huius *B*. huius *RS*. quare: igitur P_2B, ergo *KR*. et cetera *lacking in B*.

1.12.2 vero: autem *K*. qu[are]: quia P_1B. erit: est *BK*. nobilis: nobilis sicut vir *K*.

1.12.3 Hoc *lacking in B*. quia *lacking in B*. in natura omne: natura in omne natura est *R*. perfectior muliere *K*. ergo: igitur P_2B. ergo est *S*.

1.12.4 est *lacking in B*. enim videmus *R*. enim *lacking in K*. meliores: perfectiores *K*. q. operationes *lacking in K*.

1.12.5 Et preterea P_2. eiusdem nobilitatis videntur *lacking in R*.

1.12.6 ad questionem *lacking in R*. questionem illam P_2, questionem istam *K*. dicendum breviter: dicendum est *KR*. illud *lacking in BK*. Philosophus dicit: dicit Aristoteles *K*, dicit philosophus *S*. E. quod *lacking in B*, scilicet quod P_2KR. sunt *lacking in B*. exteriora: extrinseca *R*. forciorem: fortitudinem et *K*. requirunt laborem *B Colker*. operatio *corrected from* ratio *B*. operacio dirigitur *K*.

1.12.7 igitur: ergo *KR*. suas operationes P_2KR. recta regulet: regulat *K*. racione regulet *B Colker*. proportortionem *S*. licet: sed *K*.

1.12.8 mulieris: muliebris *P_2KR*. nobilitas et a (et *expunctuated*) *P_2*. discedit: deficit *P_2R*, descendit *K*.

1.12.9 respondendum *B*.

1.12.10 ita *lacking in P_2*. hoc: hic *R*. hoc est verum *P_2BKRS*. loquendo sed non (sed *expunctuated*) *P_2*.

1.12.11 alterius: utriusque *K*. non queritur: non querit *P_2KR*, querit *BS*. numquam: non *B*, non quod *S*. *After* mulier: Ad rationem secundam superius iam est dictum *K*.

Chapter 13 *P_1 240vC.20; P_2 14r.24; B 319r.21; K 198rA.22; R 241r.10; S 186vC.36.*

Title *K*; Questio *in margin of P2*; Quinto queritur utrum aliquis puer sit nobilis *Thomas (A.); lacking in P_1BRS Colker.*

Marginalia in P_1 *asterism at 1.13.5.* ***In R*** Nota *1.13.1.*

1.13.1 [C]onsequenter: Onsequenter *P_1 with guide letter* c; Consequenter *S with guide letter* c; Consequens *P_2*; Onsequens *R*; Quinto *BK Thomas (A.) Colker*, *with guide letter* q *in B*. queritur: questio est *P_2R*. nobilis? (*punctus interrogativus*) *P_2*.

1.13.2 Videtur: quia videtur *K*. quia ut: sicut *P_2*, sicut enim *K*, sicud *R*. dicit *lacking in K*. Philosophus: Aristoteles *K*. in *lacking in R*. libro *lacking in K*. dicere ab *K*. videtur in pueris *K*. quod possit esse: posse reperiri *K*, posse esse *S*. pueris i (i *expunctuated*) *P_2*.

1.13.3 patet per: probatum est per *P_2R*, vult *K*. proverbium vulgare *K*. dicens: dicit *R*. debet *S*.

1.13.4 dictu[m]: dictu *$P_1$$P_2$BKS*. virilem *lacking in R*.

1.13.5 istam: illam *R*. questionem *corrected from* rationem *in P_2*. imperfecto esse *K*. imperfectio *R*.

1.13.6 possunt: possint *P_2BKR Colker*. esse: osse *P_2*. ad: ad perfectionem et ad *K*. universaliter: naturaliter *K*. tamen quousque *S*. anime *corrected from* anima *S*. ad perfectam *K*.

1.13.7 Sunt igitur *P_2*, Sunt ergo *KR*. et in fieri: in *above line in P_1*, *lacking in B*. sicut sunt ... fieri viri *lacking in R*.

1.13.8 patet satis *B*.

Chapter 14 *P_1 240vC.32; P_2 14v.4; B 319r.32; K 198rB.2; R 241r.25; S 186vD.16.*

Title Questio *in margin of P_2;* Sexto queritur utrum viles per naturam possint fieri nobiles per doctrinam vel nutrimentum *Thomas (A.)*; *lacking in P_1BKRS Colker.*

Marginalia in P_2 *text at 1.14.14 (see below).*

1.14.1 [S]exto: Exto *P_1 with guide letter* s; Sexto *BS with guide letter* s; Exto *R*. possunt: possint *P_2 Thomas (A.) Colker.* vel: et *P_2*. nutrituram? (*punctus interrogativus*) *P_2*, nutrimentum *B*.

1.14.2 sicud *P_2*. dicit *B*.

1.14.3 igitur: ergo *KR*. sibi *lacking in K*.

1.14.4 Preterea: Prima P_2. Preterea opera ... **1.14.6** sufficere possit *lacking in B. First* opera: opa *R*. artis sunt P_2. autem: autem artem P_2KR, *lacking in B*. solum: sola P_2KR, *lacking in B*. artificilia P_2R. huius *RS*.

1.14.5 Nunc P_2K. sicud P_2. sicut se habet *K*. ad effectum *K*. humanum sed intellectus divinus *K*. comparatione: operacione *R*. magis est P_2. magis *lacking in K*. perfectior *K*, perfectivus P_2R. infallibilior *K*.

1.14.6 ergo: igitur P_2S, *lacking in B*. humana natura P_2KR.

1.14.7 Oppositum huius *K*. quod: quia *K*. bonam *lacking in R*. meliorantur: maliceantur (*meaning?*) *R*. actionibus suis: bonis actionibus *B*, suis actionibus *K*.

1.14.8 primam *lacking in* P_2BKR. [rac]ionem *Colker*, questionem P_1P_2BKRS. dicendum per illud P_2KR. dicit philosophus *K*. etiam superius ... scilicet quod *lacking in B*. etiam iam sepius dictum est *K*. scilicet quod: quod homini P_2, quod hominum *K*, quod hominum scilicet *R*. sunt *corrected from* sint *R*. boni sunt *K*. ita: eo *K*. natura eorum *K*. natura *lacking in B*. semper *lacking in K*. directa: perducta *K*. est directa *B*. agere naturaliter *K*. et bene *K*. et sunt naturaliter *K*.

1.14.9 natura non invenitur perfecta P_2. perfecta natura: recta ratio *B*. impedita et *K*. aliqualem: aliquam *BK*. temperiem *K*. defectus: perfectus *R*. non est ita: nec ita P_2K. emendantur per doctrinam *K*.

1.14.10 gradus hominum est *B*, hominum gradus est *K*. defecta est: deficit P_2, depravata est *B*, defectiva est *K*, indefecta est *S*. tales per: tales nec per *BKR Colker*.

1.14.11 tales inutiles sunt ad mores *K*.

1.14.12 est *corrected from* ex P_1. et ad questionem et ad rationes facile est respondere *K*. et ad rationes *lacking in B*.

1.14.13 Ad questionem igitur dicendum quod: Licet *B*. igitur: ergo *R*. dicendum est *K*. viles qui si (qui *crossed out*) P_1. qui tamen: qui cum P_2, cum *B*. per alios: palios *R*. *A hole in S extends from 187rA.13 to 19; the text is written around the hole.* aliqui qui: aliqui sunt qui *B Colker*. corrigi non possunt *K*. ut est dictum *lacking in B*. dictum est *KS*.

1.14.14 Ad rationem *B*. dico *in margin of* P_2. quod *lacking in B*. q. in illis *lacking in KR*, in illis in quibus (in quibus *expunctuated*) P_2. n. in illis *lacking in K*. n. in illis ... imperfecte natura *lacking in B*. perficiet: perficitur *K*, proficiet *RS*. imperfecte: in parte P_2, aliquam imperfectionem *B*. natura deficit perficit (deficit *expunctuated*) P_1, nutritura bene (*new folio begins*) bene perficit *K*, natura proficit *R*, natura pfic perficit (pfic *crossed out*) *S*. aliquid: aliquam *B*, ut in quibusdam ubi natura *K*, *lacking in* P_2. et aliquid ... bene perficit *lacking in* P_2. relinquit: dimittit *K*. bene perficit: bene proficit *R*. auxiliante natura *lacking in K*. Philosophus libro Politicorum septimo *S*. [disciplina] *lacking in* P_1, ars *B Colker*. natura *K*.

1.14.15 Et hoc est P_2*KR*. intelligendum est *K*. in illis: de illis *B Colker*. nec natura (nec *crossed out*) *R*. distat *BK*. in iuvando *K*.

1.14.16 omnium omnium P_2. est artifex vero minister *K*. artifex est minister: artifex et minister *B Colker*, artifex vero minister *K*. dicit *K*.

1.14.17 Ex hiis ... rationis secunde *lacking in B*.

Chapter 15 *P_1 240vD.15; P_2 15r.4; B 319v.20; K 198vC.10; R 242r.1; S 187rA.29.*

Title *K*; Questio *in margin of* P_2; Septimo queritur cui filius in nobilitate debeat assimilari, utrum patri vel matri *Thomas (A.); lacking in* P_1*BRS Colker.*

Marginalia in P_2 Nota *1.15.7; text at 1.15.6 (see below).*

1.15.1 [S]eptimo: Eptimo P_1*R*, Septimo *B with guide letter* s. assimilari debeat (debeat *above line*) P_2. similari *K*.

1.15.2 Et videtur *K*. enim *lacking in* P_2*K*. quia *lacking in* P_2. ut *lacking in K*. Philosophus: Aristoteles *K*. libro *lacking in K*. formam: fortunam *R*. hoc est: id est P_2*K*. informativam *K*. debeat: debet *R*. patri in nobilitate P_2*KR*.

1.15.3 patet in pluribus patet P_2. qui sequuntur mores matris *K*. non *inserted above line in* P_2.

1.15.4 soluit: i *inserted above line in P2*. in libro: libro *B*, in *K*. capitulo: o. *S*. [quarto]: primo P_1P_2*BKRS Colker*. de similitudine: similitudine *B*. dicens in *B*. et ex parte: et *expunctuated in B*. ex [par]te matris: [par] *destroyed by hole in* P_1. g. et: sed *R*. particulares: principales *B*.

1.15.5 Hoc est quod P_2*K*, hic est quod *R*. generativa generativa *R*. movet secundum: movet sed *R*. sed secundum quod: sed quod P_2, secundum secundum quod *R*. vel per se subsistentis *B*. vel subsistentis *lacking in K*. animate et *K*. sensibilis rationalis *B*. vel sic vel sic P_1*BS*, et sic vel sic *K*. [vel]: quod P_1. masculum vel femellam *K*.

1.15.6 autem aliqualiter est i. q. m. v. c. motibus *S*. viri aliquando *B*. aliqualiter contrariantur *K*. contrariatur *R*. aliqualiter *in margin of* P_2, *lacking in B*. virtus enim *B*. oportet quod ... enim solvuntur: fortior prevalet et debilior soluitur *B*. sequatur: sequantur P_1*KR*, *lacking in B*.

1.15.7 contingitur *B*. quando: quod quando P_2*BKR Colker*. motus: motos *R*. *Between* paterni motus *and* omnes maternos, *B inserts a citation from Quintilian; see "Sources and Analogues."* maternos motus *B*. devincunt *K*. et quando: quando *B*. quando est e converso tunc assimilatur *K*.

1.15.8 Quare *lacking in B*, Ex hiis *K*. questionem ergo *B*. dicendum est *K*. vel alteri *lacking in K*. temperie: tempore *BKS*. *After* contingit: Cuius enim motus prevalent, assimilabitur illi *B*.

1.15.9 *lacking in B*. oportet dici *K*. dictum: doctum *R*. filium faciet similem P_2, filium similem faciet *R*, filium facit sibi similem ut dictum est *K*. prevaleant filius formabitur *K*. secundum quod huiusmodi *lacking in K*. huius *RS*.

1.15.10 patet solutio *B*.

Chapter 16 *P_1 240vD.41; P_2 15r.24; B 320r.5; K 198vD.1; R 242r.27; S 187rB.23.*

Title *K;* Questio *in margin of P_2;* Octavo queritur quare homines non loquantur nisi de una specie nobilitatis, cum constet eas esse quinque *Thomas (A.); lacking in P_1BRS Colker.*

1.16.1 [O]ctavo: ctavo *P_1*, Octavo *with guide letter* o *in BS.* homines communiter *K.* loquantur: loquuntur *BKRS.* nisi: communiter nisi *P_2R.* specie qualitatis nobilitatis (qualitatis *crossed out*) *S.* sit superius determinatum: constet *B.* superius sit *P_2R.* superius determinatum sit *K.* eas: earum *K.* quinque: 5 5 (*first* 5 *malformed and crossed out*) *R. After* quinque: Ad istam questionem quia superius sufficienter de ea locuti fuimus ideo *K.* species *lacking in BK. After* species: nobilitatis ad questionem istam quia sufficienter superius locuti sumus *P_2R* (superius sufficienter *R*).

1.16.2 De hoc *lacking in K.* breviter: breviter et *K,* videtur *R.* dicendum est *K.* gentium: hominum *K.* licet quod *R.* presumptionem aliquam *K,* presumptione *R.* probabilitatem aliquam: probabilitatem *K.* levi gentes *B.* decipitur *P_2R,* decipiunt *S.* provide: providere *P_1*. provide et subtiliter *K.* sequitur: consequitur *P_2R.* dicta sequitur *K.* realitatem: racionalitatem *R.* postponens realitatem *K.* supponens *lacking in K.*

1.16.3 in *lacking in S.* dicit in topicis *K. First* est *lacking in KR. Second* est *lacking in P_2BKRS.* ut sapientes: sapientes *P_2*. et ut: ut *P_2B.*

1.16.4 est enim *BR.* qui: quia *P_2*. detrahendum de eodem *lacking in B.* eodem proposito minimo opposito *K.* loquendum oppositum *B.* minimo: nimio *BR.* movetur *P_2*.

1.16.5 nec pluribus: nec in pluribus *P_2BKR Colker.* dicit philosophus *KS.*

1.16. Unde ipse dicit quod *lacking in B. After second occurrence of* genti et civitati: quia nobilitas simpliciter est de qua superius sufficienter dictum est *KR* (fuit dictum *R*).

Chapter 17 *P_1 241rA.7; P_2 15v.5; B 320r.17; K 198vD.28; R 242v.12; S 187vC.8.*

Title *K;* Nono queritur utrum rex sit nobilior comite, vel imperator rege *Thomas (A.); lacking in P_1P_2BRS Colker.*

Marginalia in *P_1* *text at 1.17.3 (see below).*

1.17.1 [N]ono: Ono *P_1 with guide letter* n; Nono *B with guide letter* n; Ono *R.* rex r *K.* nobilior sit *KR.* rege *lacking in S.* quia hoc: istud *B,* quia hic *R.*

1.17.2 Huius *B.* potest: videtur *B.* ut: sicut *B Colker.* per predicta superius: per superius dicta *B Colker.*

1.17.3 istam *lacking in P_2KR.* istam questionem *B.* vel: et *K.* dominium tunc *K.* nobiles *in margin of P_1*. parvum eos contingat habere *K.*

1.17.4 contingit: convenit *R.* aliqui sibi sunt: aliqui sunt *P_2BKR.* sint *K.* parvis *corrected from* pero *expunctuated in B.* qui *lacking in R.* se haberent: se habent *P_2*, regerent *B.* et tales: tales *R.* et non: non *P_2R.* non equaliter: inequales *K.*

1.17.5 sint: sunt *B*. adhuc: ad hoc *R*. bene et: tamen vel P_2, bene vel *BKR*. haberent se P_2. se haberent bene vel melius *K*. nobiles sunt P_2.
1.17.6 et rationem *lacking in K.*

Chapter 18 *P_1 241rA.20; P_2 15v.15; B 320r.27; K 199rA.4; R 242v.25; S 1897vC.25.*
Title Questio *in margin of P_2;* Ultimo queritur utrum nobilitas inveniatur in aliis rebus, sicut in avibus, equis et canibus, quia hoc tenetur communis opinio *Thomas (A.); lacking in P_1BKRS Colker.*
Marginalia in P_2 *text at 1.18.7 (see below).* ***In B*** Versus *1.18.5.*
1.18.1 [U]ltimo: Ltimo *P_1R*, Ultimo *B with guide letter* u. queritur: dubitatur *K*. sicut: scilicet *K*. avibus et *K*. hoc etiam tenere videtur: hoc tenetur *B*, hoc etiam videtur tenere *K*, hoc videretur tenere *R*, hoc etiam tenetur tenetur *S*. opinio quod sic *B*.
1.18.2 Dicendum ad hoc *K*. disputatione maiori *P_2KR*. aliis *lacking in P_2R*. animalibus *lacking in K*. ab: absque *B*. dupliciter: duplex *K*. et absolute *lacking in P_2*. absolute: abstracte *B*. particulariter *corrected from* partuci *in R*. ad aliquid *lacking in R*.
1.18.3 animal dicitur *R*. dicit philosophus *BK Colker*. in *lacking in K*. animalibus scilicet *K*. quod pertinet: pertinentia *B*. opus suum: opus eius *B*, suum genus *P_2KR*.
1.18.4 animalium *lacking in R*. operantur: comperantur P_2. dicunt *S*. animalia vel ... quedam et *lacking in K*. vel nobilia: et nobilia animalia *R*. fuerunt *R*. illa: similia *B*.
1.18.5 generosa animalia: animalia generosa *K*, nobilia animalia *R*. vel nobilia: et generosa *R*. aves vel canes ordinati *B*. et canes et que ordinantur: et canes vel huiusmodi que ordinantur *P_2KR* (et c.: aut *K*, aut huiusmodi *K*, huius *R*). recreacionem aliquam P_2. qui *corrected from* que *in B*. tedio sunt affecti: cotidie sunt affecti tedio *K*. per: pro *R*, vel per *S*. longum: multum longum tempore (tempore *expunctuated*) P_2. sicud *R*. sicut enim dicit Cato ... sunt gaudia (Cato dicit *P_2KR*) (*paraphrase of Disticha Catonis III.6*): unde Cato, "Interpone tuis interdum gaudia curis" *BK* (unde Cato: sicut Catho dicit *K*, sicud enim Catho dicit *R*) (*exact citation*).
1.18.6 quandoque possunt *P_2B*. rationabiliter *lacking in K*. uti rationabiliter talibus *B*. talibus uti et usus: talibus uti unde canes et aves qui ad hoc ordinantur nobiles possunt dici et usus *P_2KR* (qui: que *KR*, usus: osus *R*). sic: sit *R*.
1.18.7 nimis *in margin, corrected from* niuus *lined out in P_2*. delectetur *B*. in talibus delectetur *K*. hiis: eis *K*. que ad ... fatuitatem converti: nobilitatis negligat tunc talis usus vilis est *B*. [vi]litatem: utilitatem *P_1S*, *lacking in B;* utilitatem et con (con *crossed out*) *S*. bestialem fatuitatem converti: bestialitatem pertinere *K*. *Hole in S extends from 187vD.13 to 19; text written around the*

hole. After converti P_2R *or* pertinere *K:* et propter hoc dixi aliquando et non frequenter debent nobiles talibus uti P_2KR (dixi *corrected from* dixit P_2, quod aliquando *KR*).

1.18.8 ut fuit dictum *lacking in B*, ut superius dictum est *K*. oper[a]: operi P_1. frequentari nobilium P_2.

1.18.9 hiis igitur *K*, hiis ergo *R*. librum primum *KR*. sit determinatum in tantum: tantum dictum sit *B*.

Part 2

Prologue *P_1 241rA.44; P_2 16r.1; B 320v.11; K 199rA.37; R 243r.17; S 187vD.20.*

Incipit *K; lacking in P_1P_2BRS Thomas (A.) Colker.*

2.0.1 [P]ars: Ars P_1 *without guide letter*; Pars *B with guide letter* p; Ars *R*. huius libri *R*. et tutas *lacking in B*. lecturas: sententias *B*. quilibet sive *lacking in B*. nobilis sive: nobilis vel *B*. cognoscitur *B*. perfectissime cognoscetur *K*.

2.0.2 capitula qua quibus (qua *expunctuated*) P_2. harum *lacking in B*, horum *K*. et: seu *B*. de oppositis earumdem: earumdem oppositarum *B*, de opposito earumdem *Thomas (A.)*.

Chapter 1 *P_1 241rA.49; P_2 16r.4; B 320v.14; K 199rB.3; R 243r.22; S 187vD.25.*

Title *K; lacking in P_1P_2BRS Thomas (A.) Colker.*

Marginalia in P_1 *asterism at 2.1.4.* ***In P_2*** Aristoteles *2.1.1*, Hermes *2.1.2*, Plato *2.1.3*, Alfraganus *2.1.4*, Nota *2.1.7*; *text at 2.1.10 (see below).*

2.1.1 [S]ecundum: ecundum P_1 *with guide letter* s, Ecundum est quod *R*. disputat et *lacking in P_2*. sufficienter: suf (*blank space*) ficienter (*written around a hole or tear*) *B*. intelligere: intendere *Thomas (A.)*. in prohemio *K*. scit: sit *Thomas (A.)*. difficillima: diffi (*blank space*) cillima (*written around a hole or tear*) *B*. causam: causas et *K*.

2.1.2 in *lacking in P_2R*. quindecim: .5. *S*. quod *lacking in P_2BKR*. cognoscit res *BK*.

2.1.3 libro *K*, libello dicit suo (dicit *crossed out*) *R*. quod sapiens *K*. preter *B*.

2.1.4 quod *lacking in B*. et sapiens *BK*. tempore *K*.

2.1.5 quia bonorum omnium fons est et *B*. et sui ... omne bonum *lacking in P_2*. suo *K*.

2.1.6 bonis bonis *K*. contingerit *B*, contingant *K*.

2.1.7 defidit *K*.

2.1.8 de bonis et malis bona elicit P_2KR, *faint in B*.

2.1.9 respicit: despicit *B*.

2.1.10 Et sapiens se et alios cognoscat P_2, sapiens se et omnes alios cognoscit omnes *B*. est *lacking in R*, et etiam exemplar *S*. exemplar *in margin, corrected from* exar *lined out in P_2*.

2.1.11 et *lacking in KS*. nobilissimus P_2KR.

Chapter 2 *P_1 241rB.15; P_2 16r.20; B 320v.30; K 199rB.32; R 243v.9; S 188rA.14.*

Title De proverbiis nobilitatis anime *K; lacking in P_1P_2BRS Thomas (A.) Colker.*

Marginalia in P_1 *asterism at 2.1.2.* ***In P_2*** Pholomeus *2.2.1,* Willanus *2.2.3,* Demostenes *2.2.6; text at 2.2.2 (see below).*

2.2.1 [P]tholomeus: tholomeus *P_1 with guide letter* p; Ptholomeus *B with guide letter* p; tholomeus *R.* proverbiis: proverbiis suis *B Thomas (A.) Colker.* quod *lacking in B Thomas (A.).* Insipiens: Sapiens *K.*

2.2.2 Salomo: Secundo *P_2KR,* Item *B.* vero *lacking in B.* dicit *lacking in KR.* quod *lacking in P_2BKR.* respondeat *BS.* audit *S.* dignus *inserted in margin of P_2.* est *lacking in BKS.*

2.2.3 Willanus: Villanus *KRS.* quod *lacking in B.* quod stultus est *lacking in R.* pedem *S.* stulti: ipsi *B.*

2.2.4 hoc dictum *S.* dictum quod *lacking in B,* dictum quia *P_2.* ne haberet occasionem: quod non esset occasio *K.*

2.2.5 Stultus enim nec *B.*

2.2.6 quod *lacking in B.* stultus nobilior *P_2.* universalibus: vl'ibus *P_1KRS* (= *universalibus, cf.* **1.5.6**, **1.13.6**), u'libus *corrected to* ubilibus *P_2,* u'bilibus *B,* vilibus *Colker.* involvitur *P_2.* superhabundantiam: superbiam *K.* et sermonibus *lacking in B.* inhonestis sermonibus *K.* propter velocitatem: velocitate *K.*

2.2.7 Salomon intelligit *S.* dicit quod *P_2KR.* Deus et cetera *P_2B.*

2.2.8 est *lacking in B.*

2.2.9 Stultus est qui **2.2.10** parum scit *P_1BS Colker* (est *lacking in B);* Stultus est qui [ubique suam stulticiam ostendit **2.2.10** Stultus] parum scit *P_2KR* (est: e *P_2,* est qui *lacking in K,* est *R,* stulticiam suam *R).*

2.2.11 Et *lacking in P_2BKR.* inter stultum insipientem et ignarum et malum: inter insipientem et stultum et inter insipientem et ignarum *P_2,* inter stultum et insipientem ignarum *BR Thomas (A.),* inter stultum et malum et sapientem et ignarum sit aliqua *K.* aliqua: alia *S.* accipiamus *K.*

Chapter 3 *P_1 241rB.31; P_2 16v.2; B 321r.11; K 199vC.18; R 243v.28; S 188rB.1.*

Title *K; lacking in P_1P_2BRS Thomas (A.) Colker.*

Marginalia in P_1 Versus *2.3.3.*

2.3.1 [D]e: E *P_1 with guide letter* d; De *B with guide letter* d; E *R.* plurium ordo philosophorum: plurimi philosophorum *B,* plurium philosophorum ordo *K.* Fulco Marsiliensis: Fulco mgr' (= *magister*) Siliensis *B,* Fulco magister siluensis *S.* dicit ut *P_2KR.* Si *lacking in K.* proportionetur bene *K.* in muliere sive in viro *P_2.* muliere *corrected from* mulire *P_1.*

2.3.2 Et hoc: Hoc idem *K.* hoc: hic *R.* Philosophus intelligere *P_2K.* parte: perfeccione *P_2KR.* forme *lacking in S.*

2.3.3 unde: hunc (*?*) *R*. dicit *S*. v[ul]tus: virtus P_1*S*; vultus *above line, corrected from* multus P_2; vultis *K*. qualis *KS*.
2.3.4 *lacking in* P_1P_2*BRS Colker.*
2.3.5 dicut *S*. quod *lacking in B*. nisi corpus intrinsecus P_2*KR.*
2.3.6 quod *lacking in B*. absque *lacking in* P_2. vilitas: utilitas P_2.
2.3.7 Gaufridus: Graufedus *R*, Gaufredus *S*. Bodel *K*. dicit *BK*. laudent *R*. fortitudine: forma *B*. racio *corrected from* non *B*. gerat: teneat *K*, gerit *S*, regat *Thomas (A.)*. frenum teneat *K*.
2.3.8 Odantagalus dicit quod: Item quidem alter *B*, Odontagalus dixit dum *K*, ad antagalus dicit quod *R*. corporis promptitudo P_2*KR*. dominium: du'iu' *(= dubium?)* P_2. pedum habet *K*. sed: tunc *K*. erit: est *K*.
2.3.9 Omnes virtutes corporee corpus generaliter perfecte *K*. operationibus *BK*.

Chapter 4 *P_1 241rB.47; P_2 16v.15; B 321r.24; K 199vD.3; R 244r.11; S 188rB.26.*
Title *K; lacking in P_1P_2BRS Thomas (A.) Colker.*
Marginalia in P_1 *asterism at 2.4.15.* ***In P_2*** sicut intellectus *2.4.11 (catchword at end of P_2 16v)*; Physonomia *2.4.14; text at 2.4.5, 2.4.14 (see below).*
2.4.1 [A]ntequam: Ntequam P_1 *with guide letter* a; Ntequam *R*. Antequam proverbia vili- *illegible in B*. corporum vilium P_2*KR*. occasionem contingentem *K*. complexione corporis vel compositione denotatur *S*. unde si *B*. c. vel *lacking in K*. scituata P_1, situata *corrected from* stricta *expunctuated in* P_2. secundum quod: sicut P_2*KR*. speciem *R*.
2.4.2 Unde *lacking in B*. operibus P_2*R*.
2.4.3 est *lacking in B*. duplex est P_2. uno enim modo P_2*KR*. operationibus eius cuius P_2. incorrigilibilis *S*. corrigerent: corrigerentur P_1. libenter corrigerent si esset eis possibile *K*.
2.4.4 correctio talis defectus: talis defectus correctio *K*.
2.4.5 nativitate sua *B*. vitupari P_1. debent *in margin, corrected from* debet *lined out in* P_2.
2.4.6 contingit h.: convenit *R*. defectus talis hominibus *BK*. talis *lacking in R*. sed *lacking in* P_2*KR*, secundum quod *B Colker*, sicut *S*. contingit i.: contingit eis (eis *crossed out)* P_1, *lacking in* P_2*KR*. in illis in quibus: in illis quibus P_2*KR*. pedes: pes *K*. vel huiusmodi *lacking in K*, huius aliquid *B*, huius *RS*. absciduntur P_2, abscinditur *BK*. bonitate iusticie observata: per iusticiam in ipsis observatam *K*. eis: ipsis P_2*KR*.
2.4.7 Unde propter *K*.
2.4.8 qui maliciam complexionis secuntur que: maliciam sequentes qui *B*. m maliciam (*first* m *crossed out*) *S*. posset: possit P_2*S*, possent *B*. iudicio: iudicia *R*.

2.4.9 Unde: Hinc *B*. de: in *K*. in *lacking in B*. operibus *R*. corporalibus *lacking in P_2*. posse[n]t: posset P_1, possit P_2. corrigi po ratione (po *expunctuated*) *S*.

2.4.10 maiorem: ama^{rem} (= *amatorem?*) P_2. vilitatem corporis *B*, utilitatem *S*. illa: ista P_2*BKR Colker*, ut *S*. pes os: pes caput os P_2*K*, pedes caput os *R*, pedes *B*. nasus naris auris *K*. physonomiis *corrected from* physomiis *in* P_1, phisonomis *R*, phisionomia *S*. dixerunt: defectus dixerat (defectus *crossed out*) *S*. deterior: determinatorum *B*. dignioris operationis: dignioribus *B*. convenit *R*.

2.4.11 Philosophus: Aristoteles *K*. in *lacking in B*. libro *lacking in K*. Topicorum: Topicis de oculis *K*. dixit P_2*R*. [sicut]: sed P_1 *Colker*, hoc *B*, sicud est *R*. intellectus est in *B*. in anima ... intellectus *lacking in R*. p. sicut: sicud P_2*R*. ita virtutes *R*. oculorum omnes virtutes aliorum membrorum P_2*KR*.

2.4.12 sicut *lacking in* P_2*KR*. dispositio oculi: dispositio corporis oculi (corporis *lined out*) P_1. vilescit *K*. habent[i]s: habentes P_1, *lacking in K*. nisi ... actibus: ita malicia in actibus nisi fuerit *B Colker*.

2.4.13 P_2*KR* (versus duo *K*; In constans P_2; Instans *R*), *lacking in* P_1*BS Colker*.

2.4.14 Plinius: Iplinius *K*, Plnnus (= *Plinius?*) *S*, Philosophus *Thomas (A.) Colker*. etiam *lacking in K*. sua physonomia P_2*KR*. oculus grossus P_2*KR*. rammosus: tamosus P_2, ramosus *BK Thomas (A.)*, camosus *R*. iracundum *B*. vel: significat et *K*, et *R*. ostendit *lacking in K*. cum hic *R*. hoc *in margin of* P_2. fuerit: foret P_2*R*. labia *lacking in K*, labra *Thomas (A.)*. grossum et carnosum *K*. nasus brevis P_2*KR*. sursus *R*. glutonem: gulosum *B*, glutbonem *K*, glutoneem *S*. et et (*first* et *expunctuated*) *S*. si *corrected from* sii P_1, *lacking in B*. habuerit: habent P_2*R*, haberet *K*, *lacking in S*. tybia[s]: tybia P_1*S*, tibyas P_2*BKR Thomas (A.) Colker*. tybia fuerit brevis et *S*. grossus *R*. [u]ncas: oncas P_1, ancas P_2*R*, anchas *K*, divas *S*. ad p.: et *B Thomas (A.) Colker*. in i.: et *K*, *lacking in RS*. incessum *K*. latius P_2. taquam P_2. habebit: haberet P_2*KR*, habuerit *B*. in supremo (in *rubbed out*) *K*. figuratum: dispositum *K*. adhuc: cum hoc P_2, ad hoc *R*.

2.4.15 cum *corrected from* cut *in* P_2. habuerit: haberet P_2*KR*. qualis fuit in Hanonia Bradefer *lacking in BK*. existit et: est *K*, existit *R*.

2.4.16 est *lacking in KR*. adhuc est P_2. ad hoc *R*. vilitas est *R*. magis ex cordis complexione causatur P_2*KR*. aliqui *lacking in B*. optime formati aliqui *K*. complexionate *R*. tempore: casu *K*. ullum P_2. pulchri mali *K*.

2.4.17 istis: hiis *B*. quod *lacking in B*. utrolibet *B*. apparet quod: quod apparet P_2*KR*. existerit: existit P_2*BKR Thomas (A.) Colker*, existunt *S*.

2.4.18 De et *R*. sunt *S*. hec sint *B*.

Chapter 5 *P_1 241vC.40; P_2 17r.20; B 321v.26; K 200rA.32; R 244v.24; S 188vD.11.*

Title *K; lacking in P_1P_2BRS Thomas (A.) Colker.*

2.5.1 [C]onsequenter: Osequenter P_1 *with guide letter* c; Consequenter *B with guide letter* c; Onsequenter *R*. proverbia dominorum P_2*KR*.

2.5.2 est advertendum *P_2KR*. vel sententie breves *P_2KR,* vel breves sententie *lacking in B.* dicta *lacking in K.* scilicet eorum eorum *(first* eorum *crossed out) R.* docilitatem: crudelitatem *S.* et penitenciis *lacking in K.* penitenciis: penis *B Colker*. eorum in *P_2KR.*

2.5.3 De isto: De primo *K*. Aristotiles *Colker*. scripsit in epistula *K*. in suis habere consiliis *P_2K,* in suis consiliis habere *R*. proborum virorum *K*. summe sententie *B*.

2.5.4 filium docuit *R*. largius docuit filium suum *P_2K*. fl filium (fl *crossed out*) *S*. suum *lacking in P_2R*. dicens *lacking in BK*. spreveris: sperneris *B*, tempseris *S*.

2.5.5 avariciam vitare *R*. modo *inserted above line in P_2.*

2.5.6 [Aristoteles]: Alexander *P_1BS Colker* (*italicized by Colker as the title of Walter of Châtillon's poem, for which see "Sources and Analogues"*), Oracius *K*. semper: semel *BR Colker* (*as in Walter of Châtillon*), super *K*. verumptamen: virtutum species *B Colker (as in Walter of Châtillon),* virtutes etiam *K*. ad facinus *R*.

2.5.7 dicit *B*. dixit idem *K*. est *lacking in B*. quem: quos *BK Colker (as in Walter of Châtillon),* quam *S*.

2.5.8 Unde: Hinc *B*. dicitur de dominis *B*. dicit *S*. devicti *corrected from* deducti *in P_2.*

Chapter 6 *P_1 241vD.6; P_2 17v.1; B 322r.8; K 200rB.17; R 245r.7; S 188vD.34.*
Title *K; lacking in P_1P_2BRS Thomas (A.) Colker.*

2.6.1 [N]unc: unc *P_1 with guide letter* n; Nunc *B with guide letter* n; Unc *R*. vel de servo *P_2*. et fidelis *B*. dictarum *K*.

2.6.2 dicitur *B*. [rusticus] *lacking in P_1BS,* <......> *Colker*. est non suspecta *K,* non est suspecta *S*.

2.6.3 Idem *K*. dicit quod *lacking in B,* dicitur quod *S*. multarum custodiarum *K*. custodia *B Colker.*

2.6.4 dicit quod *lacking in B*. extitit: existit *B Colker,* est *K,* exstitit *R*.

2.6.5 dicit Seneca *S*. quod *lacking in B*. piger servus *R*. est *lacking in B,* efficitur *P_2KR*.

2.6.6 dicit Petrus Vitalis *K*. quod *lacking in B*. p. est servi et valor est *B*. servi valor *S*. silvester et *lacking in S*. iracundos *R*. separetur: se separet *B*.

2.6.7 *Lacking in B.*

Chapter 7 *P_1 241vD.20; P_2 17v.11; B 322r.17; K 200rB.36; R 245r.19; S 189rA.12.*
Title *K; lacking in P_1P_2BRS Thomas (A.) Colker.*
Marginalia in P_2 Nota *2.7.1*, [Dyo]genes *2.7.4*.

2.7.1 [N]unc: unc *P_1 with guide letter* n; Nunc *B with guide letter* n; Unc *R*. tangamus: coniungamus *P_2KR*.

2.7.2 s. quod *lacking in B,* ita quod *P_2*. d. quod *lacking in B*. est *lacking in B*. cordi suo *P_2BKR Colker*.

2.7.3 Idem tamen: Hoc *B*. quia: quod P_2. venit rerum sufficiencia *K*. satis patuit *B Colker*. satis *lacking in* P_2.

2.7.4 dixit *K*. ipse *lacking in B*. erat *lacking in R*. vita sua et fortuna *K*. defecit *K*. cordi autem regis *K*. suffecit *K*.

2.7.5 proverbiis *lacking in B*. intendit: intelligit *K*. intendit quod *lacking in B*. est: sit P_2KR. dominium: desiderium *R*.

2.7.6 quod *lacking in B*. *After* dives: plures habet amicos *crossed out in S*. *Second* habet *lacking in* P_2KR. corpus: ipsum *B Colker.*

2.7.7 quod *lacking in B*. habet plures *KR*.

2.7.8 Dyonisius dicit ... **2.7.9** naturaliter **2.7.10** et *K*.

2.7.10 Hec ad presens sufficiant *B*. similia: consimilia P_2R. loco: capitulo P_2KR. sed: et P_2KR. propter opus *lacking in B*.

Chapter 8 *P_1 241vD.36; P_2 17v.21; B 322r.26; K 200vC.18; R 245r.31; S 189rA.29.*

Title *K; lacking in P_1P_2BRS Thomas (A.) Colker.*

Marginalia in P_1 *asterism at 2.8.2.* ***In P_2*** Dyogenes *2.8.5; text at 2.8.5 (see below).* ***In R*** *after* sibi *2.8.2*, de pauper[tate] (*catchword at end of folio 245r).*

2.8.1 [H]iis: iis P_1 *with unclear guide letter*; Hiis *B with guide letter* h; Iis *R*. habitis *lacking in K*. est *lacking in R*. paupe[re]: paupe P_1, paupertate *K*.

2.8.2 In historiis grecorum invenitur *K*. inquesivit *K*. Philosophus: Aristoteles *K*. ait: dixit *K*.

2.8.3 quo: aliquo *K*. s. respondet *B*. respondit quod sive quia sive large *K*. quia: quod P_2. quia sive ... verum respondit *lacking in S*. v. respondet *B*. sciencie et *lacking in B*.

2.8.4 hoc: hoc idem P_2R, idem *K*. qui dicit: dicens *K*. quod *lacking in B*. pauper non (non *expunctuated*) *B*. large *corrected from* larga *in R*.

2.8.5 Dyogenos *S*. laudabat *R*. div[i]ciarum: diuciarum P_1. scilicet quia *BS*. scilicet *lacking in P_2*, sibi *R*. et salvat P_2KR. facit gratum statum P_2. [primum] *illegible in P_1*. providendo: providencia *S*. secundum per P_2K. facit temperancia *S*. pauperi nec ... **2.8.6** O preclara *in lower margin of P_2 with sketch of a hand, index finger pointing; sketch repeated in margin of the body.* rapiat *corrected from* rapit P_2.

2.8.6 O preclara mortalium beatitudo et cetera *P_1BS Colker* (et cetera ut supra *S*). preclara: clara *lined out in P_2*. quam cum: quam si *K*.

2.8.7 Et cantabat: Et iterum cantabat *B*, Et cantat *K*.

2.8.8 consulit *B*. filio suo *K*. Infantem nudum et cetera *P_1S Colker.* dum: cum P_2K. Infantem nudum ... ferre memento *lacking in B*.

2.8.9 et precipit *repeated in P_2, lacking in B*. precipit etiam *K*. [dilige] *lacking in P_1 Colker.* [sed parce dilige formam]: et cetera *P_1S Colker.* usum et non *K*. sed *lacking in K.* sed largus: largus autem *K*.

2.8.10 Sine dubio *lacking in B.* et eorum rationes *K.* fuerunt superius P_2*BKR.* solo: stilo *S.* poterant: potuerunt *K.* fortuite: fortune *BK.* mihi *lacking in K.* omni[a]: omnium P_1. paupertate: auctoritate *R.* non *lacking in S.*

2.8.11 Et *lacking in K.* quod *lacking in B.* usus rerum P_2*KR.* satis *lacking in BK.* subtilius *K.*

Chapter 9 *P_1 242rA.14; P_2 18r.8; B 322v.14; K 200vD.21; R 245v.27; S 189rB.24.*

Title *K*; De gloriosis *in margin of R; lacking in P_1P_2BS Thomas (A.) Colker.*

Marginalia in P_2 S[ocrates] *2.9.2*, Nota *2.9.3*.

2.9.1 [N]unc: Unc P_1 *with guide letter* n; Nunc *B with guide letter* n; Unc *R.*

2.9.2 dixit *B.* quod Valerius: Valerius *B,* quod secundum Valerium *K.* narrat *lacking in K,* narravit P_2. *Second* quod *lacking in BK.* talibus *R.* operacionibus *K.* cupiunt hominibus P_2.

2.9.3 idem T. i. l. D. O. dicit P_2*R,* idem T. D. O. dicit *K.* Tulius *S.* in libro *lacking in K.* quod *lacking in B.* est *lacking in B.* qualis qualis *R.* cupit: desiderat P_2*KR.*

2.9.4 veram supple non vanam gloriam *lacking in B.* vera non supple vana gloria si curas *K.* vana gloria P_2*R.*

2.9.5 fama vel: famalis *K.* appreciatur: aspiciatur P_2, appreciantur (n *expunctuated*) *S.* gentes sapientes (gentes *expunctuated*) P_2. eo quod: quia *B.* inter gentes ... haberi quia *lacking in B.* pa[u]cissimi: pacissimi P_1. recte de bonis hominibus iudicent *B.* iudicent: iudicetur P_2. qua quia (qua *lined out*) *R.* esse *lacking in K.* sciant: sciunt *B.* livoris: nimium *K.* occasionem *R.*

2.9.6 Ad hoc *K.* magna vi: magni P_2*KRS.* tumoris: timoris P_2*BS Thomas (A.) Colker.* vacuitatis: vanitatis P_2*KR Thomas (A.).* quare: quia *K.*

Chapter 10 *P_1 242rA.29; P_2 18r.18; B 322v.23; K 200v.40; R 246r.9; S 189vC.4.*

Title De proverbiis vani *(new folio begins)* De vanigloriosis *K,* De vaniglosis *in margin of R; lacking in P_1P_2BS Thomas (A.) Colker.*

2.10.1 Ultimo *B with guide letter* u; Ultimum *K.* de vanigloriosis est dicendum *B Thomas (A.).* E vanigloriosis ultimo dicendum est *R.*

2.10.2 consequende: convenientis P_2*KR,* conveniende *B,* cōnfide *(= confingende?)* *S.* laudes convenientis P_2.

2.10.3 filio suo *K.* [nec te ... vexat inanis]: et cetera *P_1P_2S Colker,* nec te vituperes ipse *B.*

2.10.4 Et *lacking in B.* omnes *lacking in R.* alios *K.* et ad hoc ipsi *S.*

2.10.5 Quare: Unde *K.* [Plato] dicit: dicit *P_1BS Colker*, ipse dicit P_2*R,* dicit ipse *K.* sunt similes *K.* qui: qui et P_2, et *K.* tempestati: in tempestate *B.* dimittunt *S.* quod *lacking in B.* gloria est *B.* bonos: vanos *R.*

2.10.6 consimiles *K.* dixerunt sapientes *B Colker*. nobilis: sive nobilis P_2*R,* sapiens *K.* huc diximus: diximus hoc P_2*KR,* diximus *B,* hoc diximus *S.* scribendum P_2*KR.* igitur quod dictum est: ergo quod dictum est *KR,* hec dixisse *B.*

2.10.7 Laudetur altissimus ... licet pauca: a quo domino largiente (a quo *expunctuated*) *B.* altissimos *R.* concessit hec P_2R. scribere concessit *K.* pauca apud quem est et *K.* f. omnis *lacking in B.* et *lacking in K.* quem: quo P_2R.

Explicit Explicit de nobilitate animi liber *B Colker;* Explicit libellus de nobilitate animi *K;* Explicit liber de nobilitate animi editus a magistro Guillermo de Arrogonia *R.*

Colophon Versus: Hic lectura petit quisnam sit lector et unde, Ne careat titulis ut peregrinus suis, Hic est Willemus medicine sorte magister; Regis Arrogonie de dicione fuit P_2; *lacking in* P_1*BKRS Colker. Another work by Guillelmus de Aragonia, the* Commentum in Boetium, *MS Erfurt, Amplonianische Sammlungen, f. 358, reads the same except for* Hec ... peregrina ... Guilhelmus; *see Pack 238, n. 8, and Terbille, I, 2* (Haec).

Sources and Analogues

Part 1

Prologue

1.0.1 Compare Aristotle, *Ethica Nicomachea* 1.1 (Bekker 1094a1–2), translated by R. Grosseteste, *AL* 26.1–3, fasc. 3, p. 141, lines 5–7, or the anonymous reviser, fasc. 4, p. 375, lines 4–6: "Omnis ars et omnis doctrina, similiter autem et actus et eleccio, bonum quoddam appetere videtur. Ideo bene enunciaverunt bonum, quod omnia appetunt." (Every art and every inquiry, and similarly every action and choice, is thought to aim at some good; and for this reason the good has rightly been declared to be that at which all things aim [*CW* 1729].)

1.0.4 *Nichil disgregat visum nisi quod albedinem habet.* Compare Aristotle, *Metaphysica* 10.2 (Bekker 1053b29–1053b35), translated by Guillelmus de Moerbeke, *AL* 25.3.2, p. 200, lines 132–138: "At uero et in coloribus est aliquid quod color unus, puta albus, deinde alii ex hoc et nigro uidentur geniti, nigrum uero priuatio albi est, ut et lucis tenebra (hec enim est priuatio lucis). Quare si entia essent colores, essent utique numerus quidam entia. Sed quorum? Palam utique quia colorum; et ipsum unum esset utique aliquid unum puta album." (But in colours the one is a colour, e.g. white—the other colours are observed to be produced out of this and black, and black is the privation of white, as darkness of light. Therefore if all existent things were colours, existent things would have been a number, indeed, but of what? Clearly of colours; and the "one" would have been a particular "one", e.g. white [*CW* 1664].) Pseudo-Augustinus Belgicus, *Sermons* (composed after 1168), ed. A. Mai, *Nova Patrum Bibliotheca* (Rome, 1852), 1:161.4, cited in *TLL*, s.v. "albedo": "Albedo fundamentum colorum" (Whiteness is the foundation of colors). Petrus Iohannis Olivi, *Quodlibeta quinque*, 3, quaestio 5, *Collectio Oliviana* 7 (St. Defraia, 2002), 182, line 75, quoted from *LLT*: "Albedo est mensura colorum" (Whiteness is the measure of colors). (Olivi wrote *Quodlibet* 3 at Montpellier in 1289–1292, according to

LLT.) On the idea that whiteness "disgregat visum" (differentiates vision), compare Aristotle, *Topica* 7.3 (Bekker 153a), translated by Boethius, *AL* 5.1, p. 150, line 9: "Et differentias autem contrarias de contrariis probamus praedicari, velut albo et nigro; nam hoc quidem disgregativum illud autem congregativum visus." (And we claim that contrary differentiae are predicated of contraries, e.g., of white and black, for the one disperses the vision, while the other compresses it [*CW* 257].) Boethius's "disgregativum ... visus," literally "dispersive ... of vision," is closer to our text's "disgregat visum" than the language of the *Translatio Anonyma*, which uses "discretivum ... visionis" (*AL* 5.1, p. 282, lines 16–18).

Chapter 1

1.1.4 *Illa sunt in se vilia*. Colker compares Brunetto Latini, *Li livres dou tresor* 2.54.7, ed. Baldwin and Barrette 208: "& por ce que la fobleice des homes est deceable a vices, Seneques dit: ha! come li hom est vil choses & desprisables." Trans. Barrette and Baldwin 197: "Because the weakness of man is susceptible to vice, Seneca says: Ha! How vile and despicable a thing is man."

Chapter 3

1.3.3 Colker compares Aristotle, *Politica* 7.13 (Bekker 1332b), translated by G. de Moerbeke, ed. F. Susemihl, *Aristotelis Politicorum Libri Octo cum Vetusta Translatione Guilelmi de Moerbeka* (Leipzig, 1872), 301: "Alia quidem igitur animalium maxime quidem natura vivunt, parva autem quaedam et consuetudinibus, homo autem et ratione: solum enim habet rationem." (Animals lead for the most part a life of nature, although in lesser particulars some are influenced by habit as well. Man has reason, in addition, and man only [*CW* 2114].) Seneca, *Epistles* 9.76.9; *Lettres à Lucilius*, ed. F. Préchac, 3:57: "In homine optimum quid est? Ratio; hac antecedit animalia, deos sequitur. Ratio ergo perfecta proprium bonum est, cetera illi cum animalibus satisque communia sunt." (What is best in man? Reason, by which he surpasses the animals and follows the gods. Therefore perfect reason is his particular good; the others are common to him along with animals and plants.)

1.3.10 "*Secundum intellectum operans* ..." Aristotle, *Ethica Nicomachea* 10.9 (Bekker 1179a23–4), translated by R. Grosseteste, *AL* 26.1–3, fasc. 3, p. 364, lines 5–7, or the anonymous reviser, fasc. 4, p. 582, lines 3–4: "Secundum intellectum autem operans et hunc curans et dispositus optime, et dei amantissimus videtur esse" (Now he who exercises his intellect and cultivates it seems to be both in the best state and most dear to the gods [*CW* 1863]).

1.3.12 "*Res intelligunt prout sunt.*" "Liber Hermetis De Quindecim Stellis Quindecim Lapidibus Quindecim Herbis et Quindecim Imaginibus," *Textes latins et vieux français relatifs aux Cyranides*, ed. L. Delatte (Liège, 1942), 241, lines 14–15: "Sapiens autem est qui res cognoscit prout sunt et recte probari possunt." (The wise man is he who knows things as they are and can be rightly proven.) The text, attributed to Hermes Trismegistus, exists in an anonymous Latin translation of an Arabic version; "ce serait peine perdue de ... rechercher soit l'époque du traducteur latin, soit celle de l'éditeur arabe, soit enfin celle de l'auteur qui se cache sous le nom d'Hermès" (Delatte 237–238).

1.3.17 "*Dum iuvenis es ...*" Compare Galen, *De Placitis Hippocratis et Platonis* 5.5, ed. C. G. Kühn, *Claudii Galeni Opera Omnia* 5 (1821; repr., Hildesheim, 2001), 465–466: "Sic autem et ab initio hominem ad optimum conformare oportet, ante omnia quidem ipsorum seminum ratione habita, deinde victus, quo gravida utetur, et in alimentis et potionibus, et exercitiis et quiete, et somno et vigilia; de quibus omnibus Plato accuratissime disseruit." (But thus it is necessary even from the beginning to shape a man for the best, indeed before all [his traits] are received by reason of their seeds, then of nourishment that the pregnant [mother] takes, both in food and drink, and in exercise and rest, and sleep and waking; about all of which Plato spoke most accurately.)

1.3.18 Boethius, *Philosophiae consolatio* 1, meter 7.20–31; ed. L. Bieler (Turnholt, 1957), 16–17.

1.3.19 *Disticha Catonis* 2.4, ed. M. Boas (Amsterdam, 1952), 101. Boas reads, "ne possis" (so that you cannot).

1.3.20 Algazel, *Logica* 2, lines 78–80, 87–89; ed. C. H. Lohr, "Logica Algazelis: Introduction and Critical Text," *Traditio* 21 (1965): 241–242: "Munditia animae est, ut expietur a sordidis moribus et sanctificetur a phantasiis turpibus. [...] Anima enim speculum est; nam depinguntur in ea formae totius esse, cum mundata et tersa fuerit a sordidis moribus." (The cleanliness of the soul is to be expiated of sordid habits and sanctified of filthy fantasies. [...] For the soul is a mirror; in it are depicted the forms of all being, when it has been cleansed and wiped free of sordid habits.) Algazel or al-Gazzali, an Islamic theologian, died in 1111. The Latin version of his *Logica* was "known from the second half of the twelfth century"; it was a fundamental source for Christian writers in the thirteenth, but use of it declined in the fourteenth and fifteenth centuries (Lohr, 228–231).

1.3.23 Aristotle, *Ethica Nicomachea* 3.7 (Bekker 1114b4–8), translated by R. Grossteste, *AL* 26.1–3, fasc. 3, p. 189, lines 22–24, or the anonymous reviser, fasc. 4, p. 420, lines 1–3: "Si autem nullus sibi causa eius quod est malefacere, set propter ignoranciam finis hec operatur, per hec existimans sibi optimum fore" (Everyone does evil acts through ignorance of the end, thinking that by these he will get what is best [*CW* 1759]).

1.3.27 Aristotle, *De historia animalium* 8.1, according to Bekker (588a26), 7.1, according to G. de Moerbeke, translated by G. de Moerbeke, *AL* 17.2.1.2, ed. P. Beullens and F. Bossier, available through *ALD*-2: "Manifestum autem est de quibus dicimus ad puerorum etatem respicientibus; in hiis enim habituum posterius futurorum est videre velut vestigia et semina, differt autem nichil ut est dicere anima a bestiarum anima secundum tempus hoc." (In children may be observed the traces and seeds of what will one day be settled habits, though psychologically a child hardly differs for the time being from an animal [*CW* 922].)

1.3.29 Seneca, *Epistles* 1.5.8, ed. Préchac, 1:16: "Cogitationes in longinqua praemittimus." (We project our thoughts into the distant future.)

Chapter 4

1.4.2 This statement derives ultimately from Euripides, who wrote a line in his play *Aeolus* (which survives only in fragments) that may be translated, "First a beauty [*eidos*] worthy of absolute power." Euripides' line was quoted by Porphyry in a commentary, the *Isagoge*, or "Explanation," on Aristotle, in which Porphyry distinguished two senses of *eidos*, the first meaning "beauty" and the second "species," and illustrated the first with this line before going on to explain Aristotle's concept of species in relation to genus. Porphyry's commentary was translated by Boethius, who rendered this line faithfully as "Primum quidem species digna imperio"; Greek *eidos* is translated as Latin *species*, the meanings of which range from "visual appearance" to "beauty" to "a subdivision of any class or kind, a sort, species" (*OLD*), so the Boethian version meant "First, indeed, a visual appearance (or beauty or species), worthy of absolute power." Boethius's version was then misunderstood by scribes who copied *Primum* as *Priami*, producing a new meaning: "Priam's appearance (or beauty or species), worthy of absolute power." A florilegium, the *Auctoritates Aristotelis*, transmitted the misunderstanding (*Auctoritates* 30.6), adding the word *forma*, which has a similar range of meanings, from "visible form" to "beauty" to "kind, sort, variety" (*OLD*): "Species est forma uniuscujusque rei secundum quam species Priami dicta est digna imperio." (A visual appearance [or beauty or species] is a form [or beauty or sort] of every thing individually, in which sense the appearance [or beauty or species] of Priam has been called worthy of empire.) In this passage of *De nobilitate animi*, *species* refers to nobility of the body, including its beauty, strength, and agility (see the following sentence).

Boethius's translation of the *Isagoge* 3.21–4.2 is in *AL* 1.6–7, p. 8, and *Porphyry the Phoenician: Isagoge*, trans. E. W. Warren (Toronto, 1975), 34. Warren identifies the source of the poetic line in Euripides, *Aeolus* 15.2. See A. Nauck, *Tragicorum Graecorum Fragmenta*, rev. Bruno Snell (Hildesheim, 1964), 367.

1.4.10 Sallust narrates the history of Marius but does not figure in it himself.

1.4.12 Sallust, *Bellum Iugurthinum* 85.25, in *Sallust*, ed. J. C. Rolfe (Cambridge, Mass., 1965), 316. Marius speaks: "Mihi nova nobilitas est, quam certe peperisse melius est quam acceptam corrupisse." (Mine is a new nobility; surely to have begotten it is better than to have inherited and corrupted it.)

1.4.13 Reference to the *Bellum Catilinae*, in which Sallust depicts unworthy sons of noble families ("filii familiarum, quorum ex nobilitate maxuma pars erat," 43.2, ed. Rolfe, 74) who conspired with Catiline to murder their fathers.

Chapter 5

1.5.3 Boethius, *Philosophiae consolatio* 4.6.7, ed. Bieler 79.

1.5.4 See the following.

1.5.5a *Magis dicitur esse fatum.* Boethius, *Philosophiae consolatio* 4.6.8, ed. Bieler 79: "Qui modus cum in ipsa diuinae intellegentiae puritate conspicitur, prouidentia nominatur; cum uero ad ea quae mouet atque disponit refertur, fatum a ueteribus appellatum est." *The Consolation of Philosophy*, trans. I.T. (1609), rev. H. F. Stewart, (Cambridge, Mass., 1962), 341: "Which ways [i.e., manifold ways of doing things] being considered in the purity of God's understanding, are named Providence, but being referred to those things which He moveth and disposeth, they are by the ancients called Fate."

1.5.5b *A for, faris dictum.* Compare Isidore, *Etymologiae* 8.11.90, ed. W. M. Lindsay, *Isidori Hispalensis Episcopi Etymologiarum sive Originum Libri XX* (Oxford, 1911): "A fando igitur fatum dicunt" (Therefore they say "fate" from "speaking"). The verb *for, fari*, "to speak, foretell, predict" has the past participle *fatus*, "spoken, foretold," whence the noun *fatum*, "a foretelling, what has been foretold; fate."

1.5.6 *Fatum dicitur ...* Boethius, *Philosophiae consolatio* 4.6.9, ed. Bieler 79: "Nam prouidentia est ipsa illa diuina ratio in summo omnium principe constituta quae cuncta disponit, fatum uero inhaerens rebus mobilibus dispositio per quam prouidentia suis quaeque nectit ordinibus." *Consolation*, trans. I.T. (1609) rev. Stewart, 341: "For Providence is the very Divine reason itself, seated in the highest Prince, which disposeth all things. But Fate is a disposition inherent in changeable things, by which Providence connecteth all things in their due order."

1.5.7 *Anthologia latina* 792, ed. A. Riese (Leipzig, 1906; repr., 1972), 1, part 2, 270. Dated thirteenth century by Riese 270n. Walther 2879b: "Clotho colum baiulat, Lachesis net [sic], et Atropos occat."

1.5.12 Aristotle, *Physica* 2.4 (Bekker 195b31); Translatio Vetus, *AL* 7.1, fasc. 2, p. 63, lines 3–4: "Dicitur autem et fortuna et casus causarum, et multa et esse et fieri propter fortunam et propter casum." (But chance and spontaneity are also reckoned among causes: many things are said both to be and to come to be as a result of chance and spontaneity [*CW* 334].) The Translatio Vetus was produced by Iacobus Veneticus, who was active 1136–1148. See L. Minio-Paluello, "Iacobus Veneticus Grecus: Canonist and Translator of Aristotle," *Traditio* 8 (1952): 265–304. The Translatio Vaticana (*AL* 7.2) does not include this passage.

1.5.14 Aristotle, *Physica* 2.5 (Bekker 197a5–8), Translatio Vetus, *AL* 7.1, fasc. 2, p. 70, lines 7–10: "Manifestum itaque est quod fortuna causa sit secundum accidens in his que in minori sunt secundum propositum eorum que propter hoc sunt." (It is clear then that chance is an accidental cause in the sphere of those actions that are among those less according to intention, among [actions] that are because of it [trans. W. Paden].) Compare *CW* 336: "It is clear then that chance is an accidental cause in the sphere of those actions for the sake of something which involve choice." The Translatio Vaticana (*AL* 7.2) does not include this passage.

Chapter 6

1.6.2 *Dominum esse naturaliter qui pre aliis viget intellectu.* Aristotle, *Politica* 1.2 (Bekker 1252a31), G. de Moerbeke, translatio imperfecta (completed 1260–1264, p. xii), *AL* 29.1, p. 4, lines 5–6: "Quidem enim potest mente previdere, principans natura et dominans natura, quod autem potest hec corpore facere, subiectum et natura servum." (For that which can foresee by the exercise of mind is by nature lord and master, and that which can with its body give effect to such foresight is a subject, and by nature a slave [*CW* 1986–1987].) *Auctoritates* 15.1: "Homines ratione et intellectu vigentes naturaliter aliorum domini sunt et rectores." (Men vigorous in reason and intellect are naturally the masters and leaders of others.)

1.6.4 Boethius, *Philosophiae consolatio* 1.4.5, ed. Bieler, 7: "Atqui tu hanc sententiam Platonis ore sanxisti: beatas fore res publicas si eas uel studiosi sapientiae regerent uel earum rectores studere sapientiae contigisset." (But you decreed this sentence by the mouth of Plato, that republics would be happy if students of wisdom ruled them, or if their rulers happened to study wisdom.) Compare Plato, *Republic* 5.473, in Plato, *CD* 712–713: "Unless, said I, either philosophers become kings in our states or those whom we now call our kings and rulers take to the pursuit of philosophy ... there can be no cessation of troubles." *Auctoritates* 25.7: "Beata est res publica cui princeps sapiens dominatur." (Blessed is the republic that a wise prince rules.) Pseudo-Walter Burley, *Liber de vita et moribus philosophorum* 52 (Plato), ed. H. Knust (Tübingen, 1886), 226: "Platonis vero elegantia quedam dicta sunt hec: Tunc vero beatus et felix dicendus est orbis terrarum cum sapientes efficiuntur reges et reges efficiuntur sapientes." (Among Plato's elegant sayings are these: Then in truth the world must be called blessed and happy, when wise men become kings and kings become wise men.)

1.6.8 Horace, *Epistles* 2.1.191, ed. H. R. Fairclough, *Horace: Satires, Epistles and Ars Poetica* (Cambridge, Mass., 1961), 412.

1.6.9 Ecclesiastes 10:16: "Vae tibi terra cuius rex est puer."

1.6.10 Psalms 48:21: "Homo cum in honore esset non intellexit. Comparatus est iumentis insipientibus, et similis factus est illis." (Man when he was in honour did not understand: he hath been compared to senseless beasts, and made like to them [DV].)

1.6.12 Aristotle, *Rhetorica* 1.5.5 (Bekker 1360b32), translated by G. de Moerbeke, *AL* 31.1–2, p. 175, lines 18–20: "Nobilitas quidem igitur est genti et civitati sui iuris antiquos esse, et presides primos insignes, et multos insignes prodiisse ex ipsis in hiis que zelantur." (Now good birth in a race or a state means that its members are indigenous or ancient; that its earliest leaders were distinguished men, and that from them have sprung many who were distinguished for qualities that we admire [*CW* 2163].) The alternative Translatio Anonyma does not match the language of G. de Aragonia as closely: *AL* 31.1–2, p. 21, lines 20–22. G. de Moerbeke completed his translation before 1269: *AL* 31.1–2, p. xxviii.

Chapter 7

1.7.4 Horace, *Epistles* 1.10.47, ed. Fairclough 318.

1.7.5 Boethius, *Philosophiae consolatio* 2.5.4, ed. Bieler 26: "Atqui haec effundendo magis quam coacervando melius nitent, si quidem auaritia semper odiosos, claros largitas facit." (But these [riches] shine better in pouring out than in piling up, for avarice always makes men odious, and generosity makes men illustrious.)

1.7.12 *Certum terminum*. Horace, *Epistles* 1.2.56, ed. Fairclough 266: "Semper avarus eget; certum voto pete finem." (The greedy man is always lacking; seek a fixed limit for your desire.)

1.7.13 Boethius, *Philosophiae consolatio* 2.5.35, ed. Bieler 28. Quoted in *Auctoritates* 25.25.

1.7.14 *Disticha Catonis* 2.6, ed. Boas, 103: "Quod nimium est fugito, parvo gaudere memento: / tuta mage est puppis, modico quae flumine fertur." (Avoid what is too great, remember to rejoice in little: safer is the ship that sails a modest stream.)

1.7.15 Horace, *Epistles* 1.10.41, ed. Fairclough 316 (reading *nesciet*, "will not know").

Chapter 8

1.8.5 Horace, *Epistles* 1.16.17, ed. Fairclough 352. Cited again in 2.9.4.

1.8.6 *Disticha Catonis* 1.14, ed. Boas, 47: "Cum te aliquis laudat, iudex tuus esse memento; / plus aliis de te quam tu tibi credere noli." (When someone praises you, remember to be your own judge; do not trust others about you more than yourself.)

1.8.10 *Disticha Catonis* 2.16, ed. Boas, 117: "Nec te conlaudes nec te culpaveris ipse: / hoc faciunt stulti, quos gloria vexat inanis." (Do not praise yourself nor blame yourself; fools do this, whom empty glory vexes.) Cited again at 2.10.3.

1.8.11 Valerius Maximus, *Memorable Doings and Sayings* 7.2, ext. 11b, ed. D. R. Shackleton Bailey (Cambridge, Mass., 2000), 2.122: "Idem Aristoteles de semet ipso<s> in neutram partem loqui debere praedicabat, quoniam laudare se vani, vituperare stulti esset." (The same Aristotle used to say that a man should speak neither well nor ill of himself, since self-praise smacked of vanity and self-censure of stupidity [translated by Shackleton Bailey].) Alexander is mentioned in the preceding anecdote, 7.2, ext. 11a, ed. Shackleton Bailey, 2.120–122: "Aristoteles autem, Callisthenen, auditorem suum, ad Alexandrum dimittens, monuit cum eo aut quam rarissime aut quam iucundissime loqueretur." (When Aristotle sen[t] his auditor Callisthenes to Alexander, he counselled him to talk with the king either as seldom or as agreeably as possible.) Pseudo-Walter Burley, *Liber de vita et moribus philosophorum* 53 (Aristotiles), ed. Knust 236: "Huius [Aristotelis] elegancia quedam dicta sunt hec: De se ipso in neutram partem loquendum est quoniam qui se laudat vanus est, qui se vituperat stultus est." (These are some of his elegant sayings: One should speak neutrally of oneself, since he who praises himself is vain, he who blames himself is a fool.) Otto, *Nachträge*, 67: "In proprias laudes odiosa iactatio est" (In praise of oneself ... boasting is odious); "In propriis laudibus, sicut dicitur, est odiosa iactatio" (In praise of oneself, as they say, boasting is odious). *Cato Novus* (end of the twelfth or beginning of the thirteenth century), 121, in *TPMA*, s.v. "Lob," 1.2.24: "Nemo sibi culpam vel laudem conferat umquam; / Convenit hoc uanis quos gloria uexat inanis." (Let no one ever give himself blame or praise; this suits vain people whom empty glory vexes.) Werner N 38: "Nemo sibi culpam nec laudem conferat umquam!" (Let no one ever give himself blame or praise). Werner N 100: "Noli tu quicquam rerum laudare tuarum, / Ni sit ab alterius ore probata prius!" (Do not praise any of your own affairs, lest it be judged first by someone else's mouth). Walther 13524a: "Laudare se vani, vituperare stulti est." (To praise oneself is a vain man's [behavior], to blame [oneself] a fool's.)

Chapter 9

1.9.1 *Tempus expostulat*: Compare "tempus postulat" (occasion demands), *Disticha Catonis* 2.5.2, ed. Boas, 102, and 2.18.1, ed. Boas, 120.

Chapter 10

1.10.12 Aristotle, *Topics* 2.2 (Bekker 110a16–18), either translated by Boethius, *AL* 5.1–3, p. 33, lines 23–26: "Utile enim et ad construendum et ad destruendum, ut quoniam nominationibus quidem res nuncupandum ut plures, quae autem rerum sunt huiusmodi vel non huiusmodi, non iam attendendum pluribus"; or from the Translatio Anonyma, dated 1120–1160 (see *AL* 5.1–3, p. xlvii), *AL* 5.1–3, p. 211, lines 25–28: "Utile enim ad astruendum et ad destruendum, velut quoniam nominibus quidem res oportet appellare quemadmodum multi, que vero rerum sunt huiusmodi aut non huiusmodi, nequaquam attendendum multis." (We ought to use our words to mean the same things as most people mean by them, but when we ask what kinds of things are or are not of such and such a kind, we should not here go with the multitude [*CW* 183].) Geoffrey of Vinsauf, *Poetria Nova* (composed 1208–1213, Faral 33), lines 1081–1082, ed. E. Faral, *Les arts poétiques du XIIe et du XIIIe siècle* (Paris, 1962), 230: "Veterum clamat doctrina: loquaris / Ut plures, sapias ut pauci." (The doctrine of the ancients proclaims: Speak as many, know as few.) *Auctoritates* 36.26: "Loquendum est ut plures, sapiendum vero ut pauci." (One should speak as the many, but know as the few.)

Chapter 11

1.11.4 Compare At de Mons (fl. 1250–1300), *Ensenhamen*, 1914–20, ed. Bernhardt 51–52: "Donc per dreg deu venir / Per la bontat del paire / O de la bona maire / E.l mon propriamen / De dieu e de las jens / Gazardos als efans. / Vers es e par a mans." (So by right, because of the goodness of the father or of the good mother, compensation in the world should properly come to the children from God and from the people. This is true and clear to many.) See also the variant in *B*: "Quia de Adam et Eva descenderunt igitur et cetera" (Since they descended from Adam and Eve, therefore, and so on).

1.11.8 Aristotle, *Politica* 1.2 (Bekker 1253a), translated by G. de Moerbeke, ed. Susemihl 10, lines 7–11: "Sicut enim perfectum optimum animalium homo est, sic et separatum a lege et iustitia pessimum omnium. Saevissima enim iniustitia habens arma: homo autem habens arma nascitur prudentia et virtute, quibus ad contraria est uti maxime." (For man, when perfected, is the best of animals, but, when separated from law and justice, he is the worst of all; since armed injustice is the more dangerous, and he is equipped at birth with arms, meant to be used by intelligence and excellence, which he may use for the worst ends [*CW* 1988].) Since G. de Aragonia writes *sevissima ... arma*, he must have used G. de Moerbeke's finished translation (*saevissima ... arma*, Susemihl), not his Translatio Imperfecta, which reads *gravissima ... arma* (*AL* 29.1, p. 6, lines 12–16). *Auctoritates* 15.10: *Saevissima injustitia est habens arma, scilicet sciendi.* "Most cruel injustice it is having arms, that is, of knowing."

1.11.14 Aristotle, *De anima* 2.9 (Bekker 421a25), translated by I. Veneticus (active 1136–1148), *AL* 12.1, ed. J. Decorte and J. Brams, available through *ALD-2*: "Fortes quidem enim carne ineptos mente, molles autem carne bene aptos esse." (Men whose flesh is hard are ill-endowed with intellect, men whose flesh is soft, well-endowed [*CW* 670].) *Auctoritates* 6.99: "Molles carne mente aptos dicimus, duros vero ineptos." (We say that those soft in flesh are well-endowed in mind, but that the hard are ill-endowed.)

1.11.16 *Diverse sunt dispositiones in corpore per diversas virtutes ipsius anime.* Anonymous, *De physiognomia* par. 2; R. Förster, *Scriptores Physiognomonici Graeci et Latini* (Leipzig, 1893; repr., 1994), 2:4: "Loxus quidem sanguinem animae habitaculum esse constituit, corpus autem omne et partes eius quae signa dant, ... dare signa diversa." (Loxus established that blood is the dwelling of the soul, but the whole body and its parts that give signs ... give diverse signs.) G. de Aragonia attributes to Aristotle the anonymous *De physiognomia*, which describes itself (par. 1, Förster, 2:3) as an introduction to the subject using the writings of Loxus the physician, Aristotle the philosopher, and Palemon the speaker. Förster, 1:cxli, dates the *De physiognomia* in the late fourth century CE.

1.11.18 *Sicut sunt elementa in corporibus, ita stelle in animabus.* Hali's commentary on Ptolemy, *Centiloquium*, in Ptolemy, [*Quadripartitum; Centiloquium cum commento Hali*] (Venice, 1484), f. 46v, col. b: "Tales sunt stelle et fortitudines ex eis manantes: et opera earum in animalibus: qualia sunt elementa corporibus." (The stars and the influences descending from them and their effects are to creatures endowed with a soul as the elements are to their bodies.) The author of this commentary has been identified as Ahmad ibn Yusuf, an Egyptian mathematician who died about 912, by F. Sezgin,

Geschichte des arabischen Schrifttums, vol. 5 (Leiden, 1974), 289. Another candidate, 'Ali ibn Ridwan, an Egyptian astrologer and physician who died in 1061 or 1067, was also mentioned by Sarton, but according to Sezgin his translation of Ptolemy was one of the *Quadripartitum*. See G. Sarton, *Introduction to the History of Science*, vol. 1 (Baltimore, 1927), 789; Sezgin, *Geschichte*, 7:44.

1.11.21 Aristotle, *De generatione animalium* 4.10 (Bekker 777a33–777b30), translated by G. de Moerbeke, *AL* 17.2.5, pp. 151–152, lines16–20, 15–18: "Gestationis autem unicuique animalium tempora determinata existunt ut quidem ad frequenter secundum vitas: eorum enim que maioris temporis et generationes rationabile esse maioris temporis ... Et enim caliditates et frigiditates usque ad commensurationem quandam faciunt generationes, post hec autem corruptiones: horum autem habent terminum et principii et consummationis motus horum astrorum." (The period of gestation is, as a matter of fact, determined generally in each animal in proportion to the length of its life. For it is reasonable that the development of the long-lived animals should take a longer time ... For heat and cold varying within certain limits make things to come into being and after this to perish, and it is the motions of the sun and moon [*G. de Moerbeke and G. de Aragonia:* of these stars] that fix the limit both of the beginning and of the end of these processes [*CW* 1202–1203].)

1.11.27a *Tales dicuntur boni [primo Ethicorum] per se.* Aristotle, *Ethica Nicomachea* 1.12 (Bekker 1101b30), translated by R. Grosseteste, *AL* 26.1–3, fasc. 3, p. 159, line 18, or the anonymous reviser, fasc. 4, p. 392, line 14: "Talem autem esse deum et per se bonum" ([Eudoxius ... thought] that this is what God and the good are [*CW* 1740]). This citation is recalled in 1.14.8.

1.11.27b *Primo Politicorum dicuntur domini per naturam.* Aristotle, *Politics* 1.6 (Bekker 1255b), G. de Moerbeke, translatio imperfecta, *AL* 29.1, p. 11, line 11: "Quod quidem igitur habet quandam rationem dubitatio, et non sunt hii quidem natura servi, hii autem liberi, palam; et quod in quibusdam determinatum est quod tale, eo quod expediat huic quidem servire, huic autem dominari, et iustum est, et oportet hoc quidem subici, hoc autem principari, ad quem nati sunt principari, quare et dominari." (We see then that there is some foundation for this difference of opinion, and that all are not either slaves by nature or freemen by nature, and also that there is in some cases a marked distinction between the two classes, rendering it expedient and right for the one to be slaves and the others to be masters: the one practising obedience, the others exercising the authority and lordship which nature intended them to have [*CW* 1992].)

1.11.29a *Primo Ethicorum dicuntur tales viri inutiles.* Aristotle, *Ethica Nicomachaea* 1.2 (Bekker 1095b11–12), translated by R. Grosseteste, *AL* 26.1–3, fasc. 3,

p. 145, lines 1–2, or the anonymous reviser, fasc. 4, p. 378, lines 15–17: "Qui autem neque ipsemet intelligit, neque alium audiens in animo ponet, hic rursus inutilis vir." (But he who neither knows, nor lays to heart / Another's wisdom, is a useless wight [*CW* 1731].)

1.11.29b *Servi iudicantur naturaliter.* See 1.6.2, with reference to Aristotle, *Politica.*

Chapter 12

1.12.3 Pseudo-Aristotle, *Physiognomica* 6 (Bekker 814a), ed. R. Förster, *Scriptores Physiognomonici Graeci et Latini*, 1:90; Bertholomaei de Messana Interpretatio Latina, 1:91: "Demonstratus est mas femina iustior et fortior et universaliter dicere melior." (The male is more upright and courageous and, in short, altogether better than the female [*CW* 1249].) Bartholomaeus de Messana was active about 1258–1266. See the *Compendium Auctorum Latinorum Medii Aevi 500–1500*, ed. M. Lapidge and others (Tavarnuzze [Florence], 2000–), 2.1, 20–22.

1.12.6 Aristotle, *Ethica Nichomachea* 8.14 (Bekker 1162a22–23), translated by R. Grosseteste, *AL* 26.1–3, fasc. 3, p. 318, lines 6–8, or the anonymous reviser, fasc. 4, p. 538, lines 13–14: "Confestim enim divisa sunt opera et sunt altera viri et uxoris; sufficiunt igitur ad invicem ad commune ponentes propria." (From the start the functions are divided, and those of man and woman are different; so they help each other by throwing their peculiar gifts into the common stock [*CW* 1836].)

Chapter 13

1.13.2 Aristotle, *De historia animalium* 8.1; the reference is repeated from 1.3.27, which reads "anima puerorum."

1.13.3 *Vulgare proverbium.* Compare Walther 1137: "Ante fuit vitulus, qui nunc fert cornua taurus" (Before it was a calf that now bears horns as a bull). Otto, *Supplement*, 217, cites Seneca, *De beneficiis* 3.27.1 ("Tauri et vituli" [bulls and calves, i.e., men and boys]); and Ovid, *Ars amatoria* 2.341 ("Quem taurum metuis, vitulum mulcere solebas" [He whom you fear as a bull, you once caressed as a calf]). Juan Ruiz, Arcipreste de Hita (1343) in *TPMA*, s.v. "Rind," 2.1.39: "En el becerillo verá home el buey que fará" (In the calf one will see the ox that it will become).

Chapter 14

1.14.2 Walther 25901. Maximian (sixth century), *Elegies* 5.54, ed. W. C. Schneider, *Die elegischen Verse von Maximian: Eine letzte Widerrede gegen die neue christliche Zeit* (Stuttgart, 2003), 187: "Quod natura negat, reddere nemo potest."

(What nature denies, no man can give.) Compare Walther 25900 = Walter of Châtillon, *Alexandreis* 7.339–40, ed. M. L. Colker, *Galteri de Castellione Alexandreis* (Padova, 1978), 187: "Quod natura negat, facinusque paratus ad omne / Non reueretur homo quod fas et iura uerentur." Trans. R. T. Pritchard, *Walter of Châtillon: The Alexandreis* (Toronto, 1986), 171: "That is why we despise the rein of reason and desire what Nature forbids, and why man is ready to commit every wickedness and does not respect what right and justice revere."

1.14.11 *Ad mores tales sunt inutiles.* Aristotle, *Ethica Nicomachea* 4.14 (Bekker 1128b1–4), translated by R. Grosseteste 26.1–3, fasc. 3, p. 224, lines 12–14, or the anonymous reviser, fasc. 4, p. 451, lines 3–4: "Agrios autem ad tales collocuciones inutilis. Nichil enim conferens in omnibus tristatur." (The boor, again, is useless for such social intercourse; for he contributes nothing and finds fault with everything [*CW* 1780].)

1.14.14a *In illis in quibus imperfecte natura perficit et aliquid imperfectum relinquit, ars bene perficit.* Compare Seneca, *Epistles* 5.49.11, ed. Préchac, 2:32: "Dociles natura nos edidit et rationem dedit inperfectam, sed quae perfici posset." (Nature brought us forth easy to teach, and gave us reason which is imperfect but can be perfected.)

1.14.14b *Quod optime dicit Philosophus ...* Aristotle, *Politica* 7.17 (Bekker 1336b), translated by G. de Moerbeke, ed. Susemihl 331, lines 7–8: "Omnis enim ars et disciplina quod deficit naturae vult supplere" (The deficiencies of nature are what art and education seek to fill up [*CW* 2120]).

1.14.16 Galen, *Tegni* 35; ed. Kühn, I, 401: "Eo quem paulo ante diximus modo naturae famulantes." Galen aus Pergamon, *Tegni*, translated by R. Peters, *Über die Heilkunst* (Hamburg, 1978), 109: "Man offenbar auf die kurz zuvor erwähnte Weise der Natur zu Diensten ist." Compare Galen, *In Hippocratis librum de alimento commentarium* 14, ed. Kühn, 15:306: "Natura omnia omnibus sufficit" (Nature provides all things to all).

Chapter 15

1.15.2 *Ut dicit Philosophus in libro* De animalibus, *pater dat formam ... et mater dat materiam corporalem.* Aristotle, *De generatione animalium* 1.20 (Bekker 729a9–11), translated by M. Scot, *De animalibus* 16, ed. A. M. I. van Oppenraaij, *Aristotle,* De animalibus: *Michael Scot's Arabic-Latin Translation* (New York, 1992), 3:48: "Vir dat formam et principium motus et femina dat corpus et materiam." The translation by G. de Moerbeke is not as close: *AL* 17.2.5, p. 35, lines 16–18: "Masculus quidem exhibet speciem et principium motus, femella autem et corpus et materiam." (What the male contributes to generation is the form and the efficient cause, while the female contributes the material [*CW* 1131].) Elsewhere, however, G. de Moerbeke associates *forma* with the father as well as *materia* with the mother. Thus “forma et species ab illo provenit per motum in materia” (Form and species come from him by movement into material), *De generatione* 1.22 (Bekker 730b), *AL* 17.2.5, p. 38, line 22. See also *De generatione animalium* 1.21 (Bekker 729a), *AL* 17.5, p. 36, line 8.

1.15.4 Aristotle, *De generatione animalium* 4.3 (Bekker 768a13–20), translated by G. de Moerbeke, *AL* 17.2.5, p. 129, lines 10–12: “Insunt autem hii quidem motuum actu, hii autem potentia: actu quidem generantis et universalium, puta hominis et animalis, potentia autem qui femelle et progenitorum.” Trans. M. Scot, ed. van Oppenraaij, 3:177–178 (Bekker 768a15–21): “Et similiter accidit in similitudine matrum etiam. Operationes autem non sunt nisi ex motibus et virtutibus, scilicet sicut virtutibus hominum et animalium. Virtus ergo filiorum et patrum et avorum faciunt tales operationes etiam. Et cum movebitur natus et alterabitur etiam movebitur ad contrarium, et virtutes quae creantur movebuntur ad virtutes propinquiores, verbi gratia si fuerit virtus generantis feminam debilis, movebitur ad formam patris, deinde movebitur ad formam lactantis, et forte mutabitur ad formam remotioris.” (Some of the movements exist actually, others potentially; actually, those of the father and the general type, as man and animal; potentially, those of the female and the remoter ancestors [*CW* 1188].) Compare the statement in Book 1.21 (Bekker 730a27), translated by M. Scot, 3:52: “Ex masculo erit principium motus et ex femina erit materia.” Trans. G. de Moerbeke, *AL* 17.2.5, p. 38: “Masculus quidem principium motus, femella autem materiam (The male contributes the principle of movement and the female the material [*CW* 1132–1133]).

1.15.7 Between *paterni motus* and *omnes maternos*, *B* inserts a note in the bottom margin of 319v: “Quintilianus in Institutione Oratoria: Laudatur in quibusdam quod geniti sunt nobiles, in aliis quod nobilitatem virtutis sunt secuti. Pulchrum est respondisse nobilitati, pulchrum genus nobilium humilium factis illustrasse.” (Quintilian in the *Institutio Oratoria*: “Some people are praised because they were born noble, others because they have followed nobility of virtue. It is beautiful to have responded to nobility; it is beautiful to have rendered the birth of humble noblemen illustrious by one’s deeds.”) See Quintilian, *Institutio Oratoria* 3.7.9–10, ed. Russell, 2:106: “Laudandum in quibusdam quod geniti inmortales, quibusdam quod inmortalitatem virtute sint consecuti ... Aut enim respondisse nobilitati pulchrum erit aut humilius genus illustrasse factis.” (Some should be praised because they were born immortal, others because they earned immortality by virtue ... There will be credit either in living up to noble birth or in lending distinction to a humble origin by achievement [trans. Russell]).

Chapter 16

1.16.3 Cited before at 1.10.12.

1.16.5 Aristotle, *Rhetorica* 1.9 (Bekker 1367b12), translated by G. de Moerbeke, *AL* 31.1–2, p. 192, lines 21–22: "Et totaliter autem honorabile inferre in honestum, quoniam videtur vicinum esse." (Everything, in fact, that is esteemed we are to represent as noble. After all, people regard the two things as much the same [*CW* 2176].) The source could also be the Translatio Anonyma, *AL* 31.1–2, p. 39, lines 11–12; but since G. de Moerbeke was the source of the citation at 1.6.12, he probably was also the source here.

1.16.6 Aristotle, *Rhetoric* 1.5.5 (Bekker 1360b32); translated by G. de Moerbeke, *AL* 31.1–2, p. 175, lines 18–20. Cited before at 1.6.12.

Chapter 18

1.18.3 Aristotle, *De historia animalium* 1.1 (Bekker 488b17–20), translated by G. de Moerbeke, *AL* 17.2.1.1, pp. 10–11, lines 145–148: "Hec [animalia] autem liberalia et virilia et eugenea, ut puta leo, hec autem generosa et indomita et insidiosa, puta lupus; eugeneum quidem enim est quod ex bono genere, generosum autem quod non egreditur a propria natura." (Others [other animals] are free and courageous and high-bred, as the lion; others are thorough-bred and wild and treacherous, as the wolf. (An animal is high-bred if it come from a good stock, and an animal is thorough-bred if it does not deflect from its natural characteristics [*CW* 778].) G. de Moerbeke completed his translation around 1262–1263: *AL* 17.2.1.1, p. xvii.

1.18.5 *Disticha Catonis* 3.6, ed. Boas, 159: "Interpone tuis interdum gaudia curis, / ut possis animo quemvis sufferre laborem" (Put joys sometimes among your cares to be able to bear any toil with spirit).

Part 2

Chapter 1

2.1.1 Aristotle, *Metaphysica* 1.1 (Bekker 981a25–981b9), translated by G. de Moerbeke, *AL* 25.3.2, p. 13, lines 47–57: "Sed tamen scire et intelligere magis arte quam experimento esse arbitramur ... Hoc autem est quia hii quidem causam sciunt, illi uero non. Experti quidem enim ipsum quia sciunt, sed propter quid nesciunt; hii autem et propter quid et causam cognoscunt ... et omnino scientis signum est posse docere." (We suppose artists to be wiser than men of experience ...; and this because the former know the cause, but the latter do not. For men of experience know that the thing is so, but do not know why, while the others know the "why" and the cause ... And in general it is a sign of the man who knows, that he can teach [*CW* 1553].) G. de Aragonia may have used any one of the four translations of the *Metaphysics* for this passage.

2.1.2 See the citation from Hermes, *De quindecim stellis*, at 1.3.12.

2.1.3 Compare Plato, *Timaeus*, translated by Chalcidius, *Platonis Timaeus interprete Chalcidio*, ed. J. Wrobel (Leipzig, 1876), 6–7: "Solis his qui pro salute omnium bella tractarent unum hoc munus iniunximus protegendae ciuitatis uel aduersum externos uel aduersum intestinos ac domesticos hostes, mitibus quidem iudiciis erga oboedientes utpote consanguineos naturaque amicos, asperis autem contra armatas acies in congressionibus Martiis. Biformi siquidem natura praeditos: in tutela patriae ciuiumque ferociores, porro in pacis officiis religione sapientes proptereaque mites suis, aduersum alienigenas feroces ... Praediximus ... uti communiter tanta, quanta satis sit occupatis erga custodiam communis salutis et a cetera functione operis cessantibus." (To only those who would wage war for the good of all did we grant this one duty of protecting the city against either external or internal and domestic enemies, with mild judgments toward the obedient, namely toward those related by blood and friends by nature, but with harsh ones against armed troops in martial encounters; we endowed them with a double nature, more harsh in protection of country and citizens, but wise [*sapientes*] in the duties of peace by religion, and therefore mild toward their own, harsh toward foreigners ... We said they should live together with as much [in wages] as suffices for those who occupy themselves with the protection of the common good and abstain from pursuing any other activity.)

2.1.4 Alfraganus or al-Farghani, Arab astronomer, born in Farghana in modern Uzbekistan, died in Egypt after 861 CE. His best-known work, *The Elements of Astronomy*, is a summary of Ptolemy's *Almagest*; he also wrote on the astrolabe. Some of his writings remain unpublished. We have found no reference to a work with the title *Secreta*; compare *secreta*, "secret writings, ciphers" (*OLD*). See Sezgin, *Geschichte des arabischen Schrifttums*, 5:259–260, 6:149–151; *Dictionary of Scientific Biography* (New York, 1970–1990), 4:541–545; *Lexikon des Mittelalters* (Munich, 1980–), 4:298. Colker (72) says that he did not find this passage in *Al Farghani Differentie Scientie Astrorum*, ed. F. J. Carmody (Berkeley, 1943).

2.1.5 *Sapiens ... diligit Deum.* Augustine, *The City of God Against the Pagans* 8.5, ed. D. S. Wiesen (Cambridge, Mass., 1968), 3:22: "Si ergo Plato Dei huius imitatorem cognitorem amatorem dixit esse sapientem, cuius participatione sit beatus ..." (If Plato, therefore, has declared that the wise man imitates, knows and loves this God and is blessed through fellowship with him ... [trans. Wiesen]). Wiesen annotates this view in Minucius Felix and in Augustine, *De vera religione*, but not in Plato. John of Salisbury, *Policraticus*, ed. C. C. I. Webb (Oxford, 1909), 2:119, lines 30–31: "Cum enim Plato sapientem dicat esse cultorem Dei ..." (Since Plato says the wise man is a worshipper of God ...). Pseudo-Walter Burley, *Liber de vita et moribus philosophorum* 52 (Plato), ed. Knust, 226: "Ideoque non dubitat hoc esse philosophari: amare Deum." (And therefore he [Plato] does not doubt that this is what it is to be a philosopher: to love God.)

2.1.6 Partial, rather distant analogue: *Solomon and Marcolf* (end of the twelfth or beginning of the thirteenth century?), ed. J. M. Ziolkowski (Cambridge, Mass., 2008), 68, Dialogus 108a: "Cor mundum nichil timet" (A pure heart fears nothing).

2.1.7 Phaedrus, *Fabulae* 3.10.1 (first century CE), in *TPMA*, s.v. "Glauben," 2.3.162: *Periculosum est credere et non credere.* "It is dangerous to believe and not to believe." Compare Seneca, *Epistles* 1.3.4, ed. Préchac, 1:9: "Utrumque enim uitium est, et omnibus credere et nulli." (It is a vice either to believe everyone or no one.) Pseudo-Seneca, *De moribus liber* (before 567 CE) 77, in *TPMA*, s.v. "Glauben," 2.3.164: "Vitium est omnia credere, vitium nihil credere" (It is a vice to believe all things, a vice to believe nothing). Hildebert de Lavardin (d. 1133), *Epistles* 334, in *TPMA*, s.v. "Glauben," 2.3.165: "Sicut Seneca testatur, et omni et nulli credere vitium est." (As Seneca attests, it is a vice to believe all and none.) Wace, *Roman de Brut* (1155) 8760, Morawski 1389: "Ne tut creire ne tut mescreire" (Neither believe everything nor disbelieve everything). *Auctoritates* 21.13: "Utrumque est vitium omni credere et nulli." (It is a vice either to believe everyone or no one.)

2.1.8 Compare Boethius, *Philosophiae consolatio* 4.6.52, ed. Bieler, 83: "Sola est enim diuina uis cui mala quoque bona sint, cum eis competenter utendo alicuius boni elicit effectum." Trans. I.T. (1609), rev. Stewart, 351: "For it is only a divine strength to which even evil things are good, when, by using them in due sort, it draweth some good effect out of them."

2.1.9 In several biblical passages it is God, not the wise man, who is said to behold the earth. Proverbs 5:21: "Respicit Dominus vias hominis et omnes gressus illius considerat." (The Lord beholdeth all the ways of man and considereth all his steps [DV].) Psalms 103:32: "Qui respicit terram, et facit eam tremere; qui tangit montes, et fumigant." (He looketh upon the earth, and maketh it tremble; he toucheth the mountains, and they smoke [DV].) Psalms 112:5–6: "Quis sicut Dominus Deus noster, qui in altis habitat, et humilia respicit in caelo et in terra?" (Who is as the Lord our God, who dwelleth on high, and looketh down on the low things in heaven and in earth? [DV])

2.1.10 For a partial analogue, see Werner Q 109: "Qui noscit sese, homo prudens noscitur esse." (He who knows himself is known to be a prudent man.)

Chapter 2

2.2.1 *Cl. Ptolemei Alexandrini Astronomorum Principis Almagesti seu Magne Constructionis Liber* (Venice, 1515), f. 1r: "Insipiens est qui sui ipsius ignorat quantitatem." Pseudo-Walter Burley, *Liber de vita et moribus philosophorum* 121 (Ptolomeus), ed. Knust, 372: "Insipiens est qui sui ipsius quantitatem ignorat."

2.2.2 Proverbs 18:13: "Qui prius respondet quam audiat, stultum se esse demonstrat et confusione dignum" (He that answereth before he heareth sheweth himself to be a fool and worthy of confusion" [DV]).

2.2.3 Ennius quoted by Cicero, *De republica* 1.18.30 and *De divinatione* 2.13.30: "Quod est ante pedes nemo spectat" (No one looks at what is before his feet). Cicero, *Tusculanae disputationes* 5.39.114: "Alii saepe, quod ante pedes esset, non viderent" (Some people often do not see what is before their feet). Lactantius, *Institutiones divinae* 2.3.16: "Non prospexerunt quid ante pedes suos esset" (They did not see what was before their feet). For these sources see Otto, no. 1389, 274; *Nachträge*, 200.

2.2.4 *Der lateinische Aesop des Romulus und die Prosa-Fassungen des Phädrus* (350–500 CE), in *TPMA*, s.v. "Reue," 1.1.1.1: "Sed post inrecuperabile factum quid iuvat paenitere?" (But after an irrecuperable event, what does it help to repent?) Guilhem de Cabestanh (after 1197), in *TPMA*, s.v. "Reue," 1.1.1.8: "E pent s'om tart pueys quan a pres lo dan" (And one repents [too] late, when one has had the harm). *Gesta Romanorum* (end of the thirteenth century), in *TPMA*, s.v. "Reue," 1.1.1.2: "Post factum non penitebis" (After the event you shall not repent). *Proverbe au villain*, no. 241, ed. A. Tobler (Leipzig, 1895), 100: "Fous est qui met s'entente, / Tant que il se repente." (He is a fool who directs his will until he repents).

2.2.5 Compare Augustine, Sermon 150, *PL* 38, 813, line 15: "Non eris inter illos qui cognoscentes deum, non sicut deum glorificauerunt, aut gratias egerunt, sed euanuerunt in cogitationibus suis, et obscuratum est insipiens cor ipsorum: dicentes enim se esse sapientes stulti facti sunt." (You will not be among those who, knowing God, did not thus glorify God or give thanks, but disappeared into their thoughts, and their unknowing heart was darkened; saying they were wise, they became fools.) Compare Psalms 13:1: "Dixit insipiens in corde suo: Non est Deus." (The fool hath said in his heart: There is no God" [DV].)

2.2.6 We have not found this sentence attributed elsewhere to Demosthenes. Compare Boethius, *Philosophiae consolatio* 1.3.14, ed. Bieler, 6: "At nos desuper irridemus uilissima rerum quaeque rapientes securi totius furiosi tumultus eoque uallo muniti quo grassanti stultitiae adspirare fas non sit." (But we, from above, laugh at them who grasp for the vilest of things, safe as we are from all their furious tumult and defended by that wall which loitering folly may not even approach.) Werner S 33: "Saepius occurrit, quod stulti decipiuntur, / Dum res pro rebus caute minus accipiuntur" (It often happens that fools are deceived when they incautiously take one thing for another). Compare 2.2.7.

2.2.7 Proverbs 6:16–18: "Sex sunt quae odit Dominus, et septimum detestatur anima eius; oculos sublimes, linguam mendacem, manus effundentes, innoxium sanguinem, cor machinans cogitationes pessimas, pedes veloces ad currendum in malum." (Six things there are, which the Lord hateth, and the seventh his soul detesteth: Haughty eyes, a lying tongue, hands that shed innocent blood, A heart that deviseth wicked plots, feet that are swift to run into mischief [DV]).

2.2.8 Compare Augustine, Sermon 250, *Sermons pour la Pâque*, ed. S. Poque (Paris, 1966), 312, line 57: "Male uiuentium multitudo turbat bene uiuentes ita perturbat, ut qui bene uiuit, stultum se esse putet." (The throng of those living badly disturbs those living well, so perturbs them that he who lives well may think he is a fool.) Morawski, 766: "Fous aime tençon" (A fool loves a quarrel).

2.2.9 Compare Walther 25460: "Quis vere stultus? Stultitiam peragens." (Who is truly foolish? One who carries his folly through to the end.) Marcabru (fl. 1130–1148) 30.78, in *TPMA*, s.v. "Narr," 2.6.131: "Mas segon dreitura / cerca fols sa follatura" (But by rights a fool seeks his folly). Bernart de Ventadorn (fl. 1150–1180 [?]) 42.29, in *TPMA*, s.v. "Narr," 2.6.132: "Mas costum' es tostemps que fols foleya" (But it is always the custom that a fool acts foolish). *Girart de Rossillon* (1155–1180) 5445, in *TPMA*, s.v. "Narr," 2.6.123: "Mais dreiz est e costume ke fouz folei" (But it is right and customary that a fool acts foolish).

2.2.10 Compare Lactantius, *Divinae institutiones* 3.6.8, in *LLT*, 188, line 16: "Arcesilas uidit adrogantes uel potius stultos esse qui putent scientiam ueritatis coniectura posse conprehendi" (Arcesilas saw that they were arrogant, or rather fools, who think knowledge of truth can be comprehended by conjecture). Werner S 196: "Stultus stultitiam semper putat esse sophiam" (A fool always thinks folly is wisdom).

Chapter 3

2.3.1 *Fulco Marsiliensis*. See "Troubadours" in the Introduction.

2.3.2 Anonymous, *De physiognomia liber* par. 11; R. Förster, *Scriptores physiognomonici Graeci et Latini*, 2:21: "Unde medium temperamentum corporis perfectum animum indicat, is autem perfectus est animus, qui pari virtute est atque sapientia." (So a medium temperament of the body indicates a perfect mind: the mind is perfect which is of equal virtue and wisdom.) Förster, 1:cxli, dates the *De physiognomia* in the late fourth century CE.

2.3.3 Cicero, *De oratore* 3.5.221, in *TPMA*, s.v. "Gesicht," 2.5: "Imago animi voltus, indices oculi" (The face is the image of the mind, the eyes its signs). Eugenius Toletensis (d. 657 CE), *Carmina* 81.2, in *TPMA*, s.v. "Gesicht," 2.8: "Qualis vultus erit, talia corda gerit" (As is the face, so is the intention). Werner V 145: "Vultu talis eris, qualia mente geris" (You will be such in your face as you bear in your mind). Walther 8018.

2.3.4 Werner D 121 (*vultum*). Walther 6026 (*vultum*).

2.3.5 *Petrus Vitalis*. See "Troubadours."

2.3.6 *Arnoldus*. See "Troubadours."

2.3.7 *Gaufridus Rodel*. See "Troubadours."

2.3.8 *Odantagalus*. See "Troubadours."

Chapter 4

2.4.11 Aristotle, *Topica* 1.17 (Bekker 108a10), Translatio Anonyma, *AL* 5.1–3, p. 206, line 27: "Sicut visio in oculo, intellectus in anima" (As sight is in the eye, so is intellect in the soul [*CW* 179]). The Translatio Anonyma was completed in 1120–1160: *AL* 5.1–3, p. xlvii. The translation by Boethius does not match as closely, substituting *mens* for *intellectus*. *AL* 5.1–3, p. 27, lines 15–16: "ut quemadmodum visus in oculo, mens in anima."

2.4.13 Walther 12215: "Inconstans animus, oculus vagus, instabilis pes: / Hec tria sunt hominis, de quo mihi nulla boni spes." (An inconstant mind, a roving eye, a wandering foot: these are three things of a man in whom I have no hope of good.) Walther 12214: "Inconstans animus, oculus vagus, instabilis pes: / Hec sunt signa satis corrupte virginitatis." (An inconstant mind, a roving eye, a wandering foot: these are signs enough of a corrupted virginity.)

2.4.14 *Inverecundum vel luxuriosum*. Compare Pliny, *Historia naturalis* 11.94.276, trans. H. Rackham (Cambridge, Mass., 1969–1989), 3:606–607: "Oculi quibus utrimque sunt longi malificos moribus esse indicant; qui carnosos a naribus angulos habent malitiae notam praebent." (If people's eyes are narrow on both sides, this shows them to be malicious in character; eyes that have fleshy corners on the side of the nostrils show a mark of maliciousness [trans. Rackham]).

2.4.17 *Montaneolus.* See "Troubadours."

Chapter 5

2.5.3 *Probos viros habere in suis consiliis.* Pseudo-Aristotle, *Rhetorica ad Alexandrum* (Bekker 1428b33–1429a21), Version Alpha: Grabmann 43: "Oportet te ... ostendere alios tuos amicos modestos existentes. Sic enim amphibologicum facies id, quod accusatur." Version Beta: Stapleton 181, fol. 41vb.35–38: "et ostendere oportet amicorum tuorum alios modestos existentes, sic enim amphibologicam facies acusationem." (You must show that others of your associates are honest men; you will thus throw doubt on the crime of which you are accused [*CW* 2284].)

2.5.4 The *Disticha Catonis* 3.10, ed. Boas, 164, read *tempseris*, "despise," for *spreveris*, but the latter occurs as a variant (Boas, 166).

2.5.5 The *Disticha Catonis* warn against avarice at 4.1 and 4.16 ("fuge nomen avari" [flee the name of miser], ed. Boas, 194 and 211) but do so without reference to greedy princes. Compare Cicero, *De officiis* 2.22.77, ed. W. Miller (Cambridge, 1968), 252: "Nullum igitur vitium taetrius est ... quam avaritia, praesertim in principibus et rem publicam gubernantibus" (Therefore no vice is more offensive ... than avarice, especially in princes and those who govern the republic). *Garin le Loherain* (end twelfth century), 1.239, in *TPMA*, s.v. "Herr," 4.4.2.144: "Nuns avers princes ne puet monter en pris" (No greedy prince can rise in merit). *Prise de Defur* (before 1257), 69, in *TPMA*, s.v. "Geiz," 6.1.262: "Ne doit on laissier terre a aver n'a felon" (One must not leave land to a greedy man or a felon). Ibid., 160, in *TPMA*, s.v. "Geiz," 6.1.263: "Mauvais hons ne avers ne doit terre tenir" (A bad man or a greedy one must not hold land).

2.5.6 Thus Aristotle speaks to his pupil Alexander in Walter of Châtillon, *Alexandreis* 1.111–114, ed. Colker, 13: "Cum semel obtinuit uiciorum mater in aula / Pestis auaritiae, que sola incarcerat omnes / Virtutum species, spreto moderamine iuris / Curritur in facinus, nec leges curia curat." Trans. Pritchard, 39: "When once that pest avarice, mother of vices, who alone imprisons every kind of virtue, has gained a foothold in a hall, men rush into evil, despising the controlling hand of justice, and the court shows no regard for the laws." Verse 114 = Walther 4789a.

2.5.7 Aristotle continues to lecture Alexander in Walter of Châtillon, *Alexandreis* 1.158, ed. Colker, 15: "Non opus est uallo quos dextera dapsilis ambit." Trans. Pritchard, 40: "Those whom a generous right hand encompasses have no need of a rampart."

2.5.8 For a similar thought in a German proverb, compare Freidank (fl. 1220–1230) in *TPMA*, 4.194, no. 184: "Reiniu milte nie verdarp, / Sô erge manege schande erwarp." (Pure generosity has never come to harm, though greed has suffered many setbacks.)

Chapter 6

2.6.2 Compare *Disticha Catonis* 3.10, ed. Boas, 164: "Utile consilium dominus ne despice servi; / nullius sensum, si prodest, tempseris unquam." (As a lord, do not despise the useful counsel of a slave; never scorn anyone's opinion, if it is good.) Already quoted above, at 2.5.4.

2.6.3 In the same general vein but without the image, compare Horace, *Epistles* 1.17.35, ed. Fairclough, 362: "Principibus placuisse viris non ultima laus est" (To have pleased their princes is not the least praise for men).

2.6.4 Compare Aristotle, *Rhetorica* 2.3 (Bekker 1380a15–17); translated by G. de Moerbeke, *AL* 31.1–2, p. 226, lines 16–19: "Signum autem in servorum castigatione; negantes quidem enim et contradicentes magis flagellamus." (The punishment of servants shows this: those who contradict us and deny their offence we punish all the more [*CW* 2198].) Compare *Auctoritates* 16.36: "Servos arrogantes et contradicentes magis flagellamus." (Servants who are arrogant and contradictory we whip all the more.) Guilhem Molinier, *Leys d'amors* 4, ed. A. F. Gatien-Arnoult, *Monumens de la littérature romane* (Toulouse, 1841–1849), 3:276: "Ergulhezir fas to sirven / Si.l tenes delicadamen" (You make your servant grow proud if you treat him gently).

2.6.5 We have not found this thought in Seneca, whose name often stands for proverbial lore in general. A. Hilka, "Altfranzösische Sprichwörter" (circa 1250–1300), *Jahresbericht der Schlesischen Gesellschaft für vaterländische Cultur* 1913, vol. 1, Part 4c, 21ff., v. 107: "Pigrum mancipium dat satis augurium" (A lazy servant gives good augury). Morawski, 1811: "Qui a mauvays serjant si a bon devin" (He who has a bad servant has a good augur).

2.6.6 *Petrus Vitalis*. See "Troubadours."

Chapter 7

2.7.4 Cicero, *Tusculanae disputationes* 5.92, ed. J. E. King (Cambridge, Mass., 1966), 518: "Et hic [Diogenes] quidem disputare solebat quanto regem Persarum vita fortunaque superaret: sibi nihil deesse, illi nihil satis umquam fore." (And in fact Diogenes, to show how far superior he was to the king of Persia in the conditions of his life, used to argue that while he had no needs, nothing would ever be enough for the king.) Seneca, *De beneficiis* 5.4.4, in *Seneca: Moral Essays*, trans. J. W. Basore (Cambridge, Mass., 1928–1935), 3:298: "[Diogenes] multo potentior, multo locupletior fuit omnia tunc possidente Alexandro; plus enim erat, quod hic nollet accipere, quam quod ille posset dare." (Far more powerful, far richer was he than Alexander, who then was master of the whole world; for what Diogenes refused to receive was even more than Alexander was able to give [trans. Basore]). Pseudo-Walter Burley, *Liber de vita et moribus philosophorum* 50 (Diogenes), ed. Knust, 198–200: "Dicebat enim Diogenes, ut dicit Tullius in libro .V. de Tusculanis questionibus, se vita et fortuna regem persarum superare eo quod sibi nil deesset, illi autem satis numquam foret." (Diogenes said, as Cicero says in Book V of the *Tusculan Disputations*, that he surpassed the king of the Persians in life and fortune, since he felt he lacked nothing, but the king never had enough.)

2.7.5 Ptolemy, *Almagestu[m] Cl. Ptolemei: Pheludiensis Alexandrini astronomo[rum] principis* (Venice, 1515), fol. 1r: "Non fuit mortuus qui scientiam vivificavit, nec fuit pauper qui intellectui dominatus est." (He was not dead who kept knowledge alive, nor was he poor who was master of the intellect.) Pseudo-Walter Burley, *Liber de vita et moribus philosophorum* 121 (Ptolomeus), ed. Knust, 372: "Pauper non est qui suo intellectui dominatur" (He is not poor who is master of his intellect).

2.7.6 *Disticha Catonis* 4.5, ed. Boas, 199: "Cum fueris locuples, corpus curare memento: / aeger dives habet nummos, se non habet ipsum." (When you are rich, remember to take care of your body: a sick, rich man owns coins, but does not own himself.)

2.7.7 Boethius, *Philosophiae consolatio* 3.5.13, ed. Bieler, 45: "An praesidio sunt amici quos non uirtus sed fortuna conciliat? Sed quem felicitas amicum fecit infortunium faciet inimicum." (Are they friends in support, whom not [our] virtue but [our] fortune brings [to us]? But whom prosperity made a friend, adversity will make an enemy.)

2.7.8 Dionysius the Pseudo-Areopagite, *De divinis nominibus* 4.18, *Dionysiaca: Recueil donnant l'ensemble des traductions latines des ouvrages attribués au Denys d'Areopage*, ed. Ph. Chevalier (Bruges, 1937–1950), 1:185, as translated by Jean le Sarrazin (ca. 1167): "Bonum et pulchrum secundum omnem causam cuncta desiderant, et non est aliquid exsistentium quod non participet pulchro et bono." Or as translated by R. Grosseteste (ca. 1235): "Bonum et pulchrum secundum omnem causam omnia appetunt, et non est aliquid entium quod non pulchro participet et bono." Trans. Chevalier: "Toutes choses demandent de toutes manières et le beau et le bon, et il n'est pas un être qui n'ait part au beau et au bon."

2.7.9 Werner L 9: "Laetitia plenus sine re fit divus egenus." (The poor man, full of joy without a thing, becomes rich.) Girard Pateg (ca. 1200–1250), *Splanamento de li Proverbi de Salamone*, in Contini, *Poeti del Duecento*, 1:576,

vv. 413–414: “Miei è un pover om a cui plas quel q’el à, / qe un rico qe vol tuto quant el vedhrá” (Better off is a poor man who is pleased by what he has than a rich man who wants everything he sees). *Trattato di Virtù* (ca. 1300), in *TPMA*, s.v. “Reich,” 5.2.1.190: “Ma quelli è ricco, che si chiama contento di ciò ch’elli àe” (He is rich who calls himself happy with what he has). Compare 2.8.4, 2.8.11.

Chapter 8

2.8.2 Pseudo-Aristotle, *Rhetorica ad Alexandrum* 18 (Bekker 1433a2), Version Alpha: Grabmann 55: “Fortassis plorabit suam penuriam, cuius non ego, sed hujus modus causa erit.” Version Beta: Stapleton 198, f. 44ra17–19: “Forsitan quidem suam penuriam plorat, cuius non ego, sed huius modus causa est.” (You can say: “Perhaps he will bewail his poverty, which is not my fault but has been caused by his own way of life” [*CW* 2291].) Pseudo-Walter Burley, *Liber de vita et moribus philosophorum* 53 (Aristotiles), ed. Knust, 238: “[Aristotiles] dicebat eciam unum se solum incommodum paupertatis pati quod non posset egentibus subvenire” ([Aristotle] said he felt only one disadvantage of poverty: that he could not help those in need).

2.8.4 Seneca, *Epistles* 1.2.6, ed. Préchac, 1:7: “Non qui parum habet, sed qui plus cupit, pauper est” (Not he who has little, but who wants more, is poor). Walther 20912: “Pauper est, cui sua non sufficiunt” (A poor man is one for whom his [possessions] are not enough). *Auctoritates* 21.11: “Non qui parum habet est pauper, sed qui plus cupit” (Not he who has little is poor, but he who wants more). Morawski, 2013: “Qui n’a soufisance il n’a rien” (He who has not enough has nothing). Compare *TPMA*, s.v. “Genug,” 1.4.1.

2.8.5 Compare John of Salisbury, *Policraticus* 8.16, ed. C. C. I. Webb, 2:340, lines 31–32: “Diogenes ait: Indigentia naturae fortunam non timet” (Diogenes says, “Nature’s indigence does not fear fortune”).

2.8.6 Boethius, *Philosophiae consolatio* 2.5.35, ed. Bieler 28. Quoted before in 1.7.14.

2.8.7 Juvenal, *Satires* 10.22, *Juvenal and Persius*, ed. S. M. Braund (Cambridge, Mass., 2004), 368, reading *cantabit*; “A traveller who is empty-handed can sing in the mugger’s face,” Braund, 369. Boethius, *Philosophiae consolatio* 2.5.34, ed. Bieler, 28: “Tu igitur, qui nunc contum gladiumque sollicitus pertimescis, si uitae huius callem uacuus uiator intrasses coram latrone cantares.” *The Consolation of Philosophy*, trans. I.T. (1609), rev. H. F. Stewart (Cambridge, Mass., 1962), 203–205: “Wherefore thou, who with much perturbation fearest now to be assailed and slain, if thous hadst entered the path of this life like a poor passenger, needest not be afraid, but mightest rejoice and sing even in the sight of most ravenous thieves.” Immediately precedes the citation in 2.8.6. The Boethian sentence is quoted in *Auctoritates* 25.24.

2.8.8 *Disticha Catonis* 1.21, ed. Boas, 57, reads *crearit* with the variant *creavit*.

2.8.9 *Disticha Catonis* 4.4, ed. Boas, 197: "Dilige denarium, sed parce dilige formam, / quam nemo sanctus nec honestus captat habere." (Love money, but love its beauty sparingly, which no holy or honest man strives to get.)

2.8.10 *Unde Salomon* ... Wisdom 7:11: "Venerunt autem mihi omnia bona pariter cum illa et innumerabilis honestas per manus illius" (Now all good things came to me together with her [the spirit of wisdom], and innumerable riches through her hands" [DV]).

2.8.11 Horace, *Epistles* 1.12.4, ed. Fairclough, 328: "Pauper enim non est cui rerum suppetit usus."

Chapter 9

2.9.2 Valerius Maximus 7.2, ext. 1b, ed. Shackleton Bailey, 2:114: "Idem [Socrates] expedita et compendiaria via eos ad gloriam pervenire dicebat qui id agerent ut quales videri vellent, tales etiam essent" ([Socrates] would say that by a clear and short path they come to glory who act so as to be as they wish to seem).

2.9.3 Cicero, *De officiis* 2.12.43, ed. W. Miller (Cambridge, Mass., 1968), 210: "Socrates hanc viam ad gloriam proximam et quasi compendiariam dicebat esse, si quis id ageret, ut, qualis haberi vellet, talis esset" (Socrates used to say that the nearest way to glory, almost a short cut, is to act so as to be as you would like to be thought).

2.9.4 Horace, *Epistles* 1.16.17, ed. Fairclough, 352. Cited before at 1.8.5; here with an interpolated comment.

Chapter 10

2.10.3 *Disticha Catonis* 2.16.1, ed. Boas, 117. Cited before at 1.8.10.

2.10.4 Seneca, *Epistles* 2.20.2, ed. Préchac, 1:81: "Aliud propositum est declamantibus et adsensionem coronae captantibus; aliud his, qui iuuenum et otiosorum aures disputatione uaria aut uolubili detinent." (They have another purpose, the declaimers and those striving to capture the consent of their circle, and they another who hold the attention of the young and idle with a varied and voluble disputation.) The passage continues as cited at 2.10.5b, below.

2.10.5a [*Plato*] is lacking in P_1BS (*Quare dicit*) and in P_2KR (*Quare ipse dicit*). Plato, *Republic* 6.488b, in Plato, *CD* 724: "Conceive the sailors to be wrangling with one another for control of the helm, each claiming that it is his right to steer though he has never learned the art." Cicero, *De officiis* 1.25.87, ed.

Miller, 88: "Praeclare apud eundem est Platonem, similiter facere eos, qui inter se contenderent, uter potius rem publicam administraret, ut si nautae certarent, quis eorum potissimum gubernaret." (Concerning this also we find a fine thought in Plato: "Those who compete against one another," he says, "to see which of two candidates shall administer the government, are like sailors quarrelling as to which one of them shall do the steering" [trans. Miller].) John of Salisbury, *Policraticus* 5.11, ed. C. C. I. Webb, 1:331, lines 23–27: "Vnde et Plato egregie quidem et luculenter (si tamen audiatur) eos qui de rei publicae gerendo magistratu contendunt, ita inter se uersari asserit ut si nautae sub adversa tempestate decertent quis eorum debeat potissimum gubernare." (So also Plato asserts uncommonly well and indeed excellently, if it may be heard, that those who contend over the office of governing the republic act like sailors who dispute, before a threatening storm, over which of them should steer the ship.) Others understand that the implicit subject of *dicit* is Seneca, as before and after. Colker (78) calls attention to Seneca, *Epistles* 11.85.30–37, ed. Préchac, 3:134–136, where Seneca discusses the pilot threatened by a storm; but Seneca defends the pilot (*Epistle* 11.85.33) rather than accusing him of vainglory, as here; nor does he speak of a pilot who chatters about steering the ship and then pilots it to disaster. The text without emendation ("Quare dicit quod similes sunt naute ...") would translate "so that he [Seneca] says that they are like a sailor," and so forth. Since Seneca does not say this, however, and Plato does, we emend to "Quare [Plato] dicit quod similes sunt naute." For further discussion, see "Affiliations" in the Introduction.

2.10.5b *Ipse dicit quod homo debet facere et non loqui.* Seneca, *Epistles* 2.20.2, ed. Préchac, 1:81: "Facere docet philosophia, non dicere" (Philosophy teaches to act, not to speak).

Bibliography

Primary Sources

Alanus de Insulis. *De fide catholica contra haereticos*. *PL* 210.305–430.

Algazel. "Logica Algazelis: Introduction and Critical Text." Edited by Charles H. Lohr. *Traditio* 21 (1965): 223–290.

Andreas Capellanus on Love. Edited by P. G. Walsh. London: Duckworth, 1982.

Anthologia latina. Edited by Franz Bücheler and Alexander Riese. 2 vols. in 4. Leipzig, 1894–1906. Reprint, Amsterdam: Hakkert, 1972–1973.

Aristoteles Latinus. Categoriarum supplementa: Porphyrii Isagoge, translatio Boethii, et anonymi fragmentum vulgo vocatum "Liber sex principiorum." Edited by Lorenzo Minio-Paluello and Bernard G. Dod. Bruges: Desclée de Brouwer, 1966. *AL* 1.6–7.

———. *De anima: Iacobus Veneticus translator Aristotelis*. Edited by J. Decorte and J. Brams. *AL* 12.1 [*ALD*], 2006.

———. *De generatione animalium: Translatio Guillelmi de Moerbeka*. Edited by H. J. Drossaart Lulofs. Bruges: Desclée de Brouwer, 1966. *AL* 17.2.5.

———. *De historia animalium, Lib. I–V: Translatio Guillelmi de Morbeka*. Edited by Pieter Beullens and Fernand Bossier. Leiden: Brill, 2000. *AL* 17.2.1.1.

———. *Ethica Nicomachea*. Edited by Renatus Antonius Gauthier. 5 vols. Leiden: Brill; Brussels: Desclée de Brouwer, 1972–1974. *AL* 26.1–3.

———. *Metaphysica Lib. I–XIV: Recensio et translatio Guillelmi de Moerbeka*. Edited by Gudrun Vuillemin-Diem. 2 vols. Leiden: Brill, 1995. *AL* 25.3.

———. *Physica: Translatio Vaticana*. Edited by Augustinus Mansion. Bruges: Desclée de Brouwer, 1957. *AL* 7.2.

———. *Physica: Translatio Vetus*. Edited by Fernand Bossier and Jozef Brams. Leiden: Brill, 1990. *AL* 7.1.2.

———. *Politica (Libri I–II.11): Translatio prior imperfecta interprete Guillelmo de Moerbeka (?)*. Edited by Petrus Michaud-Quantin. Bruges-Paris: Desclée de Brouwer, 1961. *AL* 29.1.

———. [*Politica*]. *Aristotelis Politicorum libri octo cum vetusta translatione Guilelmi de Moerbeka*. Edited by Franz Susemihl. Leipzig: Teubner, 1872. *AL* 29.2.

———. *Rhetorica: Translatio anonyma sive vetus et translatio Guillelmi de Moerbeka*. Edited by Bernhardus Schneider. Leiden: Brill, 1978. *AL* 31.1–2.

———. *Topica: Translatio Boethii, Fragmentum recensionis alteris, et Translatio anonyma*. Edited by Laurentius Minio-Paluello and Bernardus G. Dod. Brussels: Desclée de Brouwer, 1969. *AL* 5.1–3.

Aristotle. *De animalibus: Michael Scot's Arabic-Latin Translation. Part Three: Books XV–XIX: Generation of Animals*. Edited by Aafke M. I. van Oppenraaij. Aristoteles Semitico-Latinus 5. New York: Brill, 1992.

———. *Nicomachean Ethics*. Translated by Martin Ostwald. Library of Liberal Arts. Indianapolis: Bobbs-Merrill, 1962.

Aristotle (Pseudo-). *Eine lateinische Übersetzung der pseudo-aristotelischen Rhetorica ad Alexandrum aus dem 13. Jahrhundert*. Edited by Martin Grabmann. Munich: Bayerische Akademie der Wisssenschaften, 1932.

———. *Rhetorica ad Alexandrum. A Latin Translation of the Rhetorica ad Alexandrum from the Thirteenth Century*. Edited by Patricia Alice Stapleton. Dissertation, University of Illinois, 1977.

Arnaut de Mareuil. *Les Poésies du troubadour Arnaut de Mareuil*. Edited by R. C. Johnston. Paris: E. Droz, 1935.

At de Mons. *Die Werke des Trobadors N'At de Mons*. Edited by Wilhelm Bernhardt. Heilbronn: Henninger, 1887.

Augustine. *The City of God against the Pagans*. Translated by G. E. McCracken, W. M. Green, D. S. Wiesen, P. Levine, E. M. Sanford, W. C. Greene. Loeb Classical Library 411–417. 7 vols. Cambridge, Mass.: Harvard University Press, 1957–1972.

———. *Sermons pour la Pâque*. Edited by Suzanne Poque. Sources Chrétiennes 116. Paris: Éditions du Cerf, 1966.

Boethius. *Boetii De consolatione philosophiae, with the English Version Ascribed to Chaucer . . . A Reproduction of MS Ii.3.21 in the Cambridge University Library*. 2 vols. Modern Language Association of America Collection of Photographic Facsimiles no. 73. Washington, D.C.: Modern Language Association, 1928.

———. *Philosophiae consolatio*. Edited by Ludwig Bieler. Corpus Christianorum Series latina 94. Turnholt: Brepols, 1957.

———. *The Theological Tractates: The Consolation of Philosophy*. Translated by I. T. (1609). Rev. H. F. Stewart. Loeb Classical Library 74. Cambridge, Mass.: Harvard University Press, 1962.

Boetius Dacius. "Opusculum Magistri Boetii Daci: De summo bono sive de vita philosophi." In *Mittelalterliches Geistesleben*, edited by Martin Grabmann, vol. 2, 209–216. Munich: M. Hueber, 1936.

Brunetto Latini. *The Book of the Treasure (Li Livres dou Tresor)*. Translated by Paul Barrette and Spurgeon Baldwin. New York: Garland, 1993.

———. *Li Livres dou Tresor*. Edited by Spurgeon Baldwin and Paul Barrette. Tempe, Ariz.: Arizona Center for Medieval and Renaissance Studies, 2003.

———. *Text and Concordance of the Aragonese Translation of Brunetto Latini's "Li livres dou tresor": Gerona Cathedral, MS 20-a-5*. Edited by Dawn Prince. Four microfiches plus guide. Madison, Wis.: Hispanic Seminary of Medieval Studies, 1990.

Cerverí de Girona. *Obras completas del trovador Cerverí de Girona*. Edited by Martín de Riquer. Barcelona: Instituto Español de Estudios Mediterráneos, 1947.

Cicero. *De officiis*. Translated by Walter Miller. Loeb Classical Library 30. Cambridge, Mass.: Harvard University Press, 1968.

———. *Tusculanae Disputationes*. Edited by J. E. King. Loeb Classical Library 141. Cambridge, Mass.: Harvard University Press, 1966.

Dante Alighieri. *The Banquet*. Translated by Christopher Ryan. Saratoga, Calif.: ANMA Libri, 1989.

———. *De vulgari eloquentia*. Edited and translated by Steven Botterill. Cambridge Medieval Classics 5. Cambridge: Cambridge University Press, 1996.

———. *Monarchia*. Edited by Pier Giorgio Ricci. Milan: Mondadori, 1965.

Daude de Pradas. *Poésies de Daude de Pradas*. Edited by A. H. Schutz. Toulouse: Privat, 1933.

———. "Le roman de Daude de Pradas sur les quatre vertus cardinales." Edited by Peter T. Ricketts. *La France latine* 134 (2002): 131–183.

Dionysius the Pseudo-Areopagite. *Dionysiaca: Recueil donnant l'ensemble des traductions latines des ouvrages attribués au Denys d'Aréopage*. Edited by Philipe Chevallier. 2 vols. Bruges: Desclée de Brouwer, 1937–1950.

Disticha Catonis. Edited by Marcus Boas. Amsterdam: North-Holland, 1952.

Farghani. *Al Farghani Differentie scientie astrorum*. Edited by Francis J. Carmody. Berkeley, 1943.

Folquet de Marseille. *Le poesie di Folchetto di Marsiglia*. Edited by Paolo Squillacioti. Ospedaletto (Pisa): Pacini, 1999.

———. *Le troubadour Folquet de Marseille*. Edited by Stanislaw Stronski. Cracow: Academie des Sciences, 1910.

Galen. *Claudii Galeni opera omnia*. Edited by C. G. Kühn. 20 vols. in 22. Leipzig, 1821. Reprint, Hildesheim: Georg Olms, 2001.

———. *Über die Heilkunst* [*Tegni* or *Techne Iatrike*]. Translated by Reinhard Peters. Hamburg, 1978.

Guilhem de Montanhagol. *Les poésies de Guilhem de Montanhagol, troubadour provençal du XIIIe siècle*. Edited by Peter T. Ricketts. Toronto: Pontifical Institute of Mediaeval Studies, 1964.

Guillelmus de Aragonia. "De nobilitate animi." Edited by Marvin L. Colker. *Mediaeval Studies* 23 (1961): 47–79.

———. "Edición crítica de los comentarios de Guillermo de Aragón al De consolatione philosophiae de Boecio." By Carmen Olmedilla Herrero. Dissertation, Universidad Complutense de Madrid, 1997.

Guiraut Riquier. "Le tenzoni del trovatore Guiraut Riquier." Edited by Maria Pia Betti. *Studi mediolatini e volgari* 44 (1998): 7–193.

Hermes Trismegistus. "Liber Hermetis De Quindecim Stellis Quindecim Lapidibus Quindecim Herbis et Quindecim Imaginibus." *Textes latins et vieux français relatifs aux Cyranides.* Edited by Louis Delatte. Bibliothèque de la Faculté de Philosophie et Lettres de l'Université de Liège 93. Liège: Faculté de Philosophie et Lettres, 1942.

Horace. *Satires, Epistles and Ars Poetica.* Translated by H. Rushton Fairclough. Loeb Classical Library 194. Cambridge, Mass.: Harvard University Press, 1991.

Isidore of Seville. *Isidori Hispalensis episcopi Etymologiarum sive Originum libri XX.* Edited by W. M. Lindsay. 2 vols. Oxford: Clarendon Press, 1911.

Jacobus de Pistorio. "A Philosophical Treatise from Bologna Dedicated to Guido Cavalcanti: Magister Jacobus de Pistorio and His Questio de Felicitate." Edited by P. O. Kristeller. In *Medioevo e Rinascimento: Studi in onore di Bruno Nardi*, 1:425–463. Florence: G. C. Sansoni, 1955.

Johan Esteve. *Le poesie del trovatore Johan Esteve.* Edited by Sergio Vatteroni. Pisa: Pacini, 1986.

John of Salisbury. *Ioannis Saresberiensis episcopi Carnotensis Policratici sive De nvgis cvrialivm.* Edited by Clemens C. I. Webb. Oxford: Clarendon Press, 1909.

Juvenal. *Juvenal and Persius.* Edited by Susanna Morton Braund. Loeb Classical Library 91. Cambridge, Mass.: Harvard University Press, 2004.

Matieu de Quercy. *Provenzalische Inedita aus Pariser Handschriften.* Edited by Carl Appel. Wiesbaden: Sändig, 1892. 193–196.

Maximian. *Die elegischen Verse von Maximian: Eine letzte Widerrede gegen die neue christliche Zeit.* Edited by Wolfgang Christian Schneider. Stuttgart: Steiner, 2003.

Monumens de la littérature romane. Edited by Adolphe Félix Gatien-Arnoult. 4 vols. Toulouse: J.-B. Paya, 1841–1849.

[*Officium in diem festum Assumptionis Beatae Mariae.*] "Rezo antiguo de la Inmaculada Concepción." In *Monumentos antiguos de la Iglesia Compostelana*, edited by Fidel Fita [y Colomé], 92–104. Madrid: Maroto, 1882.

Paulet de Marselha. *Paulet de Marselha: Un provençal a la cort dels reis d'Aragó.* Edited by Isabel de Riquer. Barcelona: Columna, 1996.

Peire d'Alvernhe. *Poesie.* Edited by Aniello Fratta. Rome: Vecchiarelli, 1996.

Peire Vidal. *Poesie*. Edited by D'Arco Silvio Avalle. Documenti di filologia 4. 2 vols. Milan: R. Ricciardi, 1960.

———. *Les poésies de Peire Vidal*. Edited by J. Anglade. 2nd ed. Les classiques Français du Moyen Âge 11. Paris: Champion, 1966.

Plato. *Timaeus*. Translated by Chalcidius. *Platonis Timaeus interprete Chalcidio*. Edited by Joh. Wrobel. Leipzig: Teubner, 1876.

Pliny. *Natural History*. Translated by H. Rackham, W. H. S. Jones, and D. E. Eichholz. 10 vols. Loeb Classical Library 330, 352–353, 370–371, 392–394, 418–419. Cambridge, Mass.: Harvard University Press, 1969–1989.

Poeti del Duecento. Edited by Gianfranco Contini. 2 vols. La Letteratura italiana, storia e testi 2. Milan: R. Ricciardi, 1960.

Porphyry the Phoenician. *Isagoge*. Translated by Edward W. Warren. Toronto: Pontifical Institute of Mediaeval Studies, 1975.

Li Proverbe au vilain. Edited by Adolf Tobler. Leipzig: S. Hirzel, 1895.

Ptolemy. *Almagestu[m] Cl. Ptolemei: Pheludiensis Alexandrini astronomo[rum] principis. . . .* Venetijs: Petri Liechtenstein, 1515.

———. [*Quadripartitum; Centiloquium cum commento Hali*]. Venice: Erhard Ratdolt, 1484.

Publilius Syrus. *Sententiae*. Edited by Otto Friedrich. Berlin: T. Griebeni, 1880.

Quintilian. *The Orator's Education*. Edited and translated by Donald A. Russell. 5 vols. Loeb Classical Library 124–127, 494. Cambridge, Mass.: Harvard University Press, 2001.

Sallust. Translated by J. C. Rolfe. Loeb Classical Library 116. Cambridge, Mass.: Harvard University Press, 1965.

Scriptores Physiognomonici Graeci et Latini. Edited by Richardus Förster. Leipzig, 1893. Reprint, Stuttgart: Teubner, 1994.

Seneca. *De beneficiis*. In *Seneca: Moral Essays*. Translated by John W. Basore. Loeb Classical Library 310. 3 vols. Cambridge, Mass.: Harvard University Press, 1928–1935.

———. *Lettres à Lucilius*. Edited by François Préchac. Translated by Henri Noblot. 5 vols. Paris: Belles Lettres, 1969–1979.

Solomon and Marcolf. Edited by Jan M. Ziolkowski. Harvard Studies in Medieval Latin 1. Cambridge, Mass.: Department of the Classics, Harvard University, 2008.

Sordel. *Sordello: le poesie*. Edited by Marco Boni. Bologna: Palmaverde, 1954.

Stobaeus. *Florilegium*. Edited by Augustus Meineke. 4 vols. Leipzig: Teubner, 1855–1857.

Valerius Maximus. *Memorable Doings and Sayings*. Edited and translated by D. R. Shackleton Bailey. Loeb Classical Library 492–493. 2 vols. Cambridge, Mass.: Harvard University Press, 2000.

Walter Burley (Pseudo-). *Liber de vita et moribus philosophorum*. Edited by Hermann Knust. Bibliothek des litterarischen Vereins in Stuttgart 173. Tübingen: Minerva, 1886.

Walter of Châtillon. *The Alexandreis*. Translated by R. Telfryn Pritchard. Toronto: Pontifical Institute of Mediaeval Studies, 1986.

———. *Galteri de Castellione Alexandreis*. Edited by Marvin L. Colker. Padua: Antenor, 1978.

Secondary Sources

Agrimi, Jole. "La ricezione della Fisiognomica pseudoaristotelica nella Facoltà delli Arti." *AHMA* 64 (1997): 127–188.

Anglade, Joseph. "Peire Vidal et le Liber de Nobilitate Animi." *Studi Medievali*, n.s., 2 (1929): 445–446.

Arnaldez, Roger. *Averroes: A Rationalist in Islam*. Notre Dame: University of Notre Dame Press, 2000.

Asperti, Stefano. "I trovatori e la Corona d'Aragona: riflessioni per una cronologia di riferimento." *Mot, so, razo* 1 (1999): 12–31. Revised version at www.rialc.unina.it/bollettino.htm.

Atkinson, J. Keith. "A Fourteenth-Century Picard Translation-Commentary of the *Consolatio Philosophiae*." In *The Medieval Boethius: Studies in the Vernacular Translations of "De consolatione philosophiae,"* edited by Alastair J. Minnis, 32–62. Cambridge: D. S. Brewer, 1987.

Attali, Jacques. *Raison et foi: Averroès, Maïmonide, Thomas d'Aquin*. [Paris]: Bibliothèque nationale de France, 2004.

Aurell, Martin. *La noblesse en occident (Ve–XVe siècle)*. Paris: Armand Colin, 1996.

Baldinger, Kurt. *Complément bibliographique au* Provenzalische Supplement-wörterbuch *de Emil Levy: Sources—Datations*. Genève: Slatkine, 1983.

Battaglia, Salvatore. *Grande dizionario della lingua italiana*. 20 vols. to date. [Turin]: Unione tipografico-editrice torinese, 1961–.

Bisson, T. N. *The Medieval Crown of Aragon: A Short History*. Oxford: Clarendon Press, 1986.

Bolduc, Michelle. "Naming Names: Matfre Ermengaud's Use of Troubadour Quotations." *Tenso* 22 (2007): 41–75.

Bouchard, Constance Brittain. *Strong of Body, Brave and Noble: Chivalry and Society in Medieval France*. Ithaca: Cornell University Press, 1998.

Bullough, Vern L. "The Development of the Medical University at Montpellier to the End of the Fourteenth Century." In Bullough, *Universities, Medicine and Science in the Medieval West*, 15–30. Aldershot: Ashgate, 2004.

Cabré, Miriam. "Italian and Catalan Troubadours." In *Troubadours*, 127–140.

———. "Mécènes et troubadours dans la Couronne d'Aragon." *Europe* 86, nos. 950–951 (2008): 126–136.

Cappelli, Adriano. *Dizionario di abbreviature latine ed italiane*. 6th ed. Milan: Hoepli, 1967.

Chambers, Frank M. "Imitation of Form in the Old Provençal Lyric." *Romance Philology* 6 (1953): 104–120.

Cherchi, Paolo. *Andreas and the Ambiguity of Courtly Love*. Toronto: University of Toronto Press, 1994.

Cluzel, Irénée. "Princes et troubadours de la maison royale de Barcelone-Aragon." *Boletín de la Real Academia de Buenas Letras de Barcelona* 27 (1957–58): 321–373.

Compendium auctorum latinorum Medii Aevi 500–1500. Edited by Michael Lapidge and others. Tavarnuzze (Florence): SISMEL edizioni del Galluzzo, 2000–.

Conde y Delgado de Molina, Rafael. "La salva de la infanzonía aragonesa: Fueros, praxis documental y archivo." *Aragón en la edad media* 14–15.1 (1999): 313–328.

Coromines, Joan, with Joseph Gulsoy and Max Cahner. *Diccionari etimològic i complementari de la llengua catalana*. 10 vols. Barcelona: Curial, 1980–1991.

Corral Lafuente, José Luis. "Cambios estructurales en Aragón a mediados del siglo XIII." *Aragón en la edad media* 5 (1983): 95–112.

Corti, Maria. *Scritti su Cavalcanti e Dante: La felicità mentale, percorsi dell'invenzione e altri saggi*. Turin: Einaudi, 2003.

Courcelle, Pierre. "Étude critique sur les Commentaires de la Consolation de Boèce (IXe–XVe siècles)." *AHMA* 12 (1939): 5–140.

Crespo, Roberto. "Il prologo alla traduzione della 'Consolatio Philosophiae' di Jean de Meun e il commento di Guglielmo d'Aragona [sic]." In *Romanitas et Christianitas, Studia Iano Henrico Waszink . . . Oblata*, edited by W. den Boer, 55–70. Amsterdam: North-Holland, 1973.

Crouch, David. *The Birth of Nobility: Constructing Aristocracy in England and France 900–1300*. Harlow: Pearson, 2005.

Curtius, Ernst Robert. *European Literature and the Latin Middle Ages*. Translated by Willard R. Trask. New York: Harper & Row, 1963.

De Poorter, Alphonse. *Catalogue des manuscrits de la Bibliothèque publique de la ville de Bruges*. Catalogue général des manuscrits des bibliothèques de Belgique 2. Gembloux: J. Duculot, 1934.

Del Estal, Juan Manuel. "Antigüedad del concepto y denominación 'Corona de Aragon.'" *Medievalia* (Barcelona) 10 (1992): 133–168.

Del Giudice, Maria. "La Contentio de nobilitate generis et animi probitate secondo il codice di Fitalia." *Centro di Studi Filologici e Linguistici Siciliani: Bollettino* 14 (1980): 393–404.

Denomy, Alexander Joseph. "The Vocabulary of Jean de Meun's Translation of Boethius' De consolatione philosophiae." *Mediaeval Studies* 16 (1954): 19–34.

Di Girolamo, Costanzo. "L'eredità dei trovatori in Catalogna." *Filologia antica e moderna* 9 (1995): 7–21.

Dicionário da Literatura Medieval Galega e Portuguesa. Edited by Giulia Lanciani and Giuseppe Tavani. Lisbon: Caminho, 1993.

Dictionary of Scientific Biography. 18 vols. New York: Scribner, 1970–1990.

Enciclopedia Dantesca. 6 vols. Rome: Istituto della Enciclopedia Italiana, [1970–1978].

Encyclopedia of the Middle Ages. 2 vols. Edited by André Vauchez. Cambridge: Clarke, 2000.

Faral, Edmond. *Les arts poétiques du XIIe et du XIIIe siècle.* Paris: Champion, 1962.

Fluvià Escorsa, Armand de. "Los títulos nobiliarios en el Principado de Cataluña (siglo IX–1716)." *Hidalguía: La revista de genealogía, nobleza y armas* 36.207 (1988): 249–255.

Gattermann, Günter, and Heinz Finger. *Handschriftencensus Rheinland.* Wiesbaden: L. Reichert, 1993.

Gauthier, R. A. "Notes sur les débuts (1225–1240) du premier 'averroïsme.'" *Revue des sciences philosophiques et théologiques* 66 (1982): 321–374.

Gleason, M. J. "Clearing the Fields: Towards a Reassessment of Chaucer's Use of Trevet in the *Boece*." In *The Medieval Boethius: Studies in the Vernacular Translations of "De consolatione philosophiae,"* edited by Alastair J. Minnis, 89–105. Cambridge: D. S. Brewer, 1987.

González Antón, Luis. "Las Cortes aragonesas en el reinado de Jaime II." *Anuario de historia del derecho español* 47 (1977): 523–628.

———. *Las uniones aragonesas y las Cortes del reino (1283–1301).* 2 vols. Saragossa: Consejo Superior de Investigaciones Científicas, Escuela de Estudios Medievales, 1975.

Gregory, Tullio. "I sogni e gli astri." In *I sogni nel medioevo*, edited by Tullio Gregory, 111–148. Rome: Ateneo, 1985.

Die Handschriften-Verzeichnisse der Cistercienser-Stifte: Reun in Steiermark [etc.]. 2 vols. Vienna: Alfred Hölder, 1891.

Hilka, Alfons. "Altfranzösische Sprichwörter." *Jahresbericht der Schlesischen Gesellschaft für vaterländische Cultur: Sitzung der Sektion für neuere Philologie im Jahre 1913* 91, 1, pt. 4c (1914): 21–38.

Hillgarth, J. N. *The Spanish Kingdoms, 1250–1516.* 2 vols. Oxford: Clarendon Press, 1976–1978.

Huot, Sylvia. "Troubadour Lyric and Old French Narrative." In *Troubadours*, 263–278.

Jungwirth, Augustin. *Beschreibung der Handschriften des Stiftes St. Peter in Salzburg.* 6 vols. 1913. Photocopy, Ann Arbor: University Microfilms, 1983.

Kay, Sarah. "How Long is a Quotation? Quotations from the Troubadours in the Text and Manuscripts of the *Breviari d'amor.*" *Romania* 127 (2009): 1–29.

Keen, Maurice. *Chivalry.* New Haven: Yale University Press, 1984.

Keller, Hans-Erich. "*La Cort d'Amors* de Raimon Vidal et ses citations." In *Literatur, Geschichte und Verstehen: Festschrift für Ulrich Mölk zum 60. Geburtstag*, edited by Hinrich Hudde, Udo Schöning, and Friedrich Wolfzettel, 185–192. Studia Romanica 87. Heidelberg: Winter, 1997.

Klingebiel, Kathryn. "Lost Literature of the Troubadours: A Proposed Catalogue." *Tenso* 13, no.1 (1997): 1–23.

Kolsen, Adolf. "25 bisher unedierte provenzalische Anonyma." *Zeitschrift für romanische Philologie* 38 (1914–1917): 281–310.

Lacombe, George. *Aristoteles Latinus: Codices.* 3 vols. Rome: Libreria dello stato, 1939–1961.

Laliena Corbera, Carlos, and María Teresa Iranzo Muñío. "Poder, honor y linaje en las estrategias de la nobleza urbana aragonesa: siglos XIV–XV." *Revista d'història medieval* 9 (1998): 41–80.

Levy, Emil. *Petit dictionnaire provençal-français.* Heidelberg: C. Winter, 1909.

Lexikon des Mittelalters. Edited by Robert Auty and others. 9 vols. Munich: Artemis-Verlag, 1980–.

McDonald, William C. "The Nobility of Soul: Uncharted Echoes of the Peraldean Tradition in Late Medieval German Literature." *Deutsche Vierteljarhrsschrift für Literaturwissenschaft und Geistesgeschichte* 60 (1986): 543–571.

Meneghetti, Maria Luisa. "Intertextuality and Dialogism in the Troubadours." *Troubadours*, 181–196.

Minio-Paluello, Lorenzo. "Iacobus Veneticus Grecus: Canonist and Translator of Aristotle." *Traditio* 8 (1952): 265–304.

Minnis, Alastair J.; A. Brian Scott; and David Wallace. *Medieval Literary Theory and Criticism c. 1100–c. 1375: The Commentary-Tradition.* Oxford: Clarendon Press, 1988.

Monson, Don A. *Andreas Capellanus, Scholasticism, and the Courtly Tradition.* Washington, D.C.: Catholic University of America Press, 2005.

Moran i Ocerinjauregui, Josèp. "Inicio y desarrollo del Catalán escrito." *Medioevo romanzo* 27 (2003): 311–319.

Moxó Montoliu, Francisco de. "Jaime II y la nueva concesión de títulos nobiliarios en la España del siglo XIV." *Anales de la Universidad de Alicante: Historia medieval* 9 (1992–1993): 133–143.

Nardi, Bruno. "L'amore e i medici medievali." In *Saggi e note di critica dantesca*, 238–267. Milan: R. Ricciardi, 1966.

Nauck, August. *Tragicorum graecorum fragmenta.* Revised by Bruno Snell. Hildesheim: Olms, 1964.

Nelson, Deborah H. "Northern France." In *Handbook*, 255–261.

Olmedilla Herrero, Carmen. "Un accessus medieval: el comentario de Guillermo de Aragón al *De consolatione Philosophiae* de Boecio." *Actas: II Congreso Hispánico de Latín Medieval (León, 11-14 de Noviembre de 1997)*, 2:709–720. León: Universidad de León, Secretariado de Publicaciones, 1998.

———. "Commentaire de Guillaume d'Aragon sur *De Consolatione Philosophiae* de Boèce." In *L'Orphée de Boèce au Moyen Age: Traductions françaises et commentaires latins (XIIe-XV siècles)*, edited by Béatrice M. Atherton and J. Keith Atkinson, 181–196. Verona: Fiorini, 2000.

———. "Commentarios a la Consolatio Philosophiae de Boecio: Guillermo de Aragón y la versión castellana anónima del comentario de Nicolás de Trevet." *Cuadernos de filologia clásica* (Madrid) 2 (1992): 277–288.

Ottman, Jennifer, and Rega Wood. "Walter Burley: His Life and Works." *Vivarium* 37 (1999): 1–24.

Pack, Roger A. "Auctoris incerti De Physiognomia libellus." *AHMA* 41 (1974): 113–138.

Paden, William D. *An Introduction to Old Occitan.* New York: Modern Language Association of America, 1998.

———. "Old Occitan as a Lyric Language: The Insertions from Occitan in Three Thirteenth-Century French Romances." *Speculum* 68 (1993): 36–53.

Parkes, M. B. *English Cursive Book Hands, 1250-1500.* Oxford, 1969. Reprint, Berkeley: University of California Press, 1979.

Paterson, Linda. "*Fin'amor* and the Development of the Courtly Canso." *Troubadours*, 28–46.

Pérez Lasheras, Antonio. *La literatura del reino de Aragón hasta el siglo XVI.* Saragossa: Ibercaja-Institución Fernando el Católico, 2003.

Porcher, Jean. "Nouvelles acquisitions latines et françaises du Département des Manuscrits de la Bibliothèque Nationale pendant les années 1941–1945." *Bibliothèque de l'Ecole des Chartes* 106 (1945–1946): 225–281.

Prosser, Gareth. "The Later Medieval French Noblesse." In *France in the Later Middle Ages, 1200-1500*, edited by David Potter, 182–209. Oxford: Oxford University Press, 2002.

Recueil des Historiens des Gaules et de la France. 24 vols. in 25. Paris: Aux dépens des librairies, 1738–1904.

Ricketts, Peter T. *Concordance de l'occitan médiéval: COM2, Les troubadours, Les textes narratifs en vers.* CD-ROM. Turnhout: Brepols, 2005.

Riquer, Isabel de. "Presencia trovadoresca en la Corona de Aragón." *Anuario de estudios medievales* 26 (1996): 933–966.

Riquer, Martí de. "Els Trobadors catalans." In *Història de la literatura catalana: Part antiga*, vol. 1, 24–196. Barcelona: Ariel, 1964.

———. *Los trovadores: Historia literaria y textos*. 3 vols. Barcelona: Planeta, 1975.

Rodrigo Estevan, María Luz. *La ciudad de Daroca a fines de la edad media: Selección documental, 1328–1526*. Daroca: Centro de Estudios Darocenses, Institución "Fernando el Católico," 1999.

Rubinstein, Nicolai. *Studies in Italian History in the Middle Ages and the Renaissance*. Vol. 1, *Political Thought and the Language of Politics*. Edited by Giovanni Ciappelli. Rome: Edizioni di Storia e Letteratura, 2004.

Sarasa Sánchez, Esteban. *El Privilegio general de Aragón: la defensa de las libertades aragonesas en la Edad Media, estudio y edición*. [Saragossa]: Cortes de Aragón, [1984].

Sarton, George. *Introduction to the History of Science*. 3 vols. in 5. Baltimore: Carnegie Institution of Washington, 1927–1948.

Schmitt, Charles B., and Dilwyn Knox. *Pseudo-Aristoteles Latinus: A Guide to Latin Works Falsely Attributed to Aristotle before 1500*. London: Warburg Institute, University of London, 1985.

Senner, Walter. "Der vollständige Kommentar des Guillelmus de Aragonia über die Consolatio Philosophiae." *Bulletin de philosophie médiévale* 22 (1980): 98–100.

Sesma Muñoz, José Ángel. *La Corona de Aragón: Una introducción crítica*. Saragossa: Caja de Ahorros de la Inmaculada de Aragón, 2000.

Sezgin, Fuat. *Geschichte des arabischen Schrifttums*. 9 vols. Leiden: Brill, 1967–1984.

Snow, Joseph T. "The Iberian Peninsula." In *Handbook*, 271–278.

Soldevila, Ferran. *Vida de Pere el Gran i d'Alfons el Liberal*. Barcelona: Aedos, 1963.

Taylor, Archer. "The Wisdom of Many and the Wit of One." In *Selected Writings on Proverbs*, by Archer Taylor, edited by Wolfgang Mieder, 68–73. Helsinki: Suomalainen Tiedeakatemia, 1975.

Thorndike, Lynn. *A History of Magic and Experimental Science*. 8 vols. New York: Columbia University Press, 1958.

Thorndike, Lynn, and Pearl Kibre. *A Catalogue of Incipits of Mediaeval Scientific Writings in Latin*. Revised and augmented edition. London: Mediaeval Academy of America, 1963.

Trésor de la langue française. Edited by Paul Imbs. 16 vols. Paris: Éditions du Centre national de la recherche scientifique, 1971–1994.

Ullmann, Walter. "Some Observations on the Medieval Evaluation of the Homo Naturalis and the Christianus." In *L'homme et son destin, d'après les penseurs du Moyen Age: Actes du Premier Congrès International de Philosophie Médiévale. Louvain-Bruxelles, 28 août–4 septembre 1958*, 145–151. Louvain: Nauwelaerts, 1960.

Val Naval, Paula. "Autoría y datación de la *Summa supra Phisonomiam Aristotelis*." *Studium: Revista de humanidades* 12 (2006): 127–140.

Van D'Elden, Stephanie Cain. "The Minnesingers." In *Handbook*, 262–270.

Vanhamel, W. "Biobibliographie de Guillaume de Moerbeke." In *Guillaume de Moerbeke: Recueil d'études à l'occasion du 700e anniversaire de sa mort (1286)*, edited by J. Brams and W. Vanhamel, 301–383. Leuven: Leuven University Press, 1989.

Vielliard, Françoise. "Auteur et autorité dans la littérature occitane médiévale non lyrique." In *Auctor et auctoritas: Invention et conformisme dans l'écriture médiévale: Actes du colloque tenu à l'Université de Versailles-Saint-Quentin-en-Yvelines, 14–16 juin 1999*, edited by Michel Zimmermann, 375–389. Paris: Ecole des Chartes, 2001.

Watson, Andrew G. *Catalogue of Dated and Datable Manuscripts c. 700–1600 in the Department of Manuscripts, the British Library*. 2 vols. London: British Library, 1979.

Index of Sources and Analogues

Parentheses ( ) indicate sources or analogues that are implicit.

This book was composed by Ivy Livingston
(Department of the Classics, Harvard University)
and manufactured by Sheridan Books, Ann Arbor, MI.

The cover was designed by Joni Godlove (big*bang creative).

The typeface is Gentium Plus, designed by Victor Gaultney
and distributed by SIL International.